Confronting Whiteness

CONFRONTING WHITENESS

A Spiritual Journey of Reflection, Conversation, and Transformation

W. Benjamin Boswell

ORBIS BOOKS
Maryknoll, New York 10545

Founded in 1970, Orbis Books endeavors to publish works that enlighten the mind, nourish the spirit, and challenge the conscience. The publishing arm of the Maryknoll Fathers and Brothers, Orbis seeks to explore the global dimensions of the Christian faith and mission, to invite dialogue with diverse cultures and religious traditions, and to serve the cause of reconciliation and peace. The books published reflect the views of their authors and do not represent the official position of the Maryknoll Society. To learn more about Maryknoll and Orbis Books, please visit our website at www.orbisbooks.com.

Manufactured in the United States of America.

Library of Congress Cataloging-in-Publication Data

Names: Boswell, W. Benjamin, author.
Title: Confronting whiteness : a spiritual journey of reflection, conversation, and transformation / W. Benjamin Boswell.
Description: Maryknoll, NY : Orbis Books, [2024] | Includes bibliographical references.
Identifiers: LCCN 2023037963 (print) | LCCN 2023037964 (ebook) | ISBN 9781626985568 (trade paperback) | ISBN 9798888660140 (epub)
Subjects: LCSH: White people—Race identity. | White people—Attitudes. | White people—Psychology. | Anti-racism.
Classification: LCC HT1575. B67 2023 (print) | LCC HT1575 (ebook) | DDC 305.809—dc23/eng/20230906
LC record available at https://lccn.loc.gov/2023037963
LC ebook record available at https://lccn.loc.gov/2023037964

To my daughter Lucy Joy,
the light of my life and the inspiration for my awakening.

To Myers Park Baptist Church,
the beloved community in which this course was born and raised.

To all the participants and facilitators
of "What Does It Mean to Be White?"
who bravely journeyed with me into the heart of Whiteness.

Contents

Foreword

Gerardo Martí

In November 2020 in the midst of the COVID-19 pandemic I found myself in a Zoom session with twelve other people, all of them members of Myers Park Baptist Church, all of them living in the Charlotte area, and all of them identifying themselves as White. Their pastor, Benjamin Boswell, had created "a journey of spiritual reflection" titled *What Does It Mean to Be White?* and had already led dozens of people through an experience of looking at their own racial identity. As a participant in the church who is also a professor of race and religion in America, I decided to sign up, hoping not just to sit back as an observer but rather to take this as a unique opportunity to examine my own Whiteness.

My parents are refugees from Cuba who met and married in Boston, Massachusetts. I was born there, and we soon moved to California, where I grew up between two cultures: an enclave of Cuban exiles and a surge of Southern and Midwestern migrants pursuing economic opportunities in the expanding suburbs of Orange County. Spanish was my first language, yet I grew up in a segregated White community, largely oblivious to racial tensions and critical events happening in the Black, Latino, and Asian communities that surrounded my family. My education did little to correct this blindness, and much of my teaching and scholarship since becoming a professor of sociology—especially my recent book, appropriately titled *American Blindspot* (2020)—has grown out of my efforts to overcome my own ignorance.

As the Whiteness class started, our cameras streamed our faces, and stories about realizing our own sense of having a racial self poured from our lives. Even with the limitations of being entirely online, we were

___

Gerardo Martí is William R. Kenan Jr. Professor of Sociology at Davidson College.

learning so much from one another! The group was kept small to allow interaction, and we all expressed gratitude that everyone was willing to be so intimate, thoughtful, and vulnerable. We soon learned that there were a lot of people who wanted to join a group like ours, but the church could not yet accommodate everyone. Hundreds attempted to reserve a spot. More groups were launched, and facilitators who had already journeyed through the experience were brought on board. People from the greater Charlotte area were calling the church and trying to get into a Whiteness group. *How can I join? When is the next one?* Yet the church simply could not offer enough classes to meet the demand.

With so much discomfort on racial issues, so many questions about Christians and their commitments, and so much distrust of strangers, why were so many White people eager to commit several weeks meeting with other White people just to talk about their Whiteness?

In the years leading up to Pastor Boswell's formation of this reflective group experience, Americans repeatedly witnessed an unmistakable and profound trauma inflicted on Black people. Although the United States elected a Black president in 2008, racialized polarization continued to grow. Racial incidents multiplied, becoming even more prominent with the ubiquity of social media and 24/7 news cycles. Any optimism that the United States might have finally become a "post-racial" country was quickly smothered with an aggressive Islamophobia stemming from the attacks of 9/11, continued agitation against immigrants from countries beyond our southern border, and stubborn inequalities of employment, income, and wealth among African Americans.

Competing policies, political ambitions, and provocative rhetoric about how to address racial issues stirred up misinformation and mistrust, obscuring potential solutions. Streaming platforms provided fodder that fed divisions at the daily water cooler and our own kitchen tables. The general malaise regarding Black progress on jobs, education, and health was further exaggerated by mounting reports produced by sociologists, political scientists, and survey researchers of increased racial animosity, with fresh data presented every day. While some Americans continued to insist on a color-blind ideology—believing that the American Dream was accessible to anyone willing to work for it—reality revealed that this was less truth and more myth.

Most dramatically, even with a Black president in the White House, our American awareness of racial discomfort shifted abruptly from an emphasis on racial differences to a focus on outright racial violence. In 2012, seventeen-year-old Trayvon Martin was fatally shot by a neighborhood-watch captain convinced that this Black teenager was "up to no good," sparking outrage over the assumed threat of African Americans. Polarizing responses forced African Americans to reframe their discussions, finding ways to communicate their circumstances and to promote greater understanding.

The following year the Twitter hashtag #BlackLivesMatter went viral on social media after Martin's killer was acquitted. But overshadowing any attempts to confront issues of race was more racial violence. A spate of police killings of unarmed Black men followed: Eric Garner (New York City), Michael Brown (Ferguson, Missouri), and Tamir Rice (Cleveland) all died in 2014. The next year Freddie Gray and Sandra Bland died while in police custody. In that year a White supremacist entered Emanuel AME Church in Charleston, South Carolina, and murdered nine Black members during a weekly Bible study. The following year Alton Sterling and Philando Castile were fatally shot by police.

Then, in 2016, in Charlotte, North Carolina, Keith Lamont Scott was waiting for his son's school bus. Charlotte-Mecklenburg police arrived at the apartment complex on a warrant, saw Scott in his car, and thought he was holding a handgun. While demanding he exit the vehicle and drop his weapon—and as his wife was yelling, "Don't shoot him!"—police fired, killing Scott immediately. Riots in uptown Charlotte lasted three days, the largest protests in its history. Pastor Boswell, still in his first year as senior pastor of Myers Park Baptist, said: "I came out of 2016 thinking conversations about race in the church were not working. They seemed so shallow and hollow."

The visible and reported violence against Black people continued, and Boswell dedicated more attention in his ministry to addressing racial justice. The culmination came with another series of incidents in 2020, just months before our group's "Whiteness" class. In Georgia, Ahmaud Arbery was jogging in a White neighborhood when he was chased down by three White men in cars and shot at point-blank range. In Kentucky, Breonna Taylor was killed with a flurry of gunfire in a botched police raid in her own apartment. And in Minnesota, George Floyd was suspected of using a counterfeit twenty-dollar bill and restrained on the street outside the store by local police. One officer knelt on Floyd's neck for over nine minutes, while onlookers used their cell phones to record the scene, pleading to let him go. "I can't breathe," he said. "I can't breathe. I can't breathe." In his final breaths Floyd called out for his mother. Floyd died on the street. Protests immediately broke out on those same streets.

George Floyd's horrific and heartrending death was captured on video and struck a deep chord across the country. As summer heated up, so did protests in cities and towns across the nation. I remember at my local Target store a lone Black man stood silently at the entrance with a handmade cardboard sign: "Is This the Best We Can Do?" Floyd's murder by police stirred something deep, and people took to the streets. It was not just a few advocates and agitators following a routine. These protests brought in people who had never protested before. Americans who had never held up a protest sign in their lives were motivated to march together and demonstrate their outrage. In the summer of 2020 people of all colors and faiths, old and young, participated in the greatest mass protest movement in American history. Parents even brought their children to be witnesses to this history and to express their sympathy for the dead.

In Charlotte the protests for George Floyd expanded to include the names of other recently dead, including the city's own Keith Lamont Scott. These deaths remained fresh, and the angst about the future of race was deeply felt. Many were asking, "What can I do?" Pastor Boswell's answer was to mobilize the members of his predominantly White congregation to take a harder look at their own racial selves. He believes that achieving racial justice necessitates a more deliberate action by those racialized as White to reflect on the nature of Whiteness as a source of identity and as a source of power. In addition to learning Black history and Black achievements, this intentional reflexivity involves reading Black voices describing Whiteness through the lens of their Black experience. By engaging writers like James Baldwin, Toni Morrison, and Malcolm X, his White congregants would encounter new perspectives on themselves, stimulating a profound revelation of what had been kept invisible to them their entire lives.

For Boswell, Whiteness is not merely a form of power; it is a destructive force. With this conclusion, he agrees with many deeply religious people who have come before him. Former slave Frederick Douglass said, "The true problem is not the negro, but the nation. Not the law-abiding blacks of the South, but the white men of that section, who by fraud, violence, and persecution, are breaking the law, trampling on the Constitution, corrupting the ballot-box, and defeating the ends of justice."[1] Later, the Rev. Dr. Martin Luther King Jr. said: "Whites, it must frankly be said, are not putting in a similar mass effort to reeducate themselves out of their racial ignorance. It is an aspect of their sense of superiority that the white people of America believe they have so little to learn."[2] And Trappist monk Thomas Merton, who thought deeply about America's seemingly intractable racial divide, once wrote, "As long as white society persists in clinging to its present condition and its own image of itself as the only acceptable reality, then the problem will remain without reasonable solution, and there will inevitably be violence."[3]

Whiteness is a form of power, yet it is largely invisible to most White people. The steps laid out in the following pages will allow you and others to process the reality of race, not only as a source of identity but also as a source of comfort, privilege, and existential certainty. Not all White people have a lot of material wealth or income. But Whiteness has been a force that has shaped you, your family, your neighbors, and your friends. Sociologist W.E.B. Du Bois argued that Whiteness has long served as a "public and psychological wage," a sort of compensation for the lack of wealth that provides even the most impoverished White person a valuable source of social status. The history of the United States repeatedly shows how White people align with one another, agreeing even without explicitly saying so that they will work together to keep their world agreeable and comfortable for White people. When people of color introduce racial issues, they are judged to be the disruptors, the agitators, the misfits, and the troublemakers. Yet Du Bois clearly documented the lawlessness and destruction inflicted by White people using White-centered organizations, White-dominant systems, and White-promoting terrorist groups. White people have been willing to push, restrain, and even kill Black people and others across the colorline to maintain a societal order that seems best in their own eyes.

This book and the group process that goes with it offer a mirror for examining ourselves. Consider the words of Lamentations chapter 3:

---

[1] Frederick Douglass, "The Race Problem," speech, Bethel Literary and Historical Association, Metropolitan A.M.E. Church, Washington DC, October 21, 1890.

[2] Martin Luther King Jr., *Where Do We Go from Here: Chaos or Community* (1967), goodreads.com.

[3] Thomas Merton, "Letters to a White Liberal" (1963).

> Let us examine our ways and test them.
> And let us return to the Lord.

Personal examination is a spiritual practice that strengthens our faith. In the humility of such introspection, illuminated by voices of the oppressed, accomplished in communion with others in the church, and bringing our spirits in line with the Spirit, we join together with the many who are taking firm steps forward toward the grand ambition of racial justice.

Preface

Why Whiteness?

In 2008, conservative and liberal commentators celebrated the election of Barack Obama as the first Black president of the United States as a sign that America had become a "post-racial" society. For example, the conservative radio host Lou Dobbs said, "We are now in a twenty-first-century post-partisan, post-racial society."[1] MSNBC host Chris Matthews said President Obama "is post-racial by all appearances. You know, I forgot he was Black tonight for an hour."[2] Dobbs and Matthews were not alone in their perspective. Opinion pieces in the *Boston Globe, Wall Street Journal,* and *New York Times* all used the buzzword *post-racial* to describe the election and to define "Obama's America." Polls, however, indicated that White Americans were far more likely than Black Americans to believe they were now living in a post-racial society.

The idea of a post-racial society was consistent with the beliefs most White Americans held for over a decade: that African Americans had achieved, or would soon achieve, racial equality in the United States despite substantial evidence to the contrary. Eduardo Bonilla-Silva states: "The white commonsense view on racial matters is that racists are few and far between, that discrimination has all but disappeared since the sixties, and most whites are color blind. . . . Whites seem to be collectively shouting, 'We have a black president, so we are finally beyond race.'"[3] Declaring Obama's election to be the advent of a post-racial society was

[1] Media Matters Staff, "Dobbs Calls on Listeners to Rise Above 'Partisan and Racial Element That Dominates Politics,'" *Media Matters for America*, November 12, 2009, online video.

[2] Rachel Weiner, "Chris Matthews on Obama: 'I forgot he was black for an hour,'" *The Washington Post* online, January 28, 2010.

[3] Eduardo Bonilla-Silva, *Racism without Racists: Color-Blind Racism and the Persistence of Racial Inequality in America,* 4th ed. (Lanham, MD: Rowman and Littlefield, 2014), 25.

both false optimism and a denial of the problem of race. It not only proved to be false but performed a rebranding of the insidious myth of color-blind racism.

White Americans were living in denial, desperately hoping that the issue of racism had simply gone away. Unfortunately, few organizations or institutions were more susceptible to this false hope than the church, which clung to the myth of a post-racial color-blind society and fell victim to what Bonilla-Silva defines as the "sweet enchantment" of color-blind racism.[4] Commentators frequently quote Dr. Martin Luther King Jr.'s observation that the most segregated hour of Christian America is eleven o'clock on Sunday morning.

In an unprecedented nationwide survey sociologists Michael O. Emerson and Christian Smith found that the cause of division in American churches is the color-blind racism of White Christians. When they probed the grassroots of White Christian America, they found that despite recent efforts by some Christian leaders to address the problem of racial discrimination, White evangelicals are preserving America's racial chasm. In fact, they discovered that most White evangelicals do not believe there is any systematic discrimination against Blacks. Emerson and Smith contend that it is not active racism that prevents White evangelicals from recognizing ongoing problems in American society; rather, the movement's emphasis on individualism, free will, and personal relationships with God obscures the pervasive injustice that perpetuates racial inequality. The subjects told the researchers they believe that most racial problems can be solved by repentance and the conversion of the sinful individuals, a naive and deluded view.

Emerson and Smith determined that despite some positive trends and the best intentions of White evangelical leaders, true racial healing remains far off:

> We stand at a divide. White evangelicals' cultural tools and racial isolation direct them to see the world individualistically and as a series of discrete incidents. They also direct them to desire a color-blind society. Black evangelicals tend to see the racial world very

---

[4] Eduardo Bonilla-Silva and David Dietrich, "The Sweet Enchantment of Color-Blind Racism in Obamerica," *The Annals of the American Academy of Political and Social Science* 634, no. 1 (March 2011): 190–206.

differently. Ironically, evangelicalism's cultural tools lead people in different social and geographical realities to assess the race problem in divergent and nonreconciliatory ways. This large gulf in understanding is perhaps part of the race problem's core, and most certainly contributes to the entrenchment of the racialized society.[5]

Emerson and Smith's survey of evangelical churchgoers was revolutionary because it revealed that eleven o'clock on Sunday remains the most segregated hour due in large part to the color-blind racial attitudes of White American Christians. *Color-blind racism* is a term developed by sociologist Eduardo Bonilla-Silva to label an ideology that "explains contemporary racial inequality as the outcome of nonracial dynamics . . . [where] whites rationalize minorities' contemporary status as the product of market dynamics, naturally occurring phenomena, and blacks' imputed cultural limitations."[6] However, church segregation is not confined to White evangelical congregations; it also influences White mainline denominations and the larger church in America.

In *The Color of Compromise,* Jemar Tisby argues that the American church has been and remains complicit in all forms of racism.[7] However, many White-dominant congregations are reluctant to accept their role in the creation, development, and implementation of White supremacy in America. White congregations continue to perpetuate a White supremacist ideology by simply refusing to acknowledge their complicity in racism or by operating from a naive and dangerous color-blind racist perspective. Meanwhile Black communities in America continue to be affected by policies laden with White ideology. Color-blind racism often masks White racial identity and prevents White congregations from identifying their own Whiteness, thereby disabling any understanding of the complex realities of systematic racism or the way it continues to permeate the church and the other institutions of American society.

Over the past twenty years I have served as senior minister of three different churches in the Southern United States. All these churches

---

[5] Michael O. Emerson and Christian Smith, *Divided by Faith: Evangelical Religion and the Problem of Race in America* (New York: Oxford University Press, 2000), 91.

[6] Bonilla-Silva, *Racism without Racists,* 2.

[7] Jemar Tisby, *The Color of Compromise: The Truth about the American Church's Complicity in Racism* (Grand Rapids, MI: Zondervan, 2019).

have been White-dominant congregations, and in every context, the concept of racism has been a frequent topic of conversation as well as a critical factor affecting our ministry. In 2009, my wife and I entered a transracial adoption process and welcomed a Black daughter into our family. Becoming the father of a Black daughter radically changed my personal experience of race and my professional engagement with racial identity as a minister. In addition, it altered the understanding I had of my own racial identity and increasingly intensified my conversations about race as a leader in church, as well as my engagement on issues of racial justice in the wider community.

While I was experiencing my racial awakening, America had its own awakening to the continued impact of White supremacy and racial injustice. The same year my daughter was born, Michelle Alexander published *The New Jim Crow: Mass Incarceration in the Age of Colorblindness.* Between 2009 and 2015, videos of the police killing Black citizens like Oscar Grant, Trayvon Martin, Sandra Bland, Eric Garner, Michael Brown, Philando Castile, Alton Sterling, Tamir Rice, Freddie Gray, and many others horrified the nation and gave birth to the Black Lives Matter movement.[8] Then, on June 17, 2015, a White supremacist killed the pastor and eight members of the historically Black Mother Emanuel AME Church in Charleston, South Carolina. This heinous act sparked a nationwide debate about the impact of White supremacy that evolved into strong opposition to the persistence of the symbolic vestiges of slavery, such as Confederate flags and monuments throughout the South.

During this violent and tumultuous time in our nation, I was leading conversations about race as a pastor in the White-dominant congregations I served. In 2015, I accepted the call to become the sixth senior minister of a large historic and influential progressive Baptist church in Charlotte, North Carolina. Even though the church was predominantly White in membership, the congregation had a reputation as a staunch proponent of racial justice whose members were trailblazers in the civil

---

[8] Black Lives Matter was founded in 2013 by three radical Black organizers—Alicia Garza, Patrisse Cullors, and Opal Tometi—as a Black-centered political will-building and movement-building project called #BlackLivesMatter in response to the acquittal of Trayvon Martin's murderer, George Zimmerman. Today the Black Lives Matter Global Network is a chapter-based, member-led organization whose mission is to build local power and to intervene in violence inflicted on Black communities by the state and vigilantes.

rights movement, challenged the White supremacy of Jim Crow, and even championed forced busing to integrate the city's public schools. However, the church's reality was not always consistent with its reputation. Most of the church's positions and efforts on racial justice had been initiated by its clergy. Many members participated in these efforts and held similar positions, but other members remained free to maintain their own racist views. Therefore, the congregation was rarely forced to confront its own racial ideas or wrestle with its own racial identity. Further, during the long interim period between pastors, the church had become complacent, and its stamina for conversations about race and the work of racial justice had atrophied in the years leading up to my arrival. Many members were content to rest on their storied history and progressive reputation, imagining that the work of racial justice was something the church had already completed.

Recognizing these challenges as an opportunity for growth, one of our associate ministers, Rev. Chrissy Williamson, and I began developing a year-long faith formation program called "Awakening to Racial Injustice" that would include monthly events to help reeducate the congregation on racial justice for the twenty-first century. In addition to planning the church's formation journey, Rev. Williamson and I began preparing ourselves for the work ahead by attending a racial-justice training led by the Racial Equity Institute.[9] The training was transformative. However, the experience gained even more power and urgency because an African American man named Keith Lamont Scott was fatally shot by the Charlotte city police the same day we completed the training—and the morning before the kickoff of our Awakening to Racial Injustice series. In the following weeks civic leaders refused to release the video of the shooting, protests erupted in the streets, an uprising of activism took place, the city shut down, and the National Guard was be called in to protect buildings and property. None of our training had prepared us for this crisis and how it would affect the church.

The crisis in our city increased the interest in our Awakening to Racial Injustice series and elicited a desire for more serious conversations about

---

[9] The Racial Equity Institute is an alliance of trainers, organizers, and institutional leaders who have devoted themselves to the work of creating racially equitable organizations and systems by helping individuals and organizations develop tools to challenge patterns of power and grow equity.

race in our church and around the city. However, despite the passion and seriousness with which White people pursued these conversations, they were impeded by fundamental issues such as color-blind racism that went unacknowledged by the participants.

According to Bonilla-Silva, color-blind racism has become the dominant racial ideology in America, and it serves to reproduce racial inequality through subtle, institutional, and supposedly nonracial practices that oppress Black people and other minorities. Color-blind racism makes conversations about race in White-dominant congregations extremely difficult. As Bonilla-Silva explains, "Color-blind racism forms an impregnable yet elastic ideological wall that barricades Whites off from America's racial reality . . . because it provides them a safe (color-blind) way to state racial views without appearing to be irrational or rabidly racist folks."[10] Practically, color-blind racism is evident in White individuals who say things like "I don't see color" or "We live in a post-racial society" or "We've made a lot of progress on the issue of race."

On the heels of the uprising over the police shooting of Keith Lamont Scott, in the middle of a year of racial awakening for the city and the church, Donald J. Trump was elected president of the United States of America. Trump ran an openly White-supremacist campaign, and his election presented a crisis of conscience for our progressive White-dominant congregation, which came to a head at an event that took place five days after the election. Months earlier I had invited Dr. William J. Barber—former president of the NAACP, prominent civil rights leader, and founder of the Moral Monday movement—to lead a revival and preach a "National Sermon on Race" at our church on the Sunday after the election.[11] Nearly one thousand people showed up to the service looking for some sense of meaning and hope, but afterward the church erupted.

Dr. Barber preached for an hour and a half, and the service lasted nearly three hours. In his sermon Barber attacked the color-blind racism of Americans that led to Trump's election. He quoted directly from Eduardo Bonilla-Silva's *Racism without Racists* and narrated the long

---

[10] Bonilla-Silva, *Racism without Racists,* 234.

[11] William J. Barber II, "Resiliency, Revival, and Redemption after Rejection," sermon, Myers Park Baptist Church, Charlotte, North Carolina, November 13, 2016.

lineage of White supremacy in American history. He reminded listeners that President Woodrow Wilson had hosted a viewing of the KKK propaganda film *Birth of a Nation* at the White House, and Dr. Barber challenged racial disparities in education, healthcare, housing, and financial well-being. Barber explicitly condemned Trump's campaign as racist, misogynist, xenophobic, and un-Christian. He portrayed the American people as Israel in Samuel 8, longing for a king to be like the other nations. Then he compared Barack Obama to the prophet Samuel and Donald Trump to King Saul. Afterward he invited me forward to the center of the chancel, anointed me with oil for the work of resistance, and then asked me to help him invite all the other ministers first and then anyone else to come forward to be anointed as well.

Dr. Barber's sermon elicited a wide range of strong reactions, including White fragility, White guilt, and vehement White rage that surprised many leaders of Myers Park Baptist who imagined the church had dealt with race many years ago. At a regularly scheduled deacons meeting the day after Dr. Barber's sermon, church leaders denounced his message as a partisan political speech that was not appropriate for our church. A handful of deacons suggested the church should publicly forbid Dr. Barber from ever preaching there again. Many were upset about the way Dr. Barber had talked about President Trump, presumably because some of them had just voted for him five days prior to the service. I knew the deacons were going to need to have a serious in-depth conversation about why Dr. Barber's sermon caused such a negative reaction in a church that had a long history of working for racial justice.

In preparation for leading the deacons through this conversation, I remembered that we had a guest preacher back in October who had said in his sermon that Trump was "a narcissistic sociopath who wants to die alone in his own arms." The guest preacher's words about Trump were far more inflammatory than Dr. Barber's, but only one person contacted me after that sermon. The reaction to the two sermons was wildly divergent, and I believed the key difference was the race of the person who delivered the message: the guest preacher was a White professor and Dr. William Barber is a Black civil rights leader. Before the next deacons meeting I sent copies of both sermons to all the deacons and asked them to study them in preparation for discussion. At the meeting I began by reminding the deacons of our church's longstanding commitment to the concept of a free pulpit, which originated as a component of the concept of religious freedom and the liberty of conscience with early Baptist pioneers John Smyth and Thomas Helwys. In establishing this concept at Myers Park Baptist, the church's first senior minister said: "A free pulpit is the very essence of religious and political democracy; . . . a free pulpit means a stimulating ministry; a free pulpit means encouragement to break new trails in thought and action; a free pulpit is a great bulwark against tyranny."[12] Drawing on the historic Baptist principle and the church's own conception of the free pulpit, I facilitated a discussion about the two sermons, admitting that I found some faults in both, and I asked the deacons to explain why they thought people reacted so differently to the two sermons. Some said it was the timing around the election, and some said Barber's sermon was more overtly partisan, but many said they simply did not know.

Finally, one brave deacon stood up and said, "Isn't it obvious? One is White and the other is Black—that's what made the difference here." His remark turned the entire conversation as the deacons had to reflect on the possibility that their own implicit racism may have been what caused the divergent reaction to the two sermons. At that point one of the oldest and wisest deacons stood up and reaffirmed the concept of the free pulpit and recounted the congregation's history of empowering soul liberty and the freedom of conscience in former senior ministers, as well as the story of Dr. Owens's support of the lesbian feminist theologian and Episcopal priest the Rev. Dr. Carter Heyward, who was invited to preach at Myers Park Baptist in the late seventies. The deacon then noted that the free pulpit existed as an idea in the mind of some members but had never been formally written as a statement for the congregation, so he proposed a team of deacons should write a formal statement reaffirming the church's belief in the freedom of the pulpit. This turned the meeting around and led the deacons to establish a taskforce charged with drafting of a formal statement on the free pulpit, which was approved by the congregation one year later.

The experiences I had leading the congregation during this time of racial reawakening led directly to the development of this spiritual formation and anti-racism training course. As the new senior minister of

---

[12] Marion Ellis, *By a Dream Possessed: Myers Park Baptist Church* (Charlotte, NC: Myers Park Baptist Church, 1997). See also Myers Park Baptist's "Statement Affirming the Free Pulpit and Pew," approved December 11, 2017.

this historic liberal congregation that had been at the forefront of civil rights and the battle for desegregation in Charlotte, I saw that many issues surrounding race had yet to be identified. Most significant, we were suffering from blindness to our own Whiteness, including the way it undergirds and influences our faith as followers of Jesus. We needed a new conversation about race and racism. However, I thought it was important for this conversation not to be about racism in general, a sociological and historical phenomenon. Rather it should help members of a White-dominant church identify their own racial history and wrestle with what it means to be White. Therefore, I developed an intentional spiritual journey of anti-racism to aid people racialized as White to identify their Whiteness.

This course seeks to identify the persistent habits of Whiteness that are embedded in the practice of Christianity in White-dominant congregations. As Eduardo Bonilla-Silva claims:

> High levels of social and spatial segregation and isolation from minorities creates what I label as a "white habitus," a racialized, uninterrupted socialization process that conditions and creates whites' racial taste, perceptions, feelings, and emotions and their views on racial matters. . . . One of the central consequences of the white habitus is that it promotes a sense of group belonging (a white culture of solidarity) and negative views about nonwhites.[13]

Tragically, White individuals and churches are often blissfully unaware of this white habitus and how it shapes their own identities, languages, spaces, spiritual practices, and congregational life, as well as their social and ethical relations with the community at large.

According to Mary McClintock Fulkerson and Marcia Mount Shoop, "Without intentional work by white faith communities to explore how we embody privilege and racialized biases in the habits of our faith, the transformative possibilities will be diminished and trivialized."[14] In order to explore White habits, Fulkerson and Shoop recommend "new postures for white churches [that] involve looking inward at the congregation

---

[13] Bonilla-Silva, *Racism without Racists,* 151.

[14] Mary McClintock Fulkerson and Marcia W. Mount Shoop, *A Body Broken, A Body Betrayed: Race, Memory, and Eucharist in White-Dominant Churches* (Eugene, OR: Cascade, 2015), 18.

itself instead of waiting for people of color to make real work on race possible."[15] They claim that "a new gesture might be to take an open stance toward exploring what it means to be white in American culture. These same gestures can be extended into congregations."[16] The concept of introducing "new postures" and "new gestures" that explore and identify Whiteness in the lives of individuals, the church community, and the culture holds tremendous promise.

Confronting Whiteness is intended as a new posture or gesture for the people of faith and the church. Participants will be exposed to personal postures and gestures embedded in the spiritual-formation process, such as the practices of contemplation and confession. These spiritual practices will help participants engage in and develop alternative habits that confront the White habitus and expose and undermine the power of Whiteness.

This course was born from my own personal spiritual journey of confronting Whiteness as a person, pastor, and father. During the journey I participated in the two-year Academy for Spiritual Formation through The Upper Room and a doctor of ministry program with St. Paul's School of Theology in Kansas City. All these experiences shaped this course, which has now been experienced by more than three hundred people. I am excited and prayerful for you to begin *Confronting Whiteness.*

---

[15] Fulkerson and Shoop, 19.
[16] Fulkerson and Shoop, 19.

Acknowledgments and Permissions

Confronting Whiteness was born out of my collective experiences as a father, friend, and pastor. I'm grateful for my daughter Lucy Joy whose life and future animate my passion for the work of racial justice. I must also express my gratitude to Myers Park Baptist Church for providing the soil in which this work could be planted and cultivated, and for the "Magnificent Eleven" who were the original participants in the "What Does It Mean to Be White?" qualitative research study that became my doctoral thesis, "Identifying Whiteness: Discerning Race through Spiritual Practice in the White Dominant Church." I want to thank my D.Min advisers, Dr. James Brandt and Dr. Sherry McGlaughlin, who guided me in the development and writing of my project. I'd also like to thank my good friends Greg and Helms Jarrell of QC Family, my collaborators and co-conspirators. They partnered with me to pilot this course for the Charlotte community in 2020 immediately after the murder of George Floyd and have talked through many aspects of this work over pints of beer. I want to thank the Upper Room staff, the Academy for Spiritual Formation, and especially Academy #39 for encouraging me to take a journey of deep soul work. I offer my gratitude for Dr. Lucretia Berry and Dr. Gerardo Martí for being incredible colleagues and conversation partners along the way. I want to thank every person who participated in the "What Does It Mean to Be White?" version of this course before it was published, especially Rev. Carrie Veal and all the facilitators who have been selflessly offering their time and talents to help White people be accountable and take responsibility for their Whiteness. I'd like to thank Mother and Father for being my first anti-racist teachers and my biggest cheerleaders, and my brother for always supporting me no matter what I was getting myself into. Finally, I'd like to thank my wife, Andi, for her countless words of affirmation, encouragement, and love.

PERMISSIONS

"Representing Whiteness in the Black Imagination" by bell hooks is republished with permission of Taylor & Francis Group LLC from Cultural Studies, eds. Lawrence Grossberg, Cary Nelson, and Paula A. Treichler, New York: Routledge, 1992; permission conveyed through Copyright Clearance Center, Inc.

Excerpts from "Whiteness as Property" by Cheryl I. Harris are republished with permission of Harvard Law Review Publishing Association from *Harvard Law Review* 106, no. 8 (June 1993); permission conveyed through Copyright Clearance Center, Inc.

Excerpts from *When the Word Is Given . . . : A Report on Elijah Muhammad, Malcolm X, and the Black Muslim World* by Louis E. Lomax, copyright © 1963 by Louis E. Lomax. Used by permission of Signet, an imprint of Penguin Publishing Group, a division of Penguin Random House LLC. All rights reserved.

"What Is Whiteness" by Nell Irvin Painter is reprinted from *The New York Times.* © 2015 The New York Times Company. All rights reserved. Used under license.

"Can White People Be Saved? Reflections on the Relationship of Missions and Whiteness" and "To Be a Christian Intellectual" by Willie James Jennings are reprinted by permission of the author.

"The First White President [originally published in *The Atlantic*, October 2017]" from *We Were Eight Years in Power: An American Tragedy* by Ta-Nehisi Coates, copyright © 2017 by BCP Literary, Inc. Used by permission of One World, an imprint of Random House, a division of Penguin Random House LLC. All rights reserved.

"What Does Jesus Have to Do with Whiteness" by Kelly Brown Douglas is reprinted by permission of the author. The Very Rev. Dr. Kelly Brown Douglas is the interim president of Episcopal Divinity School.

"Making America White Again" by Toni Morrison. Copyright © 2016 by Toni Morrison. Reprinted by permission of ICM Partners.

Statement on Capitalization and Language

Confronting Whiteness follows the 17th edition of *The Chicago Manual of Style,* section 8.38, by capitalizing the words *Black* and *Blackness* as well as *White* and *Whiteness.* This practice of capitalization may be unfamiliar to some readers or strike them as odd upon first reading. However, the purpose of capitalizing racial designations is to convey that they are not words that describe natural, innate, or biological realities but are words that describe social constructions of collective identity. Capitalizing racial designations is not intended to elevate, center, or essentialize Whiteness or Blackness but to situate these terms historically while also highlighting the artificiality of race. Traditionally, we have downgraded Black racial identity and Blackness while hiding White racial identity and Whiteness by disguising all racial designations as nouns or adjectives, treating Blackness negatively and Whiteness as if it were normative, invisible, or nonexistent. Capitalizing *White* and *Whiteness* brings the culturally dominant, socially constructed racial ideology out of the shadows and into the light, offering us the opportunity not only to see it and name it but to take responsibility for it as well. Please note that quotations and excerpts maintain their original capitalization.

Confronting Whiteness contains language that may be violent, disturbing, offensive, triggering, or re-traumatizing to some readers. We have intentionally stayed true to the original language the authors, intellectuals, and creatives used in the readings and films of this curriculum to respect the author's intent and, pedagogically, to create a more realistic and profound experience for the participants. Many of the readings and films contain gender-exclusive language and terms previously used for Black people such as *Negro* or *Colored,* as well as racial epithets that we would not consider acceptable today. In addition, some of the authors and filmmakers use explicit language, swear words, slang, and other words and phrases that may be potentially offensive and disturbing. We encourage you to proceed with caution, give yourself grace and time to process the material, and take breaks from the course as needed for your own self-care and development.

For more information on the capitalization of racial designations, see these articles:

Kwame Anthony Appiah, "The Case for Capitalizing the *B* in Black," *The Atlantic*, June 18, 2020.

Editors, "From black and white to Black and White," *The Christian Century*, September 23, 2020.

Kristen Mack and John Palfrey, "Capitalizing Black and White: Grammatical Justice and Equity," *The MacArthur Foundation* blog, August 26, 2020.

University of Chicago Press Editorial Staff, "Black and White: A Matter of Capitalization," *CMOS Shop Talk* blog, June 22, 2020.

1

Orientation for the Journey

Work out your own salvation with fear and trembling; for it is God who is at work in you, enabling you both to will and to work for his good pleasure.

—Philippians 2:12–13

Present your bodies as a living sacrifice, holy and acceptable to God, which is your spiritual worship. Do not be conformed to this world, but be transformed by the renewing of your minds.

—Romans 12:1–2

White America remains unable to believe that black America's grievances are real; they are unable to believe this because they cannot face what this fact says about themselves and their country.

—James Baldwin, *No Name in the Street*

PREPARATION FOR SESSION 1

White-dominant congregations in America struggle to talk about race and racism. While several models have been created for facilitating conversations about race in a congregational context, few are specifically designed to help White participants identify and confront their own Whiteness. In addition, few models engage participants in small groups with the goal of reflecting spiritually and theologically on how

Whiteness affects their stories, their faith, their lives, their neighbors, and the world around them. In working with congregations, Christian schools, and denominations, I have found that attending to Whiteness in a spiritual context illuminates why White-dominant congregations and organizations have difficulty talking about race. This focus helps deepen the self-awareness of Whites about our own race and racism, strengthen our capacity for healthy participation in racial dialogue, and offer White-dominant congregations new tools for identifying Whiteness in their own contexts and talking about the problem of racism.

Confronting Whiteness is a journey of spiritual formation designed for a predominantly White congregation. It is intended to offer clergy and lay leaders the opportunity to identify and overcome the pervasive ideology of color-blind racism. The objectives of the course are for participants to grow in understanding their own White racial identity, to shift the way they engage in conversations about race to include an account of Whiteness, and ultimately to transform the way they live and work in church and society. To achieve these objectives the course combines specific practices of spiritual formation with an anti-racist curriculum.

In the conclusion of *Racism without Racists,* Eduardo Bonilla-Silva suggests that the work for White people is to challenge "color-blind nonsense" by nurturing a large cohort of anti-racist Whites who confess their collective denial of the true nature of race relations; undressing White claims of color blindness before a huge mirror; and engaging in a struggle to end the habits, practices, and ideology that maintain White supremacy.[1] One recommendation that Bonilla-Silva has for helping White people overcome color-blind racism is "to challenge whiteness wherever it exists; regardless of the social organization in which whiteness manifests itself (universities, corporations, schools, neighborhoods, *churches*), those committed to racial equality must develop a personal practice to challenge it."[2]

One of the most transformative elements in my own spiritual and theological development toward identifying my own White racial identity came from sitting at the feet of Black intellectuals, scholars, writers, and poets who describe and define Whiteness. After years of engagement with the Black intellectual and artistic tradition, I found

---

[1] Eduardo Bonilla-Silva, *Racism without Racists: Color-Blind Racism and the Persistence of Racial Inequality in America,* 4th ed. (Lanham, MD: Rowman and Littlefield, 2016), 307.

[2] Bonilla-Silva, 308, emphasis added.

inspiration in David Roediger's book *Black on White: Black Writers on What It Means to Be White* and began developing a curriculum of Black authors, intellectuals, and creatives who discuss the beliefs, practices, and habits of Whiteness.[3] This curriculum was designed to be a mirror for White people to see the hidden wound of Whiteness or an "X-ray" to show White people the deepest parts of themselves through the eyes of people of color. The goal is to expose the concept of Whiteness and challenge our color-blind racist ideology.

The first session is an introduction to the course and a sharing of racial autobiographies. The second session is about "The Fire Next Time" by James Baldwin. All succeeding sessions have readings and viewings from Black authors and filmmakers centered around a particular thematic definition of Whiteness. The six themes are "Whiteness as Power," "Whiteness as Evil," "Whiteness as Mythology," "Whiteness as Terror," "Whiteness as Principality," and "Whiteness as Nationalism." The authors and themes selected do not offer a comprehensive definition of Whiteness—no selection could—but they provide organization and continuity to the overall spiritual journey and will aid the participants in finding meaning and connections among the readings in the curriculum.

All the authors and filmmakers are Black, but I intentionally chose selections from a diverse group of creatives. Some identify as male, and others as female; some are Christian theologians, and others are from different religious traditions or are nonreligious. There is a variety of different styles of writing, such as law review articles, academic essays, sermons, speeches, government reports, theological treatises, op-eds, poetry, and longform journalism. The films include documentaries, historical fiction, autobiography, fantasy, and psychological thrillers. The films and readings also represent different times and cultural sensibilities, covering a range of more than one hundred years of American history.

These essays and films were selected to help White people see themselves through the eyes of Black people, to identify Whiteness, and to understand their participation in that culture. To that end this curriculum amplifies the words and creativity of Black leaders, intellectuals, and artists who have offered unique insights throughout history about the nature of Whiteness. As White people, learning to understand Whiteness is where the journey of becoming anti-racist begins. This curriculum

---

[3] David Roediger, *Black on White: Black Writers on What It Means to Be White* (New York: Schocken, 1998).

requires a significant commitment of time and effort; however, Whiteness is an invisible bleeding wound on our backs, and we need help to see it—we need friends, guides, mirrors, and possibly even a metaphorical X-ray machine. Dr. King once wrote: "For too long the depth of racism in American life has been underestimated. The surgery to extract it is necessarily complex and detailed. As a beginning it is important to X-ray our history and reveal the full extent of the disease."[4]

Ultimately, the goal is to develop the emotional and spiritual stamina to gaze into the mirror longer and longer without needing to look away and succumb to denial or abdication. Through the exercise of gazing into the mirror or turning on the X-ray machine, this course has the potential to change the way the participants see the world and stimulate a radical conversion.

BIOGRAPHICAL SKETCHES OF OUR TEACHERS, MIRROR HOLDERS, AND X-RAY TECHNICIANS

James Baldwin (1924–87) was one of the greatest writers of the twentieth century. Baldwin wrote three plays, six novels, nine collections of essays, and many poems. He grew up in Harlem with his mother and his stepfather, who was a Baptist preacher. As a teenager Baldwin followed in his stepfather's footsteps by becoming a preacher himself; however, by the age of seventeen he became disillusioned with the church for reinforcing the system of American slavery. His novels and essays explore the intricacies of masculinity, sexuality, race, and class with exceptional prose, unflinching honesty, and profound soul-searching responsibility.[5]

Ta-Nehisi Coates (1975–present) is an American journalist and bestselling author who gained wide readership during his time as national correspondent at *The Atlantic,* where his writing focused on cultural, social, and political issues relating to African Americans and White supremacy. He is the author of dozens of comics; three nonfiction books; and the novel *Between the World and Me,* which won the National Book Award for

---

[4] Martin Luther King Jr., *Why We Can't Wait* (New York: Signet Classics, 2000), 146.

[5] The landmark work *Baldwin—Collected Essays*, selected by Toni Morrison (New York: Library of America, 1998), is available in its entirety online.

fiction in 2015, was a finalist for the Pulitzer Prize in 2016, and was ranked seventh on *The Guardian*'s list of the 100 best books of the twenty-first century. His 2014 article "The Case for Reparations" rekindled a national debate about reparations for slavery and led to his testimony before the House Judiciary Committee on June 19, 2019, about H.R. 40, legislation that would create a commission to address the effects of slavery.

Ryan Coogler (1986–present) is an award-winning American screenwriter, director, and producer who has written and directed four feature films, including *Fruitvale Station* (2013) and *Black Panther* (2018). He shares producing credits on four other films, including *Judas and the Black Messiah* (2021). His work is notable for its representation of Black people and themes of Afrofuturism. In 2018, at the age of thirty-two, he was named the runner-up of *Time*'s Person of the Year and included in the annual *Time* 100 list of the most influential people in the world.

Kelly Brown Douglas (1952–present) is an Episcopal priest, womanist American theologian, inaugural dean of the Episcopal Divinity School at Union Theological Seminary, and the canon theologian at the Washington National Cathedral. In 2015 a controversy emerged over two stained-glass windows in the National Cathedral that honored "Stonewall" Jackson and Robert E. Lee. Douglas was part of a taskforce assigned to study the issue and make recommendations on what to do with the windows. After two years of discussions the cathedral chapter voted to remove the windows. Douglas is widely considered one of the leading scholars on womanist theology, racial reconciliation, and sexuality and the Black church. She is the author of numerous articles and five books, including *Stand Your Ground: Black Bodies and the Justice of God* (2015).

W.E.B. Du Bois (1868–1963) was the preeminent academic intellectual of the early twentieth century and scholar of Reconstruction. Originally from Massachusetts, he was the first African American to earn a doctorate from Harvard University. He was a professor of history, sociology, and economics at Atlanta University and one of the founders of the National Association for the Advancement of Colored People (NAACP). Du Bois wrote more than twenty books, including *The Souls of Black Folks* (1903), *John Brown: A Biography* (1909), *Black Reconstruction in America* (1935), and *Darkwater* (1920). Though not personally religious, Du Bois's spiritually inspired generations of intellectuals, artists, and activists.

Ava DuVernay (1972–pessent) is a versatile and award-winning American filmmaker and producer who grew up near Compton, California. She is the director of four documentary series, four documentary films, two television series, three short films, and four full-length features. Her work focuses on the stories of African Americans and their struggle for freedom and justice in the United States. Most notable are *Selma* (2014), *13th* (2016), *When They See Us* (2019), and *Colin in Black & White* (2021).

Cheryl Harris (1952–present) is a lawyer, critical-race theorist, and professor of civil rights and civil liberties at the UCLA School of Law. Harris is widely known for her article "Whiteness as Property," published in the June 1993 edition of the *Harvard Law Review,* which remains one the most important descriptions of the way Whiteness was ensconced in the legal codes of the United States. She is also the mother of American rapper, songwriter, and record producer Earl Sweatshirt.

bell hooks (1952–2021)was an American public intellectual, feminist, author, professor, and social activist from Hopkinsville, Kentucky, who focused her work specifically on the intersection of gender, race, and capitalism. She coined the phrase "imperialist white supremacist capitalist patriarchy" to describe the power structure underlying the global social order, and she was the author of more than thirty books (including five children's books) and many articles. She appeared in more than a dozen films.

Willie James Jennings (1961–present) is an ordained Baptist minister and American theologian who currently serves as associate professor for systematic theology and Africana studies at Yale University. He is the author of numerous articles and three books, including *The Christian Imagination: Theology and the Origins of Race* (2010), which won the American Academy of Religion Award of Excellence in the Study of Religion in 2015 and the Grawemeyer Award in Religion. He is also the author of *After Whiteness: An Education in Belonging* (2020).

Spike Lee (1957–present) is an award-winning American film director, producer, screenwriter, actor, and professor, and the owner of his own production company 40 Acres and a Mule, which has produced more than thirty-five films since 1983. Lee's films examine race relations and colorism in the Black community, urban crime, poverty, and other political issues. Four of Lee's films—*Do the Right Thing* (1983), *Malcolm X* (1992), *4 Little Girls* (1997), and *She's Gotta Have It* (1986)—were selected by the Library of Congress for preservation in the National Film Registry for being culturally, historically, or aesthetically significant.

Toni Morrison (1931–2019), one of the most renowned writers and novelists in American history, helped to expand the range of classic American literature to include works by Black women. She wrote ten works of nonfiction, including *Playing in the Dark: Whiteness in the Literary Imagination* (1992). Morrison also wrote eight children's books and eleven novels, including *Beloved* (1987), which won the Pulitzer Prize in literature in 1988 and was later adapted for cinema. Among the countless awards she received are the Presidential Medal of Freedom, the National Humanities Medal, and the Nobel Prize in Literature.

Nell Irvin Painter (1942–present) is a leading American historian who holds the Edwards Professorship in American History, Emerita, at Princeton University. She is a prolific and award-winning scholar who is most notable for her work in the history of the South in nineteenth-century America. Painter is the author of numerous articles and seven books, including the *New York Times* bestseller *The History of White People* (2010).

Raoul Peck (1953–present) is an award-winning Haitian filmmaker who has produced more than twenty films and six television series since 1987. He served for a brief period as minister of culture in Haiti and is known for using historical and political characters, as well as his own family, to document social issues and events. His artistic philosophy and objectives are to change the way the viewer sees history, and he seeks to provoke his audience rather than simply to entertain them. Some of his most notable work includes *Lumumba: Death of a Prophet* (1990), *I Am Not Your Negro* (2016), and *Exterminate All the Brutes* (2021).

Jordan Peele (1979–present) is an award-winning American actor, director, comedian, and filmmaker from New York City who is known for his work in the genres of horror and comedy. He was a cast member on the Fox television show *Mad TV* and joined forces with Keegan-Michael

Key to create the Comedy Central sketch comedy series *Key & Peele*. He has produced seven movies, including *Get Out* (2017), *BlacKKKlansman* (2018), *Us* (2019), *Candyman* (2021), and *Nope* (2022). Many of his films use the genre of horror and haunting to confront issues of systemic racism.

Roy Wilkins (1901–81) and **Edward W. Brooke III** (1919–2015) were the only two African Americans to serve on the National Advisory Commission on Civil Disorders (the Kerner Commission). Brooke was a native of Washington, DC. He served as an infantry officer in World War II and in 1966 became the first African American elected to the United States Senate, serving the state of Massachusetts. Wilkins was a prominent civil rights leader, cofounder of the Leadership Council of Civil Rights (LCCR), and served as executive director of the National Association for the Advancement of Colored People (NAACP). Wilkins was often referred to later in life as the senior statesman of the civil rights movement and is mentioned in Gil Scott-Heron's famous poem "The Revolution Will Not Be Televised."

Malcolm X (1925–65), a Muslim minister, preacher, prophet, and human rights activist, was a critical leader in the civil rights and Black freedom movements in America. For part of his ministry he was the most famous spokesperson for the Nation of Islam, but he broke with it in 1964. Originally from Omaha, Nebraska, Malcolm X was a formidable advocate for Black freedom and liberation as well as a critic of Martin Luther King Jr. and White liberals. He was assassinated by fellow Black Muslims who were participating in a conspiracy created by the Federal Bureau of Investigation (FBI) and the Nation of Islam. His life and teachings inspired the Black Power movement, the creation of the Black Panther Party, Black Lives Matter, and many organizers and activists throughout American history.

SPIRITUAL PRACTICES FOR THE INNER
AND OUTER WORK OF ANTI-RACISM

We live in a world born from a toxic philosophy of segregation and compartmentalization. This inhuman philosophy divided our humanity, our lives, and our reality into self-contained silos for the purpose of deeper examination. However, in doing so we separated body from soul, head from heart, material from spiritual, physical from metaphysical, political from theological, land from people, creation from humanity. The result is that our understanding of the human persona and our view of reality have been segmented like the diagram of a pig that is used to determine the most prime parts to cut.

This philosophy of segregation and compartmentalization stands in opposition to the wholeness and oneness of our created reality. Humans were not intended to be divided into parts. We cannot understand ourselves or humanity by partitioning off different aspects of the person and then studying the parts. We must work to integrate into a holistic anthropology the parts of the human person and our reality that have been segregated and compartmentalized.

One of the most dangerous bifurcations Christians have made throughout history is separating spirituality from social concerns or religion from politics. This separation does not exist in scripture or the teachings of Jesus, and this false duality makes it incredibly challenging to properly interpret the Gospels. For Jesus, and for the average first-century Jew, the spiritual was always moral, and the moral was always social and political. Spiritual formation is anti-racism, and anti-racism is spiritual formation. Spiritual formation and anti-racism require both deep inner soul work and the outer work of social justice—both are mutually informed by contemplation and action. This course was designed to engage participants in the deep soul work of anti-racism and spiritual formation practices that will inform and empower action in the world.

Six spiritual practices are key components of this course: creating a circle of grace, writing a racial autobiography (journaling), anchoring our bodies in conflict, *lectio divina* (close reading of the articles) and *visio divina* (close viewing of the films), silent meditation (mindfulness), and the daily examen (confession). While this journey was designed for small groups of eight to ten participants, it may also be used as an individual journey. Individuals can engage in all the spiritual practices except the creation of a circle of grace, which requires the presence of other participants. However, offering ourselves grace at the beginning of this journey is critical for ensuring we have the freedom necessary to learn, change, and grow. Therefore, individual participants are encouraged to adapt the grace space guidelines.

Creating a Circle of Grace

The guidelines for creating grace space are adapted from "What LIES between Us: Fostering First Steps toward Racial Healing."[6] They were developed by educator, author, and cofounder of the Brownicity learning community, Lucretia Carter Berry. The guidelines for creating grace space are intended to foster and maintain an atmosphere where healing and growth can occur in a small-group setting. They are as follows:

1. Listen. Hear what is being shared. Be open to hearing perspectives and experiences that are different from yours.

2. Show respect and dignity. Regard participants and their experiences as valuable and worthy of time and attention.

3. Embrace discomfort. It is okay to experience discomfort. The tension you feel now may be creating space for growth.

4. Participate. Fully engage the session activities and your journal. Speak up during meetings, but don't drown out the voices of others.

5. Be free from guilt, shame, and condemnation. Being socialized by race ideology is not a criminal offense.

6. Use "I" not "we." Avoid making statements that imply group representation. Speak for yourself, not "our people" or "my people."

7. Avoid debating. Back-and-forth personal debating indicates that someone is not listening and is counterproductive to a grace space.

8. Keep a confidential table. If someone in your group says something that upsets you, please don't out them in public spaces.

9. Focus on the USA. For the sake of staying on task, limit your scope to the USA's issues.

10.   Respect the process. There is no quick fix. The process consists of many steps and cycles—learning, lamenting, deconstructing, healing, restoring, building.

Writing a Racial Autobiography

The purpose of writing a racial autobiography is to delve into our stories that contain both our deepest wounds and our strongest medicine

---

[6] Lucretia Carter Berry, *What LIES between Us: Fostering First Steps toward Racial Healing*, 2nd ed. (CreateSpace Independent Publishing Platform, February 23, 2017).

for healing. Journaling is a long-held spiritual practice that allows us to engage in critical reflection on the story of our lives, noticing where we have felt the presence of God. Racial autobiographies are a form of journaling that helps us to cultivate deep self-awareness about our own racial identity. Writing a racial autobiography helps us to remember the roles race has played throughout our lives, discover our racial formation, and grow in our understanding and awareness of our racial identity—specifically the ways that Whiteness has affected our lives and our world.

Begin writing a personal racial history of your life, an autobiography of the development of your individual racial identity. This should include your early formative experiences of race—perceptions and perspectives on race you inherited from your family of origin and childhood, as well as experiences with race in school, extracurricular activities, work, and church. Describe the emergence of your self-awareness of your own race. The goal is not to be comprehensive but to create a basic timeline using short stories and vignettes as snapshots of your most memorable experiences and discoveries of race at different points throughout your life.

Writing your racial autobiography is one of the most important and practical tools for engaging in the deep inner work of confronting Whiteness. Consider your racial autobiography a work in progress. The most powerful racial autobiographies are living spiritual documents to which we add stories during our journey together and long after the course is completed. You will be invited to share parts of your racial autobiography in the first and last sessions of the course, but you are also encouraged to allow your stories to inform your responses to the curriculum of readings and cinema in each session. Additionally, stories from your racial autobiography can function as a confession or acknowledgment of Whiteness at the end of each session.

Anchoring Our Bodies in Conflict

The racialized trauma and moral injury of Whiteness, or what Resmaa Menakem calls "White-body supremacy," resides in our bodies.[7] Racial stress is not simply an emotional reaction to the work of anti-racism; it is

---

[7] Resmaa Menakem, *My Grandmother's Hands: Racialized Trauma and the Pathway to Mending Our Hearts and Bodies* (Las Vegas, NV: Central Recovery Press, 2017), xiii.

a visceral response. Therefore, Menakem suggests we need to prepare our bodies for the *Confronting Whiteness* program or any anti-racism journey by anchoring ourselves in the present in our bodies. In *My Grandmother's Hands* Menakem provides five anchors for when one senses a conflict building or feels growing discomfort. I recommend engaging with these anchors before reading or watching the assignments in the curriculum, as well as before every grace-space session:

- Anchor 1: Soothe yourself to quiet your mind, calm your heart, and settle your body.
- Anchor 2: Simply notice the sensations, vibrations, and emotions in your body instead of reacting to them.
- Anchor 3: Accept the discomfort—and notice when it changes—instead of trying to flee from it.
- Anchor 4: Stay present and in your body as you move through the unfolding experience, with all its ambiguity and uncertainty, and respond from the best parts of yourself.
- Anchor 5: Safely discharge any energy that remains.[8]

Lectio Divina *and* Visio Divina

"Divine reading" and "divine viewing," as the above terms are translated from Latin, are often reserved for sacred texts like the Bible or and sacred art like *The Lord's Supper*. However, the practice simply involves giving a text or piece of art a close, slow, prayerful, sometimes repetitive, and contemplative reading or viewing. It can be applied to any text or artistic work. In 2015 some Harvard Divinity School students created a very popular podcast where they use the tools of *lectio divina* to read the *Harry Potter* novels as sacred texts.[9]

One person's secular art is another person's sacred art; one person's sacred text is another person's secular text. The determination of what is sacred is subjective. Are the words of Martin Luther King Jr. or the paintings of Jean-Michel Basquiat sacred? You are encouraged to practice *lectio divina* and *visio divina* with the curriculum of readings and films. The sacred personal stories from the authors and creators, as well as the

---

[8] Menakem, 167–68.

[9] Vanessa Zoltan, Casper ter Kuile, and Matthew Potts, "Our Story," *Harry Potter and the Sacred Text* website.

frequent engagement with the idea of God and religion, make these works the perfect subject matter to meditate on deeply and give a close, slow, prayerful, and contemplative reading or viewing.

Silent Meditation

The inclusion of silent meditation in *Confronting Whiteness* arises from my work in the two-year Academy of Spiritual Formation, where I participated in regular periods of silent meditation and maintained silence for twelve hours a day. These experiences helped me understand the transformative power of silence as a spiritual practice and see silence as a necessary part of conversations about stressful topics like race and Whiteness. Identifying Whiteness is intellectual, emotional, and spiritual labor. Therefore, I believe all aspects of a person (heart, mind, body, and soul) must be addressed during the small-group process. The intellectual aspect will primarily be met through engagement with an extensive course curriculum. The emotional and spiritual aspects will primarily be engaged through the practice of silence and confession. However, every element of the process is intended to engage the whole person of each participant. Specifically, spiritual practices like writing a racial autobiography and silent meditation engage the soul as well as the heart and body, while the readings and the movies engage the mind, heart, and soul. The entire process is intended to be deep, embodied soul work.

The purpose of engaging in silence at the beginning and throughout each session is to reduce the tension and alleviate the stress caused by reading painful and agitating descriptions of Whiteness. In addition, silent meditation offers us the time to decompress, breathe, relax, and prepare for deep listening to our own hearts and to one another. One of the reasons the practice of silence can increase our ability to participate in healthy racial dialogue and create opportunities for White people to identify our own Whiteness is that silence can deepen our self-awareness. In "Whiteness on the Couch," clinical psychologist Natasha Stovall defines Whiteness as a psychopathology and argues that meditation and mindfulness practices may be a potential avenue for White people to become more aware of their racial identity and attitudes.[10]

---

[10] Natasha Stovall, "Whiteness on the Couch," *Longreads* online (August 2019).

For Stovall, interventions like meditation and mindfulness could have the kind of impact and effectiveness that cognitive-behavioral therapy has on racial psychology. Stovall writes, "Meditation and mindfulness practices are the keys to the realm of greater awareness, and methods like legal scholar Rhonda Magee's techniques for using meditation to help law students dismantle their racial bias have shown promising results . . . [because] meditation-based practices work on the interaction of thoughts, feelings and behavior."[11] Rhonda V. Magee, a professor of law at the University of San Francisco, was trained in mindfulness-based stress reduction and has pioneered the development of contemplative pedagogy, mindfulness education for social justice and transformation, and the use of meditation practices for overcoming racial bias. Magee claims that psychologists have noted that a major dimension of the experience of Whiteness is its transparency or invisibility to those sharing the experience—Whiteness is difficult to see. Therefore, Magee suggests that the work of examining the role and implications of race for someone who has been racialized as White is particularly challenging and that a great deal of compassion and patience is required to walk with people racialized as White as they learn to see Whiteness. Magee notes that most White people too often take comfort in the notion of color blindness, hoping that ignoring racial difference as much as possible and leaving history aside will enable them to overcome racism without having to do much work.[12]

Magee has found that mindfulness practices like silent meditation are most effective at helping White people to examine racism, Whiteness, and the implications of racial identity on our lives and the world:

> By helping us to wake up to the illusory nature of race, and to the attachments and aversions that fuel racism, mindfulness meditation and the allied disciplines may help us with the aspects of the project of minimizing our reliance on race and racial categorizations that present themselves in our own lives . . . in ways that reflect the aspirations to justice behind the intention of "never again,"

---

[11] Stovall.

[12] Rhonda V. Magee, "Teaching Mindfulness with Mindfulness of Race and Other Forms of Diversity," in *Resources for Teaching Mindfulness: An International Handbook,* ed. Donald McCown, Diane Reibel, and Mark S. Micozzi (Cham, Switzerland: Springer, 2016).

and demonstrate the application of mindfulness as a means of dismantling race and racism.[13]

In *The Inner Work of Racial Justice: Healing Ourselves and Transforming Our Communities through Mindfulness,* Magee expands this idea by demonstrating how mindfulness enables those of us racialized as White to develop the inner resources to accept what we cannot change long enough to approach the things we might be able to change. Magee believes that meditation techniques help White people move from simply accepting the reality of racism to exploring ways they learn more about, confront, and disrupt it. Through mindfulness,

> we move from simply witnessing bias to figuring out how to be a resource for those fighting to end racism. We move from avoiding our sadness or burying it with distractions and addictive substances, to allowing the pain to guide us toward more emotionally intelligent, healthier, and generative relationships with ourselves and others. Thus mindfulness and compassion practices help us to identify and take wise, ethical action in the world, putting us on the path to our own freedom and toward the greater liberation of others.[14]

Magee's groundbreaking research on using meditation and mindfulness practices to help people racialized as White identify their Whiteness directly informed the inclusion of the practice of silent meditation in every session of *Confronting Whiteness.*

Confession

The final spiritual practice is confession and absolution, which has long been an important spiritual practice for Abrahamic religious traditions. In *Confronting Whiteness* the practice of confession complements the racial autobiography. At the end of each session you will be invited to

---

[13] Rhonda V. Magee, "Taking and Making Refuge in Racial [Whiteness] Awareness in Racial Justice Work," in *Buddhism and Whiteness: Critical Reflections*, ed. George Yancy and Emily McRae (Lanham, MD: Lexington Books, 2019).

[14] Rhonda V. Magee, *The Inner Work of Racial Justice: Healing Ourselves and Transforming Our Communities through Mindfulness* (New York: Tarcher Perigee, 2019), 329.

share stories or vignettes from your racial autobiography or experiences from daily life as a confession or acknowledgment of Whiteness. The act of confession is not only cathartic but also a spiritually transformative move toward repentance and redemption. The ritual of confession allows people racialized as White to practice acknowledging the harm, owning their privilege, being accountable, and taking responsibility for their actions and for creating a more just and equitable future.

The daily examen is part of the practice of confession in the weekly sessions; it helps with paying particular attention to the ways that race and Whiteness appear throughout the day. The examen is an ancient practice developed by Ignatius of Loyola in his *Spiritual Exercises* as a method for reviewing one's day in the presence of God.[15] It is a technique of prayerful reflection on the events of the day that typically uses the practice of journaling to acknowledge our consolations and desolations and to detect God's presence and direction for our lives. The examen requires fifteen to twenty minutes a day. While there are many versions and variations on the examen, I suggest the following steps:

1. Ask God for light: Look at your day with God's eyes, not merely your own.

2. Give thanks: The day you just lived is a gift from God. Be grateful for it.

3. Review the day: Carefully look back on the day just completed and allow yourself to be guided by the Spirit.

4. Face your shortcomings: Acknowledge what is wrong in yourself and your life.

5. Look toward the future: Ask where you will need God in the day to come.

I chose this version of the daily examen because it contains a confessional act of facing one's shortcomings each day. I hope that combining this practice with the study of Whiteness will develop a daily spiritual practice of processing color-blind attitudes and repenting of our participation in racial injustice.

---

[15] Ignatius of Loyola, *Spiritual Exercises and Selected Works*, Classics of Christian Spirituality (New York: Paulist Press, 1991).

2

What Does It Mean to Be White?

The thief comes only to steal and kill and destroy. I came that they may have life, and have it abundantly.

—JOHN 10:10

You will know the truth, and the truth will make you free.

—JOHN 8:32

White children, in the main, and whether they grow up rich or poor, grow up with a grasp of reality so feeble that they can very accurately be described as deluded—about themselves and the world they live in. . . . The reason for this, at bottom, is that the doctrine of white supremacy, which still controls most white people, is itself a stupendous delusion: but to be black in America is an immediate, a mortal challenge. People who cling to their delusions find it difficult, if not impossible, to learn anything worth learning.

—JAMES BALDWIN, *NO NAME IN THE STREET*

PREPARATION FOR SESSION 2

Whiteness is a lie. Whiteness is a delusion. Whiteness is an invention. Whiteness is a mythology. Whiteness is the most successful conspiracy

17

in the history of the world. What does it mean to have one's identity built entirely on a lie? What does it mean to be trapped in a delusion? This is what it means to be White.

Before we understand that being White is to be trapped in a lie, it is bliss. Ignorance is bliss, right? But when we begin to see that our identity is based in a big lie and a grand conspiracy, it causes an earth-shaking existential, spiritual, emotional, political, philosophical, and theological crisis. At least that is what happened to me.

I truly imagined that I was anti-racist, but I came to learn that I was color-blind. Color-blind racism is the ideology that imagines we are living in a post-racial society where skin color no longer determines the livelihood and rights of human beings. It attempts to explain all racial inequality as the outcome of nonracial dynamics such as market factors, naturally occurring phenomena, the lack of personal responsibility, or certain racial groups' cultural limitations. Politically, color blindness has been used over the past forty years to justify dismantling the government's capacity to challenge discrimination, to roll back Black advancement, and to undermine the welfare state.

I was raised in a White family of Methodist ministers on my mother's side. My parents were college professors and educators. They specifically raised me to be not racist, but for the most part that meant to be color-blind. My first career was an infantry officer in the Army National Guard in Lumberton, North Carolina. I later went to seminary at Duke and then went on to work on a doctoral degree in moral theology and ethics at the Catholic University of America in Washington, DC. I was the pastor of liberal Protestant churches. I was a well-educated White liberal Christian who thought he knew about race and racism. But I was severely mistaken. My real education began with the advent of the Black Lives Matter movement, the transracial adoption of my daughter, Lucy, and the frustrations I experienced trying to pastor predominantly White churches as the father of a Black daughter during White America's racial awakening of the last ten years.

Over the years I became increasingly frustrated that the churches I was pastoring were having conversations about race that were not going anywhere. They were shallow, paternalistic, unproductive, and sometimes even harmful. I was perplexed by this phenomenon and did not have any easy answers. Hoping that God might help me with my frustrations, I decided to embark on a spiritual and educational journey to try to figure out what the problem was, and I found out it was I. I was the obstacle keeping my congregations from going deeper. I had not done the hard work of examining and confronting my own Whiteness spiritually and theologically. You cannot lead people where you have not been yourself. I discovered that I did not know how to lead my people because I had not yet tried to understand my Whiteness. So I girded my loins and started doing the work. To be honest, I went into the process hoping to find something redeemable about Whiteness. I assumed that Whiteness was something neutral or benign that had been corrupted, but I was wrong. I found I was trapped in a lie, and that there is nothing redeemable about Whiteness. The most humbling revelation, however, was that while Whiteness is not redeemable, people like me who were assigned Whiteness *are* redeemable with a lifetime of work.

Whiteness is the thing we White people ignore, avoid, and never talk about. It is also the very thing that inhibits deep racial dialogue and stands in the way of racial justice. Whiteness is the largest impediment to dismantling White supremacy. I learned this by sitting at the feet of Black pastors and leaders, and by reading Black authors, intellectuals, and creatives like W.E.B. Du Bois, Malcolm X, James Baldwin, Toni Morrison, and Nell Irvin Painter. James Baldwin said that White people are "still trapped in a history which they do not understand; and until they understand it, they cannot be released from it."[1]

I learned that Whiteness is not neutral or benign. It not a God-given skin color, a biological category, or an ethnicity. Whiteness, like race, is a social construct. It is a lie, a mythology, a delusion, a conspiracy. There are no truly White people. There are, as Baldwin said, only people who think they are White, people who were assigned Whiteness at birth and have lived into a social construct that has become our social contract. Some White people understand this reality, yet we rarely ask why Whiteness was created. Whiteness is a lie that European Christians invented to steal things from others, specifically, to steal people, land, labor, resources, money, and power. The lie of Whiteness is the hierarchy of human value—the lie that some people are superior because of the color of their skin. We need to be honest about this lie and tell that story. But the problem is Whiteness is hidden, unmarked, unspoken,

---

[1] James Baldwin, "The Fire Next Time," in *James Baldwin: Collected Works*, ed. Toni Morrison (New York: Library of America, 1998), 295.

avoided, ignored, and in the shadows because it is the dominant culture, the water in which we swim.

As I did my own work, I began to see that White people almost never talk about what it means to be White. When we talk about racism our conversations are often shallow discussions that discuss the subject of race is if we were detached from it. What we are detached from is reality. We discuss race as if it is an abstract, external issue others are struggling through. We imagine that race is something other people possess that we do not have. We tend to participate in conversations about race as detached subjects without ever discussing or addressing our own racial identity. Because White people are a part of the dominant culture, we imagine we are "normal" and do not have a race. Therefore, most White people are living in a constant state of denial about our own history, our own racial identity, and the ongoing legacy of White supremacy and systemic racism in our society. Denial is our reality.

However, White people not only have a racial identity, but we invented the concept of race intentionally—by which I mean we invented the concept of Whiteness. So, I began to wonder if a curriculum that was like the journey I had been on myself—where White people of faith could spend time looking at Whiteness and our participation in it—might help change the conversation about race and shift the burden of responsibility for racism back to White people where it belongs.

Responsibility is an important word, because Whiteness is not only the process of living a lie and being trapped in a pathological cycle of denial about that lie. Whiteness is being unwilling to take responsibility for the lie and the harm it has caused so many people throughout history. Whiteness is abdication.

One of the most troubling aspects of Whiteness is that it functions as an anti-Black ideology of domination and oppression. Whiteness establishes its power through anti-Blackness, creating a hierarchy of color with Whites on the top, Blacks on the bottom, and everyone else situated in proximity to White domination or Black oppression. Therefore, it is no wonder that White people do not want to look at Whiteness. To do so is to disrupt and disturb our identities in ways that cause an existential crisis. That is unbearable for us; therefore, we willingly become blind to it, ignore it, hide it, avoid it, or live in denial. Denial is the primary emotional state of White people in America. It is a privilege to be able to live in denial. It is only possible to avoid this conversation because we are the dominant culture that has benefited from the long legacy of White terror and oppression of Black people.

So, what happens in White-dominant settings like churches, schools, and businesses where we are working on diversity, equity, and inclusion? What are we diversifying? What are we including people into? Whiteness? We have White people living in denial who are working in proximity with Black people who are experiencing constant trauma. Think about that for a second: White denial and Black trauma. Denial and trauma do not communicate well. Denial does not know what to do with trauma. Trauma is a threat to denial. Denial threatens to traumatize further those who are in trauma. Those who are in denial must be the ones who take the first step. You don't ask people who have been abused by their spouses to sit down and talk nicely with their abusers. You go to therapy for trauma, and you go to anger management for your violence. As White people we must understand our history, so we know we have almost always been the abusers.

Color-blind racism is another form of White abdication from moral responsibility. Because we are trapped in a lie that is tied directly to our identity, White people avoid responsibility at all costs. Yet it is exactly through taking responsibility for our history and our Whiteness that we can find a way forward out of denial and into truth.

James Baldwin wrote to Angela Davis, "They will never, so long as their whiteness puts so sinister a distance between themselves and their own experience and the experience of others, feel themselves sufficiently human, *sufficiently worthwhile*, to become responsible for themselves, their leaders, their country, their children, or their fate."[2] Loss of reality and the loss of responsibility result in the loss of our humanity. When we dehumanized and degraded others, we dehumanized and degraded ourselves. We lost our humanity.

I created this course to give White people a crisis of identity and conscience like the one I experienced. Put up the mirror and do the deep soul work of looking at ourselves through the lens of the Black intellectual and artistic tradition. This course challenges White people to learn the history and development of Whiteness—how it was invented, how it works, how it harms people—and discern what we can do about it.

---

[2] James Baldwin, "An Open Letter to My Sister, Miss Angela Davis" (January 7, 1971), *New York Review of Books* online.

We must take responsibility by learning our own brutal history of oppression and dehumanization; acknowledging the systemic racism that pervades every aspect of American life; and facing the violence, oppression, and death that continue to this day. Then we can atone for what we did and begin to repair the damage. To regain our humanity White people must put Black lives before our own—before our own safety and desires, before our own politics and religion, before our own bank accounts and 401(k)s. It's not enough to be anti-racist; we must be *for* Black people, *for* people of color. We must give up our power and money and follow their lead.

One of the defining characteristics of Whiteness in the United States is anti-Blackness, but it was really created to oppress not only Black people but also poor White people. Rich landowning European men in Virginia were already settler-colonists, and they needed a way to keep the poor White people from aligning themselves with the poor free Blacks and slaves. Whiteness was the perfect wedge issue. By convincing poor White people that they were more like the White landowners and better than Blacks, the rich White men could ensure that the poor White population did not work together with Black people to overthrow their economic oppressors. So, Whiteness operates by setting up a hierarchy of power and value with White rich landowning males at the top, then White women, then all the way down to Black and indigenous women at the very bottom of the hierarchy. Today, many wealthy White people and political leaders continue to use racism to divide Blacks, Whites, and other people who are in the same economic class out of fear they might realize they have more in common with each other than they do with the wealthy elite and begin organizing together for their own shared economic well-being.[3]

James Weldon Johnson wrote in 1912, "I believe it to be a fact that the colored people of this country know and understand the white people better than the white people know and understand them."[4] I have found that to be true. Black people were forced to learn to understand White people to survive in a White supremacist society. By reading every

---

[3] See Theodore W. Allen, *The Invention of the White Race* (New York: Verso, 1994); Asad Haider, *Mistaken Identity: Mass Movements and Racial Identity* (New York: Verso, 2018); and Jonathan M. Metzl, *Dying of Whiteness: How the Politics of Racial Resentment Is Killing America's Heartland* (New York: Basic Books, 2019).

[4] James Weldon Johnson, *The Autobiography of an Ex-Colored Man* (Boston: Sherman, French, and Co., 1912; New York: Warbler Classics, 2020), 13.

Black author I could find who wrote about Whiteness, I learned that examining Whiteness through the eyes of Black authors, intellectuals, and creatives allows us to see ourselves more clearly. Racism and White supremacy are not problems for the Black community but are White problems—problems our ancestors created, problems we benefit from. It is our responsibility to work to eliminate racism and White supremacy for the sake of love and justice—for the sake of our own freedom and salvation from the ideology of Whiteness.

I love watching Toni Morrison's interview on The Charlie Rose Show in which she said:

> "Don't you understand that the people who do this thing, who practice racism, are bereft? There is something distorted about the psyche. It is a huge waste, a corruption, a distortion. It feels crazy. It is crazy. It has as much of a deleterious effect on white people as it does black people. . . . If you can only be tall because somebody is on their knees, then you have a serious problem. White people have a very, very serious problem, and they should start thinking about what they can do about it. Take me out of it."[5]

Every time White people try to have a conversation about racism and social injustice without dealing with our own White racial identity, we end up being harmful because we think we are doing a favor for people of color—when we are the ones with the problem.

We created this mess. White faith communities should be at the forefront of supporting and participating in efforts to address systemic racism and injustice—not just for our Black and brown neighbors but for the sake of our own humanity.

Lillian Smith called this the "grand bargain."[6] Another way to describe it would be to call it a deal with the devil. Our European ancestors from England, Scotland, Ireland, Italy, Sweden, France, Norway, Poland, Germany, and so on made a great and horrible trade. They realized that the path as an outsider in America would be very difficult. So they chose to trade their ethnic identity for Whiteness, but what they didn't know

---

[5] Toni Morrison, "Novelist Toni Morrison Looks Back on Her Youth and Family and Presents Her Newest Book, *Jazz*," interview by Charlie Rose, video, *The Charlie Rose Show*, PBS, May 7, 1993.

[6] Lillian Smith, *Killers of the Dream* (New York: Norton, 1949), 154–68.

was that they were not just giving away their ethnic identity but trading away their humanity to participate in an ideology of dehumanization and oppression. So our ancestors not only traded our ethnic identity for Whiteness but lost our humanity in the process.

Whiteness is not neutral. I've searched and searched for something positive about Whiteness or in Whiteness that can be redeemed, but it is evil. There is no hope in Whiteness. I'm a pastor and a theologian. I have no categories to describe the ideology of Whiteness other than evil. It showed its ugly face in Nazi Germany, but we like to forget that Hitler borrowed many of his ideas from American White supremacists and the segregated South. There is hope for people who currently identify as White—but there is no hope in Whiteness. White people can be redeemed, but Whiteness cannot. So we need to work toward rehumanizing White people by enlisting them in the cause of treason against Whiteness—divesting from and dismantling the very thing that they have benefited from the most. As Noel Ignatiev and John Garvey proclaimed, "Treason to whiteness is loyalty to humanity."[7] We must learn to speak this treason fluently and live as traitors to our own race.

White people will have to take responsibility for our Whiteness, to listen to Black and brown voices, histories, and experiences, and begin to understand Whiteness. We will have to confront our Whiteness and then imagine how we can dismantle Whiteness in our spheres of power and influence.

We have lost our humanity by participating in the dehumanization of our Black and brown neighbors, and so White religious communities must become places where White people can take responsibility and recover their humanity. This is our work and our responsibility.

As James Baldwin writes, "When the dream was slaughtered, and all that love and labor seemed to have come to nothing, we scattered. . . . We knew where we had been, what we had tried to do, who had cracked, gone mad, died, or been murdered around us. . . . But not everything is lost: responsibility cannot be lost, it can only be abdicated. If one refuses abdication, one begins again."[8]

---

[7] Noel Ignatiev and John Garvey, eds., *Race Traitor* (New York: Routledge, 1996), 10.

[8] James Baldwin, *Just above My Head* (New York: Delta Trade Paperbacks, 2000), 219–20.

As a pastor, I discovered that predominantly White faith communities such as the White church have never reckoned with terror and the ongoing legacy of the four-hundred-year history of anti-Black violence and oppression. White faith communities, like most White Americans, continue to live in denial about history and their own participation in Whiteness.

We have a tremendous amount of work to do. As Baldwin suggested, White faith communities can begin by seeking to understand the history and by working together to discover how to take responsibility for our Whiteness and how the ideology of White supremacy was created and sustained by White religious people.

White faith communities must understand that addressing racial and social injustice is not optional; it is our first and foremost work. I strongly recommend White religious communities in America immediately cease all other ministries, programs, or activities to devote all their time, energy, and attention to understanding and reckoning with Whiteness. Only then will we be able to address racial and social injustice and be good neighbors in building the beloved community. It will be extremely hard, painful, and soul wrenching, but it is good work. I know that White faith communities can do this work; I've seen them do it with my own eyes.

DEEP SOUL WORK

Read. *Give this book a close reading by engaging it slowly and carefully, taking time to stop and take notes as you go.*
- Read "The Fire Next Time" by James Baldwin.[9]

Meditate and Reflect. Spend some time in silent meditation after the reading and then write your answers to these questions.
1. How did the reading make you feel?
2. What was most meaningful to you?
3. What are you discovering about Whiteness?
4. Where do you see yourself in the readings and films?

---

[9] Baldwin, "The Fire Next Time," 291–347.

Acknowledge and Confess. *Examine your own life story considering the reading this week and acknowledge what arises.*

- What stories from your life experience relate to what you read this week? (Be sure to write them in your racial autobiography.)
- What did Baldwin reveal to you about what it means to be White?
- When did you first come to understand yourself as White?
- Did God create Whiteness? If not God, then who did? Why?
- Read John 10:10. If Whiteness is a lie European Christians created to steal land, people, resources, labor, and money, then how is it like the thief whom Jesus describes in John 10:10, who comes to steal, kill, and destroy and is opposed to abundant life? What might abundant life look like without the lie of Whiteness?
- Reflect on this quotation from the reading: "White people in this country will have quite enough to do in learning how to accept and love themselves and each other, and when they have achieved this—which will not be tomorrow and may very well be never—the Negro problem will no longer exist, for it will no longer be needed."
- What acknowledgments of Whiteness or personal confessions do you need to make based on this week's reading?

Repent, Turn, and Transform. *Begin trying to imagine a new creation and a new humanity for yourself and for our world.*

- Baldwin writes, "The only thing white people have that black people need, or should want, is power—and no one holds power forever." What does this mean for those of us who have been racialized as White?
- Baldwin writes, "The price of the liberation of the white people is the liberation of the blacks—the total liberation, in the cities, in the towns, before the law, and in the mind." What will the cost of this liberation be for White people?
- What kind of accountability, habits, or practices do you need in your life to better understand the history we White people are trapped in? What might freedom look like? How can the truth set us free (John 8:32)?
- What do you think would change if you apply what you've discovered this week about Whiteness in your sphere of power and influence?

3

Whiteness as Power

Jesus called them and said to them, "You know that among the Gentiles those whom they recognize as their rulers lord over them, and their great ones are tyrants over them. But it is not so among you; but whoever wishes to become great among you must be your servant."

—Mark 10:42–43

Let the same mind be in you that was in Christ Jesus, who, though he was in the form of God, did not regard equality with God as something to be exploited, but emptied himself, taking the form of a slave, being born in human likeness.

—Philippians 2:5–7

Charity is not love, certainly not the kind of love we saw as being essential to a humane society. We therefore had to learn to deal with white America on its own real terms, the terms of power.

—C. T. Vivian, *Black Power and the American Myth*

The world is not white. It never was white, cannot be white. White is a metaphor for power, and that is simply a way of describing Chase Manhattan Bank.

—James Baldwin, *I Am Not Your Negro*

PREPARATION FOR SESSION 3

In 2016, when Keith Lamont Scott was killed by a police officer in Charlotte, North Carolina, protests broke out and our city was on the national news every night for a week. After the protests, local clergy of all faiths, races, and ethnicities gathered for a conversation about how we could respond to injustice, violence, and unrest in our city. We were hoping to organize an interfaith coalition of clergy and congregations that could speak with one voice to help hold our elected leaders accountable for pursuing the common good of all people in Charlotte.

During the meeting the White pastor of a large, affluent, tall-steeple Presbyterian congregation whose members included many prominent bankers and political leaders asked, "What are we really trying to do here?" I replied, "We are trying to build power together so that we can advocate for the common good of our community." The White pastor responded, "If this is about power, then I'm out and so are my people, because Jesus was not about power, and neither are we." Then the White pastor left the meeting. The irony of this interaction was not lost on the other clergy who were gathered that day. After the meeting one of the Black pastors said, "It must be nice not to have to think about power, because you have all the power."

Regardless of our background, religion, or socioeconomic status, if we are racialized as White, we have power other people do not possess. There are many kinds of power—including physical, intellectual, spiritual, economic, and political power. However, people who are racialized as White often don't think about power. White people are the dominant culture in American society, which means we can avoid thinking about all the power we have, or the fact we have power that other people do not possess. The freedom not even to consider how much power we have is a key component of our power.

Power, in and of itself, is neither good nor evil. Power is neutral until it is exercised. The way power is used in the world with other human beings and creation determines whether power becomes good or evil. Power can be wielded for selfish gain and used to dominate, control, or exploit other people. However, power can also be exercised for the benefit of others or in support of the common good of the "least of these among us," the poor, marginalized, oppressed, all of humanity, and creation.

Contrary to the perspective of the White pastor in the story above, the gospel writers frequently discussed Jesus's possession and use of power. In Matthew, John the Baptist described Jesus as "one who is more powerful than I" who is coming to "baptize you with the Holy Spirit and fire" (Matt. 3:11). All the Gospels portray Jesus engaging in "deeds of power" and underscore the regularity by which Pharisees, scribes, and authorities interrogate and challenge Jesus's authority and power to teach, heal, eat with sinners, and break with law and tradition. Jesus also explicitly commissioned the disciples with the authority (power) to proclaim the message of the kingdom of God, drive out demons, heal the sick, raise the dead, and exercise power over "the enemy."

In addition, the Gospels and the letters of Paul offer a clear picture of the way Jesus exercised his power and taught his disciples how to use their power. Paul claims God's act of taking on flesh in human history through the bodies of Mary and Jesus was the epitome of the holy and divine use of power. In Philippians 2, Paul states that Jesus did not regard power as something to be exploited, but instead that he emptied himself of power. The act of self-emptying is an essential component of Jesus's and God's trinitarian identity. Therefore, emptying ourselves of power for the sake of other people and the world—rather than exploiting it for ourselves—is the most Christlike, godly, and holy way to think about and exercise power.

When James and John asked Jesus for positions of power in the kingdom of God, it caused great anger and division among the disciples. Jesus intervened to resolve this dispute by teaching the disciples a new way to live in community together with their power. He said, "You know that among the Gentiles those whom they recognize as their rulers lord it over them, and their great ones are tyrants over them. But it is not so among you; but whoever wishes to become great among you must be your servant" (Mark 10:42–43). Jesus's vision for the beloved community of his followers was founded on an alternative way of exercising power—not lording power over other people like the tyrannical nations of the world but using their power with and for other people through acts of selfless service.

In the words of James Baldwin quoted above, "White is a metaphor for power."[1] By this Baldwin means that Whiteness is a phenomenon

---

[1] James Baldwin, *I Am Not Your Negro* (New York: Vintage International Books, 2017), 107.

that affords certain people in our society (usually European Americans) power—particularly economic, social, legal, and political power over other people. Many American Christians imagine that racism is fundamentally about hatred, but in fact racism is fundamentally about power. Hatred is a consequence of racism, not the cause. When we use phrases like *White supremacy* or *White privilege,* we often unintentionally obscure the fact that Whiteness is about power; *Whiteness* is another word for the power that some people in our society have been given and others have been denied.

This week we will read selections from Cheryl Harris's article "Whiteness as Property" and W.E.B. Du Bois's essay "The Souls of White Folk." Harris explains how Whiteness was written into our legal codes, and Du Bois will help us understand the origins of Whiteness. We will also watch Ava DuVernay's documentary *13th* about the development of policing and imprisonment in America. The film provides historical context for understanding the problems of police brutality and mass incarceration today. Each of these selections shows us the ways that Whiteness acquired systemic political and economic power over people of color through the establishment of law and property rights.

If you struggle with the concept of Whiteness as power or property, imagine other metaphors. An alternative way to think about Whiteness is through the metaphor of credit.[2] Like Whiteness, credit is a commonly held understanding of social trust that affords certain people the economic power to purchase a car or home based on our society's perception of their ability to repay the money at a future date. Regardless of class background, Americans who are racialized as White are born with a kind of credit, and the other side of the coin (so to speak) is that people of color in America are born in debt, which gives the Lord's Prayer of Matthew 6:12—"forgive us our debts, as we also have forgiven our debtors"—a deeper meaning.

Power is a deeply moral and spiritual issue for all people, especially people of faith. Jesus said, "From everyone to whom much has been given, much will be required" (Luke 12:48). White American Christians have failed to reckon with or take responsibility for the power that we

---

[2] I first heard this metaphor from Carole Collins while she was participating in session 2 of the "What Does It Mean to Be White?" course with the staff of the Alliance of Baptists.

not only possess but have lorded over people of color for far too long. As Lord Acton's often quoted phrase puts it, "Power tends to corrupt, and absolute power corrupts absolutely." The time has come for people racialized as White to take our power seriously, not only for the sake of our neighbors whom we have failed to love but for the sake of our own souls.

DEEP SOUL WORK

Read and View. *Engage with these essays and this film slowly and carefully, taking time to stop and make notes as you go.*
- Read "White Racism or World Community?" by James Baldwin.[3]
- Read "Whiteness as Property" by Cheryl Harris.[4]
- Read "The Souls of White Folk" by W.E.B. Du Bois.[5]
- View *13th* by Ava DuVernay.[6]

Meditate and Reflect. *Spend some time in silent meditation after each of the readings and the viewing, and then write your answers to these questions:*
1. How did the readings and viewing make you feel?
2. What was most meaningful to you?
3. What are you discovering about Whiteness?
4. Where do you see yourself in the readings and film?

Acknowledge and Confess. *Examine your own life story considering the readings and viewing this week and acknowledge what arises.*
- What stories from your life experience relate to what you read and viewed this week? (Be sure to write them in your racial autobiography.)
- What acknowledgments of Whiteness or personal confessions do you need to make based on this week's readings and viewing?

---

[3] James Baldwin, "White Racism or World Community?" in *Collected Essays* (New York: Library of America, 1998), 749–56.

[4] Cheryl I. Harris, "Whiteness as Property," *Harvard Law Review* 106, no. 8 (June 1993): 1707–91.

[5] W.E.B. Du Bois, "The Souls of White Folk," in *Darkwater: Voices from within the Veil* (1920).

[6] Ava DuVernay and Jason Moran, *13th* (United States: Netflix, 2016).

- Read Mark 10:42–43 and Philippians 2:5–7. Reflect on Jesus's relationship to power and your own relationship to power.
- In what ways have you seen or experienced the power of Whiteness in your life, your community, or the world?

Repent, Turn, and Transform. *Try to imagine a new creation and a new humanity for yourself and for our world.*

- What kind of power do you have? Where did it come from? How do you exercise your power at home, work, school, and church, and in your community?
- What are the responsibilities that come with your power as a human being, a citizen, a follower of Jesus and/or person of faith?
- What kind of accountability, habits, or practices do you need in your life to help you take responsibility for the power you receive from Whiteness?
- What do you think would change if you apply what you've discovered this week about Whiteness to your sphere of power and influence?

"Whiteness as Property"

Cheryl I. Harris*

(1993)

Editor's Note:

Issues regarding race and racial identity as well as questions pertaining to property rights and ownership have been prominent in much public discourse in the United States. In "Whiteness as Property," Professor Harris contributes to this discussion by positing that racial identity and property are deeply interrelated concepts. Professor Harris examines how Whiteness, initially constructed as a form of racial identity, evolved into a form of property, historically and presently acknowledged and protected in American law. Professor Harris traces the origins of Whiteness as property in the parallel systems of domination of Black and Native American peoples out

*Assistant professor of Law, Chicago-Kent College of Law, Illinois Institute of Technology; B.A. 1973, Wellesley College; J.D. 1978, Northwestern University. My thanks for comments and support to members of the Third Midwestern People of Color Legal Scholarship Conference to whom I first presented this paper and to members of the Third and Fourth Critical Race Theory Workshops whose work and discussion inspired me to pursue this project. I especially must thank Lisa Ikemoto and Leland Ware who provided very thoughtful comments on earlier drafts. The support of Joan Steinman, Marty Malin, Steve Heyman, A. Dan Tarlock, and all the members of the faculty who provided input was most helpful. I also appreciate the encouragement offered by Gerald Torres and Linda Greene. The research assistance provided by Terry Lewis, Britt Shawver, Ron Haywood, and Jordan Marsh was also invaluable, as was the secretarial support offered by Carol Johnson and Inis Petties. This paper would not have been possible without the work and support of Derrick Bell. Beyond all reasonable expectations, Neil Gotanda has provided invaluable insights, support, and encouragement. For his contributions, I thank him most sincerely. This paper was supported by the Marshall D. Ewell Research Fund.

of which were created racially contingent forms of property and property rights. Following the period of slavery and conquest, Whiteness became the basis of racialized privilege—a type of status in which white racial identity provided the basis for allocating societal benefits both private and public in character. These arrangements were ratified and legitimated in law as a type of status property. Even as legal segregation was overturned, Whiteness as property continued to serve as a barrier to effective change as the system of racial classification operated to protect entrenched power.

Next, Professor Harris examines how the concept of Whiteness as property persists in current perceptions of racial identity, in the law's misperception of group identity and in the Court's reasoning and decisions in the arena of affirmative action. Professor Harris concludes by arguing that distortions in affirmative action doctrine can only be addressed by confronting and exposing the property interest in Whiteness and by acknowledging the distributive justification and function of affirmative action as central to that task.

The following excerpt omits Parts III and V of her article.

* * * * * *

she walked into forbidden worlds
impaled on the weapon of her own pale skin
she was a sentinel
at impromptu planning sessions
of her own destruction. . . .
—Cheryl I. Harris, *poem for alma*[1]

[P]etitioner was a citizen of the United States and a resident of the state of Louisiana of mixed descent, in the proportion of seven eighths Caucasian and one eighth African blood; that the mixture of colored blood was not discernible in him, and that he was entitled to every recognition, right, privilege and immunity secured to the citizens of the United States of the white race by its Constitution and laws . . . and thereupon entered a passenger train and took possession of a vacant seat in a coach where passengers of the white race were accommodated.
—Plessy v. Ferguson[2]

[1] Cheryl I. Harris, *poem for alma* (1990) (unpublished poem, on file at the Harvard Law School Library).
[2] 163 U.S. 537, 538 (1896).

I. INTRODUCTION

In the 1930s, some years after my mother's family became part of the great river of Black[3] migration that flowed north,[4] my Mississippi-born grandmother was confronted with the harsh matter of economic survival for herself and her two daughters. Having separated from my grandfather, who himself was trapped on the fringes of economic marginality, she took one long hard look at her choices and presented herself for employment at a major retail store in Chicago's central business district. This decision would have been unremarkable for a white woman in similar circumstances, but for my grandmother, it was an act of both great daring and self-denial, for in so doing she was presenting herself as a white woman. In the parlance of racist America, she was "passing."

Her fair skin, straight hair, and aquiline features had not spared anywhere/nowhere, Mississippi—the outskirts of Yazoo City. But in the burgeoning landscape of urban America, anonymity was possible for a Black person with "white" features. She was transgressing boundaries, crossing borders, spinning on margins, traveling between dualities of

---

[3] I use the term "Black" throughout the paper for the reasons articulated by Professor Kimberlé Crenshaw. I share her view that "Blacks, like Asians, Latinos, and other 'minorities,' constitute a specific cultural group and, as such, require denotation as a proper noun." Kimberlé W. Crenshaw, *Race, Reform, and Retrenchment: Transformation and Legitimation in Antidiscrimination Law*, 101 Harv. L. Rev. 1331, 1332 n.2 (1988). According to W.E.B. Du Bois, "[t]he word 'Negro' was used for the first time in the world's history to tie color to race and blackness to slavery and degradation." W.E. Burghardt Du Bois, The World and Africa 20 (1965). The usage of the lowercase "N" in "negro" was part of the construction of an inferior image of Blacks that provided justification for and a defense of slavery. *See* W.E.B. Du Bois, *That Capital "N," in* 2 The Seventh Son 12, 13 (Julius Lester ed., 1971). Thus, the use of the upper case and lower case in reference to racial identity has a particular political history. Although "white" and "Black" have been defined oppositionally, they are not functional opposites. "White" has incorporated Black subordination; "Black" is not based on domination. *See* discussion *infra* p. 1785. "Black" is naming that is part of counterhegemonic practice.

[4] The Great Migration of Blacks from the rural South to urban centers between 1910 and 1940 doubled the percentage of Blacks living in the North and West. *See* 1 Gunnar Myrdal, An American Dilemma 183 (1944). The second major wave of Black migration, during the 1940s, increased the Black population in Northern cities. For example, in Chicago, it increased by over 70 percent. *See* Nicholas Lemann, The Promised Land 70 (1991).

Manichean space, rigidly bifurcated into light/dark, good/bad, white/Black. No longer immediately identifiable as "Lula's daughter," she could thus enter the white world, albeit on a false passport, not merely passing, but trespassing.

Every day my grandmother rose from her bed in her house in a Black enclave on the south side of Chicago, sent her children off to a Black school, boarded a bus full of Black passengers, and rode to work. No one at her job ever asked if she was Black; the question was unthinkable. By virtue of the employment practices of the "fine establishment" in which she worked, she could not have been. Catering to the upper-middle class, understated tastes required that Blacks not be allowed.

She quietly went about her clerical tasks, not once revealing her true identity. She listened to the women with whom she worked discuss their worries—their children's illnesses, their husbands' disappointments, their boyfriends' infidelities—all of the mundane yet critical things that made up their lives. She came to know them but they did not know her, for my grandmother occupied a completely different place. That place—where white supremacy and economic domination meet—was unknown turf to her white co-workers. They remained oblivious to the worlds within worlds that existed just beyond the edge of their awareness and yet were present in their very midst.

Each evening, my grandmother, tired and worn, retraced her steps home, laid aside her mask, and reentered herself. Day in and day out, she made herself invisible, then visible again, for a price too inconsequential to do more than barely sustain her family and at a cost too precious to conceive. She left the job some years later, finding the strain too much to bear.

From time to time, as I later sat with her, she would recollect that period, and the cloud of some painful memory would pass across her face. Her voice would remain subdued, as if to contain the still remembered tension. On rare occasions she would wince, recalling some particularly racist comment made in her presence because of her presumed, shared group affiliation. Whatever retort might have been called for had been suppressed long before it reached her lips, for the price of her family's well-being was her silence. Accepting the risk of self-annihilation was the only way to survive.

Although she never would have stated it this way, the clear and ring-ing denunciations of racism she delivered from her chair when advanced arthritis had rendered her unable to work were informed by those ex-periences. The fact that self-denial had been a logical choice and had made her complicit in her own oppression at times fed the fire in her eyes when she confronted some daily outrage inflicted on Black people. Later, these painful memories forged her total identification with the civil rights movement. Learning about the world at her knee as I did, these experiences also came to inform my outlook and my understand-ing of the world.

My grandmother's story is far from unique. Indeed, there are many who crossed the color line never to return. Passing is well-known among Black people in the United States[5] and is a feature of race subordina-

---

[5] When I began to relate the subject matter of my research to Black friends and colleagues, in nearly every instance I was told, "I had an uncle. . . . I had a great aunt. . . . My grandfather's brother left Alabama to go North as a white man and we never saw or heard from him again" or other similar stories. *See also* PATRICIA J. WILLIAMS, *On Being the Object of Property*, in THE ALCHEMY OF RACE AND RIGHTS 216, 223 (1991) (recounting the story of Marjorie, Williams's godmother, who was given away by her mother at the age of six in order that her mother could "pass" and marry a white man); Gregory H. Williams, Neither Black Nor White: A Childhood on the Color Line 8 (1991) (unpublished manuscript, on file at the Harvard Law School Library) (describing the childhood of a law professor whose father passed for white, a fact unknown to his son until the age of ten).

Gunner Myrdal's discussion of the phenomenon of "passing" in his 1944 study of race illuminates the social context of my grandmother's story and the stories of many like her.

"[P]assing" means that a Negro becomes a white man, that is, moves from the lower to the higher caste. In the American caste order, this can be ac-complished only by the deception of the white people with whom the passer comes to associate and by a conspiracy of silence on the part of other Negroes who might know about it. . . . In the Northern and Border states it seems to be relatively common for light-skinned Negroes to "pass professionally" but preserve a Negro social life. Negro girls have practically no chance of getting employment as stenographers or secretaries, salesclerks in department stores, telephone operators, outside establishments run by Negroes for Negroes. In most communities their chances are slight even to become regular teach-ers, social workers, or the like, if they do not conceal their Negro ancestry. . . . Not only in these female middle class occupations but in all male and female trades where Negroes are excluded, there must be a similar incentive to attempt to "pass professionally." . . . In view of the advantages to be had by passing, it is not difficult to explain why Negroes pass, professionally or completely. It is more difficult, however, to explain why Negroes do not pass over to the white race more often than they actually do.

tion in all societies structured on white supremacy.[6] Notwithstanding the purported benefits of Black heritage in an era of affirmative action, passing is not an obsolete phenomenon that has slipped into history.[7]

The persistence of passing is related to the historical and continuing pattern of white racial domination and economic exploitation that has given passing a certain economic logic.[8] It was a given to my grandmother that being white automatically ensured higher economic returns in the short term, as well as greater economic, political, and social security in the long run. Becoming white meant gaining access to a whole set of public and private privileges that materially and permanently guaranteed basic subsistence needs and, therefore, survival. Becoming white increased the possibility of controlling critical aspects of one's life rather than being the object of others' domination.

Myrdal, *supra* note 4, at 683–86 (1944).

[6] Because of the relative privileges of whites, the principal incentive is for Blacks to pass as whites, not vice versa. *See* Marvin Harris, *Referential Ambiguity in the Calculus of Brazilian Racial Identity*, in AFRO-AMERICAN ANTHROPOLOGY: CONTEMPORARY PERSPECTIVES 75, 75–76 (Norman E. Whitten, Jr. & John F. Szwed eds., 1970) (describing the more fluid racial classification systems of the Caribbean, Brazil, and other parts of Latin America that, unlike the U.S. model that denotes as Black anyone with any known Black heritage, admits of intermediate categories of mixed blood, but still holds that "money whitens," thereby equating "white" with higher class position and reflecting that white is preferred and dominant). *See generally* MARVIN HARRIS, PATTERNS OF RACE IN THE AMERICAS 39–40, 56–59 (1964) (describing the phenomena of Indians "passing" in Mexico, and the complex racial system of Brazil). However, there have been recent accounts of "reverse passing," that is, whites attempting to be reclassified as Black or Hispanic for purposes of affirmative action programs. *See infra* note 319.

[7] *See, e.g.,* Doe v. State of Louisiana, 479 So.2d 369, 371 (La. Ct. App. 1985) (rejecting the attempt by a family whose parents had been classified as "colored" to be reclassified as white).

[8] *See* WILLIAMS, *supra* note 5, at 8 (theorizing that the author's father's masquerade as a white man was motivated by the belief that passing brought "greater job opportunities").

One recurrent image of Blacks in cinema was the "tragic mulatto" who assassinated her Black origins in order to attain a better life in the white world. Although many of the cinematic versions of this tale have been cautionary morality plays illustrative of the tragic consequences of self-denial, the underlying economic rationale for the hero(ine) to pass was so self-evident as never to be challenged nor even explicitly stated. *See generally* DONALD BOGLE, TOMS, COONS, MULATTOES, MAMMIES, AND BUCKS: AN INTERPRETIVE HISTORY OF BLACKS IN AMERICAN FILMS 9 (1989)(discussing film images of the "tragic mulatto").

My grandmother's story illustrates the valorization of whiteness as treasured property in a society structured on racial caste. In ways so embedded that it is rarely apparent, the set of assumptions, privileges, and benefits that accompany the status of being white have become a valuable asset that whites sought to protect and that those who passed sought to attain—by fraud if necessary. Whites have come to expect and rely on these benefits, and over time these expectations have been affirmed, legitimated, and protected by the law. Even though the law is neither uniform nor explicit in all instances, in protecting settled expectations based on white privilege, American law has recognized a property interest in whiteness[9] that, although unacknowledged, now forms the background against which legal disputes are framed, argued, and adjudicated.

My article investigates the relationships between concepts of race and property and reflects on how rights in property are contingent on, intertwined with, and conflated with race. Through this entangled relationship between race and property, historical forms of domination have evolved to reproduce subordination in the present. In Part II, I examine the emergence of whiteness as property and trace the evolution of whiteness from color to race to status to property as a progression historically rooted in white supremacy[10] and economic hegemony over Black and

---

[9] My exploration of this concept began in March, 1991, when I participated in a conference on "Constitution Making in a New South Africa," held at the University of the Western Cape in South Africa. (The conference was jointly sponsored by the National Conference of Black Lawyers, the National Lawyers Guild and the National Association of Democratic Lawyers in South Africa.) My paper argued that American law had implicitly recognized a property interest in whiteness. The concept resonated in the South African context because of the similar and even more extreme patterns of white domination evident there. As I later discovered, the concept of a "property interest in whiteness" is one that has been recognized in modern legal theory. Professor Bell in his chronicle, "Xerces and the Affirmative Action Myth," noted the argument advanced in Plessy v. Ferguson, 163 U.S. 537 (1896), regarding the property interest in whiteness and the extent to which affirmative action policies are seen as a threat to "property interests of identifiable whites." Derrick Bell, *Xerces and the Affirmative Action Myth*, 57 Geo. Wash. L. Rev. 1595, 1602, 1608 (1989). Finding that Professor Bell, to whom I am deeply indebted intellectually, had identified this concept before me only served to confirm my belief that further exploration of this idea is a worthwhile project.

[10] I adopt here the definition of white supremacy utilized by Frances Lee Ansley:

By "white supremacy" I do not mean to allude only to the self-conscious racism of white supremacist hate groups. I refer instead to a political, eco-

Native American peoples. The origins of whiteness as property lie in the parallel systems of domination of Black and Native American peoples out of which were created racially contingent forms of property and property rights. I further argue that whiteness shares the critical characteristics of property even as the meaning of property has changed over time. In particular, whiteness and property share a common premise—a conceptual nucleus—of a right to exclude. This conceptual nucleus has proven to be a powerful center around which whiteness as property has taken shape. Following the period of slavery and conquest, white identity became the basis of racialized privilege that was ratified and legitimated in law as a type of status property. After legalized segregation was overturned, whiteness as property evolved into a more modern form through the law's ratification of the settled expectations of relative white privilege as a legitimate and natural baseline.

Part III examines the two forms of whiteness as property—status property and modern property—that are the submerged text of two paradigmatic cases on the race question in American law, Plessy v. Ferguson[11] and Brown v. Board of Education.[12] As legal history, they illustrate an important transition from old to new forms of whiteness as property. Although these cases take opposite interpretive stances regarding the constitutional legitimacy of legalized racial segregation, the property interest in whiteness was transformed, but not discarded, in the Court's new equal protection jurisprudence.

Part IV considers the persistence of whiteness as property. I first examine how subordination is reinstituted through modern conceptions of race and identity embraced in law. Whiteness as property has taken on more subtle forms, but retains its core characteristic—the legal legitimation of expectations of power and control that enshrine the status quo as a neutral baseline, while masking the maintenance of white privilege and domination. I further identify the property interest in whiteness as

---

nomic, and cultural system in which whites overwhelmingly control power and material resources, conscious and unconscious ideas of white superiority and entitlement are widespread, and relations of white dominance and non-white subordination are daily reenacted across a broad array of institutions and social settings.

Frances L. Ansley, *Stirring the Ashes: Race, Class and the Future of Civil Rights Scholarship*, 74 Cornell L. Rev. 993, 1024 n.129 (1989).

[11] 163 U.S. 537 (1896).

[12] 347 U.S. 483 (1954).

the unspoken center of current polarities around the issue of affirmative action. As a legacy of slavery and de jure and de facto race segregation, the concept of a protectable property interest in whiteness permeates affirmative action doctrine in a manner illustrated by the reasoning of three important affirmative action cases—Regents of the University of California v. Bakke,[13] City of Richmond v. J.A. Croson & Co.,[14] and Wygant v. Jackson Board of Education.[15]

Finally, in Part V, I offer preliminary thoughts on a way out of the conundrum created by protecting whiteness as a property interest. I suggest that affirmative action, properly conceived and reconstructed, would de-legitimate the property interest in whiteness. I do not offer here a complete reformulation of affirmative action, but suggest that focusing on the distortions created by the property interest in whiteness would provoke different questions and open alternative perspectives on the affirmative action debate. The inability to see affirmative action as more than a search for the "blameworthy" among "innocent" individuals is tied to the inability to see the property interest in whiteness. Thus reconstructed, affirmative action would challenge the characterization of the unfettered right to exclude as a legitimate aspect of identity and property.

II. THE CONSTRUCTION OF RACE AND THE EMERGENCE OF WHITENESS AS PROPERTY

The racialization of identity and the racial subordination of Blacks and Native Americans provided the ideological basis for slavery and conquest.[16] Although the systems of oppression of Blacks and Native Americans differed in form—the former involving the seizure and appropriation of labor, the latter entailing the seizure and appropriation of land—undergirding both was a racialized conception of property implemented by force and ratified by law.

---

[13] 438 U.S. 265 (1978).

[14] 488 U.S. 469 (1989).

[15] 476 U.S. 267 (1986).

[16] *See* RONALD TAKAKI, IRON CAGES: RACE AND CULTURE IN 19TH-CENTURY AMERICA 11 (1990) (describing how English definitions of Blacks and Native Americans as "savage" and "instinctual" "encouraged English immigrants to appropriate Indian land and black labor as they settled and set up production in the New World, and enabled white colonists to justify the actions they had committed against both peoples").

The origins of property rights in the United States are rooted in racial domination.[17] Even in the early years of the country, it was not the concept of race alone that operated to oppress Blacks and Indians; rather, it was the interaction between conceptions of race and property that played a critical role in establishing and maintaining racial and economic subordination.

The hyper-exploitation of Black labor was accomplished by treating Black people themselves as objects of property. Race and property were thus conflated by establishing a form of property contingent on race— only Blacks were subjugated as slaves and treated as property. Similarly, the conquest, removal, and extermination of Native American life and culture were ratified by conferring and acknowledging the property rights of whites in Native American land. Only white possession and occupation of land was validated and therefore privileged as a basis for property rights. These distinct forms of exploitation each contributed in varying ways to the construction of whiteness as property.

A. Forms of Racialized Property: Relationships Between Slavery, Race, and Property

1. The Convergence of Racial and Legal Status.—Although the early colonists were cognizant of race,[18] racial lines were neither consistently

---

[17] In reviewing ROBERT WILLIAMS, THE AMERICAN INDIAN IN WESTERN LEGAL THOUGHT: THE DISCOURSE OF CONQUEST (1990), an eloquent and meticulous work on the American Indian in Western legal doctrine, Joseph William Singer draws out the organic connections between property rights and race as the pattern of conquest of native lands exemplified:

> [P]roperty and sovereignty in the United States have a racial basis. The land was taken by force by white people from peoples of color thought by the conquerors to be racially inferior. The close relation of native peoples to the land was held to be no relation at all. To the conquerors, the land was "vacant." Yet it required trickery and force to wrest it from its occupants. This means that the title of every single parcel of property in the United States can be traced to a system of racial violence.

Joseph W. Singer, *The Continuing Conquest: American Indian Nations, Property Law, and Gunsmoke*, 1 Reconstruction 97, 102 (1991); *see* Frances L. Ansley, *Race and the Core Curriculum in Legal Education*, 79 Cal. L. Rev. 1511, 1523 (1991) (citing the history of discovery and conquest of American Indian land to be illustrative of the fact that "race is at the heart of American property law").

[18] *See* WINTHROP D. JORDAN, WHITE OVER BLACK: AMERICAN ATTITUDES TOWARD THE NEGRO, 1550–1812, at 3–43 (1968) (describing early colonial racism).

nor sharply delineated among or within all social groups.[19] Captured
Africans sold in the Americas were distinguished from the population of
indentured or bond servants—"unfree" white labor—but it was not an
irrebuttable presumption that all Africans were "slaves" or that slavery
was the only appropriate status for them.[20] The distinction between
African and white indentured labor grew, however, as decreasing terms
of service were introduced for white bond servants.[21] Simultaneously,
the demand for labor intensified, resulting in a greater reliance on
African labor and a rapid increase in the number of Africans imported
into the colonies.[22]

The construction of white identity and the ideology of racial hierarchy
also were intimately tied to the evolution and expansion of the system
of chattel slavery. The further entrenchment of plantation slavery was
in part an answer to a social crisis produced by the eroding capacity of
the landed class to control the white labor population.[23] The dominant
paradigm of social relations, however, was that, although not all Africans were slaves, virtually all slaves were not white. It was their racial

---

[19] Indeed, between 1607 and 1800, racial lines among the lower classes were
quite blurred; not only were social activities between Blacks and lower class whites
sometimes racially integrated, but also political resistance in the form of urban slave
revolts sometimes included whites. *See* DAVID ROEDIGER, THE WAGES OF WHITE-
NESS 24 (1991).

[20] According to John Hope Franklin, "there is no doubt that the earliest Negroes
in Virginia occupied a position similar to that of the white servants in the colony."
JOHN H. FRANKLIN, U.S. COMM'N ON CIVIL RIGHTS, FREEDOM TO THE FREE 71
(1963), *cited in* A. LEON HIGGINBOTHAM, JR., IN THE MATTER OF COLOR: RACE
AND THE AMERICAN LEGAL PROCESS 21 (1978). The legal disabilities imposed on
Blacks were not dissimilar to those imposed on non-English servants of European
descent, as the principal line of demarcation was between Christian and non-
Christian servants. *See* Raymond T. Diamond & Robert J. Cottrol, *Codifying Caste:
Louisiana's Racial Classification Scheme and the Fourteenth Amendment*, 29 Loy. L.
Rev. 255, 259 n.19 (1983). Indeed, "the word *slave* had no meaning in English
law." THOMAS F. GOSSETT, RACE: THE HISTORY OF AN IDEA IN AMERICA 29 (1963).
Later statutory provisions prohibited Blacks who were slaves from attaining their
freedom by converting to Christianity. *See, e.g.,* HIGGINBOTHAM, *supra*, at 200
(citing a South Carolina statute of 1690 that declared "no slave shall be free by
becoming a christian").

[21] *See* GOSSETT, *supra* note 20, at 30.

[22] *See id.*

[23] *See* EDMUND S. MORGAN, AMERICAN SLAVERY, AMERICAN FREEDOM: THE
ORDEAL OF COLONIAL VIRGINIA 295–300 (1975).

otherness that came to justify the subordinated status of Blacks.[24] The result was a classification system that "key[ed] official rules of descent to national origin" so that "[m]embership in the new social category of 'Negro' became itself sufficient justification for enslaveability."[25] Although the cause of the increasing gap between the status of African and white labor is contested by historians,[26] it is clear that "[t]he economic and political interests defending Black slavery were far more powerful than those defending indentured servitude."[27]

By the 1660s, the especially degraded status of Blacks as chattel slaves was recognized by law.[28] Between 1680 and 1682, the first slave codes appeared, codifying the extreme deprivations of liberty already existing in social practice. Many laws parceled out differential treatment based on racial categories: Blacks were not permitted to travel without permits, to own property, to assemble publicly, or to own weapons; nor were they to be educated.[29] Racial identity was further merged with stratified social and legal status: "Black" racial identity marked who was subject to enslavement; "white" racial identity marked who was "free"

---

[24] *See* Neil Gotanda, *A Critique of "Our Constitution Is Colorblind,"* 44 Stan. L. Rev 1, 34 (1991).

[25] *Id.; see also* Christopher Lasch, THE WORLD OF NATIONS 17 (1974) (asserting that the concept of "Negro" emerged from "related . . . concepts of African, heathen and savage—at the very point in time when large numbers of men and women were beginning to question the moral legitimacy of slavery"). The implications are that, as the system of chattel slavery came under fire, it was rationalized by an ideology of race that further differentiated between white and Black.

[26] *Compare* GOSSETT, *supra* note 20, at 29–30 (arguing that the terms of service for white workers were decreased in order to attract white labor in the colonies) *with* Higginbotham, *supra* note 20, at 26 (citing masters' fears of a potential alliance between white indentured servants and the rapidly expanding African population). *See generally* DAVID W. GALENSON, WHITE SERVITUDE IN COLONIAL AMERICA: AN ECONOMIC ANALYSIS 159–60 (1981) (arguing that the increased demand for skilled labor, a limited pool of low-cost, skilled white labor, and the decline in the cost of training for the slave population that was increasingly born in the Americas, combined to make slave labor more economically attractive); Diamond & Cottrol, supra note 20, at 260 (advancing an argument in accord with Higginbotham).

[27] ROEDIGER, *supra* note 19, at 32.

[28] In 1661, the Maryland legislature enacted a bill providing that "All Negroes and other slaves shall serve *Durante Vita* [for life]." GOSSETT, *supra* note 20, at 30.

[29] *See* HIGGINBOTHAM, *supra* note 20, at 39–40.

or, at minimum, not a slave.[30] The ideological and rhetorical move from "slave" and "free" to "Black" and "white" as polar constructs marked an important step in the social construction of race.

2. Implications for Property.—The social relations that produced racial identity as a justification for slavery also had implications for the conceptualization of property. This result was predictable, as the institution of slavery, lying at the very core of economic relations, was bound up with the idea of property. Through slavery, race and economic domination were fused.[31]

Slavery produced a peculiar, mixed category of property and humanity—a hybrid possessing inherent instabilities that were reflected in its treatment and ratification by the law. The dual and contradictory character of slaves as property and persons was exemplified in the Representation Clause of the Constitution. Representation in the House of Representatives was apportioned on the basis of population computed by counting all persons and "three-fifths of all other persons"—slaves.[32] Gouveneur Morris's remarks before the Constitutional Convention posed the essential question: "Upon what principle is it that slaves shall be computed in the representation? Are they men? Then make them Citizens & let them vote? Are they property? Why then is no other property included?"[33]

---

[30] For a catalogue of pre-Civil War cases articulating the general rule that a Black person was presumed to be a slave, see CHARLES S. MANGUM, JR., THE LEGAL STATUS OF THE NEGRO 2 n.2 (1940).

[31] The system of racial oppression grounded in slavery was driven in large measure (although by no means exclusively) by economic concerns. *See* Morgan, *supra* note 23, at 295–315; LESLIE H. OWENS, THIS SPECIES OF PROPERTY *passim* (1976). Whether from the perspective of Southern slave owners or early Northern capitalists, the slave trade, slave labor, and the direct and indirect profits that flowed from it were central to an economic structure that benefited the nation. Thus, the tension over the issue of slavery ultimately resulted in the now well-documented set of constitutional compromises that subordinated the humanity of Black people to the economic and political interests of the white, propertied class. *See* DERRICK BELL, AND WE ARE NOT SAVED 34 (1987).

[32] U.S. CONST. art. I, § 2, cl. 3.

[33] 2 THE RECORDS OF THE FEDERAL CONVENTION OF 1787, at 222 (Max Farrand ed., 1911).

The cruel tension between property and humanity was also reflected in the law's legitimation of the use of Blackwomen's[34] bodies as a means of increasing property.[35] In 1662, the Virginia colonial assembly provided that "[c]hildren got by an Englishman upon a Negro woman shall be bond or free according to the condition of the mother. . . ."[36] In reversing the usual common law presumption that the status of the child was determined by the father, the rule facilitated the reproduction of one's own labor force.[37] Because the children of Blackwomen assumed the status of their mother, slaves were bred through Blackwomen's bodies. The economic significance of this form of exploitation of female slaves should not be underestimated. Despite Thomas Jefferson's belief that slavery should be abolished, like other slaveholders, he viewed slaves as economic assets, noting that their value could be realized more efficiently

---

[34] My use of the term "Blackwomen" is an effort to use language that more clearly reflects the unity of identity as "Black" and "woman," with neither aspect primary or subordinate to the other. It is an attempt to realize in practice what has been identified in theory—that, as Kimberlé Crenshaw notes, Blackwomen exist "at the crossroads of gender and race hierarchies." Kimberlé Crenshaw, *Whose Story Is It, Anyway? Feminist and Antiracist Appropriations of Anita Hill, in* RACE-ING JUSTICE, EN-GENDERING POWER: ESSAYS ON ANITA HILL, CLARENCE THOMAS, AND THE CONSTRUCTION OF SOCIAL REALITY 402, 403 (Toni Morrison ed., 1992). Indeed, this essay projects a powerful and complex vision of Blackwomen that forms the foundation of my construction of this term:

The particular experience of black women in the dominant cultural ideology of American society can be conceptualized as intersectional. Intersectionality captures the way in which the particular location of black women in dominant American social relations is unique and in some senses unassimilable into the discursive paradigms of gender and race domination.

Id. at 404.

[35] This use of slave women made them a type of sexual property, and particularly subject to the control of white males. *See* Margaret Burnham, *An Impossible Marriage: Slave Law and Family Law,* 5 Law & Ineq. J. 187, 197–99 (1987).

[36] HIGGINBOTHAM, *supra* note 20, at 43. By the late 1600s and early 1700s, the legislatures of various colonies adopted similar rules of classification. *See, e.g., id.* at 128 (citing a 1706 New York statute); *id.* at 252 (citing a 1755 Georgia law).

[37] *See id.* at 44. According to Paula Giddings, the Virginia statute completed "[t]he circle of denigration . . . [in] combin[ing] racism, sexism, greed, and piety" in that it "laid women open to the most vicious exploitation." She noted that "a master could save the cost of buying new slaves by impregnating his own slave, or for that matter having anyone impregnate her." PAULA GIDDINGS, WHEN AND WHERE I ENTER: THE IMPACT OF BLACK WOMEN ON RACE AND SEX IN AMERICA 37 (1984).

from breeding than from labor. A letter he wrote in 1805 stated: "I consider the labor of a breeding woman as no object, and that a child raised every 2 years is of more profit than the crop of the best laboring man."[38]

Even though there was some unease in slave law, reflective of the mixed status of slaves as humans and property, the critical nature of social relations under slavery was the commodification of human beings. Productive relations in early American society included varying forms of sale of labor capacity, many of which were highly oppressive; but slavery was distinguished from other forms of labor servitude by its permanency and the total commodification attendant to the status of the slave. Slavery as a legal institution treated slaves as property that could be transferred, assigned, inherited, or posted as collateral.[39] For example, in Johnson v. Butler,[40] the plaintiff sued the defendant for failing to pay a debt of $496 on a specified date. Because the covenant had called for payment of the debt in "money or negroes," the plaintiff contended that the defendant's tender of one negro only, although valued by the parties at an amount equivalent to the debt, could not discharge the debt. The court agreed with the plaintiff.[41] This use of Africans as a stand-in for actual currency highlights the degree to which slavery "propertized" human life.

Because the "presumption of freedom [arose] from color [white]" and the "black color of the race [raised] the presumption of slavery,"[42] whiteness became a shield from slavery, a highly volatile and unstable form of property. In the form adopted in the United States, slavery

---

[38] Letter from Thomas Jefferson to John Jordan (Dec. 21, 1805), *cited in* TAKAKI, *supra* note 16, at 44.

[39] By 1705, Virginia had classified slaves as real property. *See* HIGGINBOTHAM, *supra* note 20, at 52. In Massachusetts and South Carolina, slaves were identified as chattel. *See id.* at 78, 211.

[40] 4 Ky. (1 Bibb) 97 (1815).

[41] *Id.* at 98. The court held that the defendant was not entitled to judgment on the demurrer for three reasons, including the following:

The defendant, under the terms of the covenant, no doubt had his election to pay either in money or negroes; but in case of his choosing the latter alternative, as the covenant requires the payment to be made in *negroes*, in the plural number, the plaintiff could not be compelled to receive *one* only. The tender therefore, of a single negro, though of value equal to the amount to be paid, could not discharge the covenant.

Id.

[42] 1 THOMAS R.R. COBB, AN INQUIRY INTO THE LAW OF NEGRO SLAVERY IN THE UNITED STATES §§ 68–69, at 66–67 (1858).

made human beings market-alienable and in so doing, subjected human life and personhood—that which is most valuable—to the ultimate devaluation. Because whites could not be enslaved or held as slaves,[43] the racial line between white and Black was extremely critical; it became a line of protection and demarcation from the potential threat of commodification, and it determined the allocation of the benefits and burdens of this form of property. White identity and whiteness were sources of privilege and protection; their absence meant being the object of property.

Slavery as a system of property facilitated the merger of white identity and property. Because the system of slavery was contingent on and conflated with racial identity, it became crucial to be "white," to be identified as white, to have the property of being white.[44] Whiteness was the characteristic, the attribute, the property of free human beings.

B. Forms of Racialized Property: Relationships Between Native American Land Seizure, Race, and Property

Slavery linked the privilege of whites to the subordination of Blacks through a legal regime that attempted the conversion of Blacks into objects of property. Similarly, the settlement and seizure of Native American land supported white privilege through a system of property rights in land in which the "race" of the Native Americans rendered their first possession rights invisible and justified conquest. This racist formulation embedded the fact of white privilege into the very definition of property, marking another stage in the evolution of the property interest in whiteness. Possession—the act necessary to lay the basis for rights in property—was defined to include only the cultural practices of whites. This definition laid the foundation for the idea that whiteness—that which whites alone possess—is valuable and is property.

---

[43] *See id.* § 68, at 66.

[44] Kenneth Minogue states that property performs the critical function of identification: "[P]roperty is the concept by which we find order in things. The world is a bundle of things, and things are recognized in terms of their attributes or properties." Kenneth R. Minogue, *The Concept of Property and Its Contemporary Significance, in* NOMOS XXII: Property 3, 11 (J. Roland Pennock & John W. Chapman eds., 1980). Indeed, he suggests that it is impossible to identify anyone or anything except by reference to their properties. *See id.* at 12.

Although the Indians were the first occupants and possessors of the land of the New World, their racial and cultural otherness[45] allowed this fact to be reinterpreted and ultimately erased as a basis for asserting rights in land. Because the land had been left in its natural state, untilled and unmarked by human hands, it was "waste" and, therefore, the appropriate object of settlement and appropriation.[46] Thus, the possession maintained by the Indians was not "true" possession and could safely be ignored.[47] This interpretation of the rule of first pos-

[45] Takaki describes the construction of Native Americans as savages through political doctrine and cultural imagery—what Herman Melville called the "metaphysics of Indian hating"—as an ideology that facilitated the removal and extermination of Native Americans. *See* Takaki, *supra* note 16, at 81 (citation omitted). The "savage Indian" also served as the referential opposite by which whites defined themselves to be civilized. *See generally id.* at 56 (stating that Jefferson's efforts to civilize the Indians affirmed a definition of civilization and progress measured by distance from the savagery of the Indian); *id.* at 176–80 (describing George Custer's view of the "heathen and savage" Indians as "counterpoint[s] to civilization").

[46] Thus, the Indians' claim as first possessors was said to rest on a "questionable foundation," according to John Quincy Adams, because the right of the hunter could not preempt and provide the basis for an exclusive claim for a "few hundreds" against the needs of "millions." His argument reflected a widely held consensus. Gossett, *supra* note 20, at 230 (citations omitted). The land that lay in the common, left "wholly to nature," was the proper subject of appropriation by one's labor because these "great tracts of ground . . . [that] lie waste . . . are more than the people who dwell on it do, or can make use of." John Locke, Two Treatises of Government 137, 139 (photo. reprint 1990) (W. S. Carpenter ed., 1924) (3d ed. 1698). The forms of land use typical of Native American peoples were fluid and communal in nature. The American courts have held that governmental seizures of Indian property held under original Indian title do not offend the Takings Clause of the Fifth Amendment. Courts have reasoned that Indian property rights were not protected by the constitutional prohibition against taking private property without just compensation because the property rights of Native Americans were communal and inhered in the tribe rather than an individual. Secondly, courts have contended that Native American people had not established possession of the lands they claimed for. Although they had hunted and fished on the land, they had never enclosed it and allotted the land to individuals. *See* Joseph W. Singer, *Sovereignty and Property*, 86 Nw. U. L. Rev. 1, 17–18 (1991).

[47] According to Carol Rose, the common law made a "choice among audiences" in refusing to dismiss legal claims to Indian land based on the assertion that "the Indians . . . had never done acts on the land sufficient to establish property in it. . . . [T]he Indians had never really undertaken those acts of possession that give rise to a property right." Carol M. Rose, *Possession as the Origin of Property*, 52 U. Chi. L. Rev. 73, 85–86 (1985). She states:

session effectively rendered the rights of first possessors contingent on the race of the possessor.[48] Only particular forms of possession—those that were characteristic of white settlement—would be recognized and legitimated.[49] Indian forms of possession were perceived to be too ambiguous and unclear.

The conquest and occupation of Indian land was wrapped in the rule of law.[50] The law provided not only a defense of conquest and colonization,

---

[I]n defining the acts of possession that make up a claim to property, the law not only rewards the author of the "text"; it also puts an imprimatur on a particular symbolic system and on the audience that uses this system. Audiences that do not understand or accept the symbols are out of luck. *Id.* at 85.

[48] *See* Joseph W. Singer, *Re-reading Property*, 27 New Eng. L. Rev. 711, 720 (1992).

[49] This redefinition of possession and occupancy at the theoretical level was accompanied at the practical level by massive land dispossession that restricted Indians to reservations and designated hunting areas, established lines of demarcation by treaty that were later violated, effected land "sales" through fraud, trickery, or coercion, and led ultimately to campaigns of forced removals. *See* GOSSETT, *supra* note 20, at 228. Jefferson's Indian policy, for example, had the stated goal of "civilizing" the Indians, which resulted in their land being taken by whites for development. The objective of making the Indians "willing to sell" was achieved by the threat of force and encouraging the exchange of lands for goods pushed on them through trading houses. *See* Takaki, *supra* note 16, at 60–62. Andrew Jackson's campaign to dissolve the tribes, through both the forced removal of entire tribes and the land allotment program, was an attempt to make the Indians "citizens" and to coerce them to get rid of their lands. Under the land allotment program, Indians, as a condition of remaining on the land, were required to accept individual land grants that later were seized by land speculators through fraud or by creditors for debts. *See id.* at 92–107; *see also* ROBERT A. WILLIAMS, JR., THE AMERICAN INDIAN IN WESTERN LEGAL THOUGHT: THE DISCOURSES OF CONQUEST 274 (1990) (describing the "time-honored" policy of "waging war on the Indians in order to force a land cession").

[50] In Alexis de Tocqueville's words, "the United States ha[s] accomplished this twofold purpose [of extermination of Indians and deprivation of rights] . . . legally, philanthropically, . . . and without violating a single great principle of morality in the eyes of the world. It is impossible to destroy men with more respect for the laws of humanity." 1 ALEXIS DE TOCQUEVILLE, DEMOCRACY IN AMERICA 355 (Phillips Bradley ed. & Henry Reeve trans., 1945) (1835). As Rennard Strickland argues, these acts by the United States constituted genocide-at-law. *See* Rennard Strickland, *Genocide-at-Law: An Historic and Contemporary View of the Native American Experience*, 34 KAN. L. REV. 713, 714–15 (1986).

but also a naturalized regime of rights and disabilities, power and disadvantage that flowed from it, so that no further justifications or rationalizations were required.[51] A key decision defending the right of conquest was Johnson and Graham's *Lessee v. M'Intosh*,[52] in which both parties to the action claimed the same land through title descendant from different Indian tribes. The issue specifically presented was not merely whether Indians had the power to convey title, but to whom the conveyance could be made—to individuals or to the government that "discovered" land.[53] In holding that Indians could only convey to the latter, the Court reasoned that Indian title was subordinate to the absolute title of the sovereign that was achieved by conquest because "[c]onquest gives a title which the Courts of the conqueror cannot deny. . . ."[54] If property is understood as a delegation of sovereign power—the product of the power

---

[51] *See* Williams, *supra* note 49, at 8.

[52] 21 U.S. (8 Wheat.) 543 (1823).

[53] *See id.* at 563. Milner Ball's reinterpretation of *Johnson* rejects the traditional reading that all rights held by American Indian nations were lost in conquest. Instead, he argues that the case held only that, by conquest, Indians lost the right to convey title to any country other than the United States. *See* Milner S. Ball, *Constitution, Court, Indian Tribes*, 1987 AM. B. FOUND. RES. J. 1, 29.

[54] *Johnson*, 21 U.S. (8 Wheat.) at 588–89. According to Robert Williams, in rendering this decision, the Court "merely formalized the outcome of a political contest that the Founders had fought and resolved among themselves some forty years earlier." WILLIAMS, *supra* note 49, at 231. Before Independence, radical colonists of the "landless" states—those without Crown charters specifying the territory available for settlement under the authority of the Crown—asserted the Indians' natural law right to alienate their land to whomever they chose, without regard to approval of the sovereign. *See id.* at 229–30. On the other hand, colonists of the "landed" states, those who held original Crown charters, argued that the colonial charters, as expressions of the will of the sovereign, granted them rights to the land specified and, under the frequently broad language of the grant, rights to control the land extending to the frontier. *See id.* at 230.

However, the coherence of the views between the settlers was far more significant than their differences. Ultimately, the conflict was resolved through a political compromise reached by the Founders that allowed for frontier claims held by the landed states to be ceded to a federal sovereign that could then assert exclusive rights to eradicate Indian occupancy claims by conquest or purchase and to undertake reallocation. *See Johnson*, 21 U.S. (8 Wheat.) at 585–88. Notwithstanding the differences between the opposing settler groups, their shared assumptions were that the Indians' rights to land as first possessors were subordinate to European claims, and that therefore conquest and occupation could give rise to a right.

of the state[55]—then a fair reading of history reveals the racial oppression of Indians inherent in the American regime of property.[56]

In *Johnson* and similar cases, courts established whiteness as a prerequisite to the exercise of enforceable property rights. Not all first possession or labor gave rise to property rights; rather, the rules of first possession and labor as a basis for property rights were qualified by race.[57] This fact infused whiteness with significance and value because it was solely through being white that property could be acquired and secured under law. Only whites possessed whiteness, a highly valued and exclusive form of property.

C. Critical Characteristics of Property and Whiteness

The legal legacy of slavery and of the seizure of land from Native American peoples is not merely a regime of property law that is (mis)informed by racist and ethnocentric themes. Rather, the law has established and protected an actual property interest in whiteness itself, which shares the critical characteristics of property and accords with the many and varied theoretical descriptions of property.

---

[55] *See* Joseph W. Singer, *The Reliance Interest in Property*, 40 STAN. L. REV. 611, 650–52 (1988).

[56] *See generally* Joseph W. Singer, *Sovereignty and Property*, 86 Nw. U. L. REV. 1, 1–8 (1991) (exploring the deleterious effects of the Supreme Court's formulation of tribal property rights). Parallel to the colonization of the Americas and the removal of the indigenous peoples from the land was the colonization of Africa and the removal of Africans from the continent. European conquest effected a horrific paradigm: as Europeans took Africans from the land, control of the land was taken from the Africans who remained. The result was that Africans who were removed from the continent became people without a country, and Africans on the continent became people without the legal capacity to control the land they occupied or to reap the benefits of the land they worked. The objective of capturing and enslaving Africans was to convert Africans and their descendants into property, or more accurately, into objects of property. The land dispossession of Africans on the continent, which was a central feature of colonialization, was accompanied by the introduction of regimes of property law that ratified the results of conquest and domination. *See generally* WALTER RODNEY, HOW EUROPE UNDERDEVELOPED AFRICA *passim* (1972) (offering a historical account of the origins and impact of the slave trade and European imperialism on African development). Thus, both here and on the African continent, race domination, imperialist conquest, and property rights were organically linked.

[57] *See* Singer, *supra* note 48, at 713.

Although by popular usage property describes "things" owned by persons, or the rights of persons with respect to a thing,[58] the concept of property prevalent among most theorists, even prior to the twentieth century, is that property may "consist of rights in 'things' that are intangible, or whose existence is a matter of legal definition."[59] Property is thus said to be a right, not a thing, characterized as metaphysical, not physical.[60] The theoretical bases and conceptual descriptions of property rights are varied, ranging from first possessor rules,[61] to creation of value,[62] to Lockean labor theory, to personality theory, to utilitarian theory.[63] However disparate, these formulations of property clearly illustrate the extent to which property rights and interests embrace much more than land and personality. Thus, the fact that whiteness is not a "physical" entity does not remove it from the realm of property.

---

[58] *See* C.B. Macpherson, *The Meaning of Property, in* PROPERTY: MAINSTREAM AND CRITICAL POSITIONS 1, 3 (C.B. Macpherson ed., 1978) [hereinafter Property]. Stephen Munzer characterizes the idea of property-as- "thing" as the popular conception and property-as-relations as "the sophisticated version of property." STEPHEN R. MUNZER, A THEORY OF PROPERTY 16 (1990).

[59] Frederick G. Whelan, *Property as Artifice: Hume and Blackstone, in* NOMOS XXII: PROPERTY, *supra* note 44, at 101, 104. Whelan argues that even Blackstone was aware that property rights may pertain to things that may themselves be creations of law. *See id.* at 121–22. Thus, for example, Whelan notes that Blackstone described property in incorporeal hereditaments, which issue out of a "thing" but have "mental existence." *Id.* at 121. The distinction between property as things and property as rights, then, is not so clear.

[60] *See* JEREMY BENTHAM, THE THEORY OF LEGISLATION 111–13 (Richard Hildreth trans., 1931).

[61] *See* Richard A. Epstein, *Possession as the Root of Title*, 13 GA. L. REV. 1221, 1221–22 (1979).

[62] *See* Wendy J. Gordon, *On Owning Information: Intellectual Property and the Restitutionary Impulse*, 78 VA. L. REV. 149, 178 (1992).

[63] Margaret Radin ascribes these concepts as the principal basis for liberal property theories propounded by John Locke, Georg W. Friedrich Hegel, and Jeremy Bentham respectively. *See* Margaret J. Radin, *Property and Personhood*, 34 STAN. L. REV. 957, 958 n.3 (1982). Munzer describes the multiplicity of definitions of property as inviting the despairing conclusion that "any overarching normative theory of property is impossible." Munzer, *supra* note 58, at 17; *see* Thomas C. Grey, *The Disintegration of Property, in* NOMOS XXII: PROPERTY, *supra* note 44, at 69, 69–82.

Whiteness is not simply and solely a legally recognized property interest. It is simultaneously an aspect of self-identity and of personhood, and its relation to the law of property is complex. Whiteness has functioned as self-identity in the domain of the intrinsic, personal, and psychological; as reputation in the interstices between internal and external identity; and, as property in the extrinsic, public, and legal realms. According whiteness actual legal status converted an aspect of identity into an external object of property, moving whiteness from privileged identity to a vested interest. The law's construction of whiteness defined and affirmed critical aspects of identity (who is white); of privilege (what benefits accrue to that status); and, of property (what legal entitlements arise from that status). Whiteness at various times signifies and is deployed as identity, status, and property, sometimes singularly, sometimes in tandem. . . .

D. White Legal Identity: The Law's Acceptance and Legitimation of Whiteness as Property

The law assumed the crucial task of racial classification, and accepted and embraced the then-current theories of race as biological fact. This core precept of race as a physically defined reality allowed the law to fulfill an essential function—to "parcel out social standing according to race" and to facilitate systematic discrimination by articulating "seemingly precise definitions of racial group membership."[64] This allocation of race and rights continued a century after the abolition of slavery.[65] The law relied on bounded, objective, and scientific definitions of race—what Neil Gotanda has called "historical race"[66]—to construct whiteness as not merely race, but race plus privilege. By making race determinant and the product of rationality and science, dominant and subordinate positions within the racial hierarchy were disguised as the

---

[64] Robert J. Cottrol, *The Historical Definition of Race Law*, 21 LAW & SOC'Y REV. 865, 865 (1988).

[65] *See id.*

[66] Gotanda defines "historical race" as socially constructed formal categories predicated on race subordination that included presumed substantive characteristics relating to "ability, disadvantage, or moral culpability." Gotanda, *supra* note 24, at 4.

product of natural law and biology[67] rather than as naked preferences.[68] Whiteness as racialized privilege was then legitimated by science and was embraced in legal doctrine as "objective fact."

Case law that attempted to define race frequently struggled over the precise fractional amount of Black "blood"—traceable Black ancestry— that would defeat a claim to whiteness.[69] Although the courts applied varying fractional formulas in different jurisdictions to define "Black" or, in the terms of the day, "Negro" or "colored," the law uniformly accepted the rule of hypodescent[70]—racial identity was governed by blood, and white was preferred.[71]

---

[67] *See infra* note 139 [72 in this excerpt] and accompanying text.

[68] *See* Cass R. Sunstein, *Naked Preferences and the Constitution*, 84 COLUM. L. REV. 1689, 1693–94 (1989).

[69] See, for example, People v. Dean, 14 Mich. 406 (1866), in which the majority held that those with less than one-quarter Black blood were white within the meaning of the constitutional provision limiting the franchise to "white male citizens," *see id.* at 425. The dissent argued that a preponderance of white blood should be sufficient to accord the status of whiteness. *See id.* at 435, 438 (Martin, C.J., dissenting).

[70] "Hypodescent" is the term used by anthropologist Marvin Harris to describe the American system of racial classification in which the subordinate classification is assigned to the offspring if there is one "superordinate" and one "subordinate" parent. Under this system, the child of a Black parent and a white parent is Black. MARVIN HARRIS, PATTERNS OF RACE IN THE AMERICAS 37, 56 (1964).

[71] According to various court decisions of the nineteenth and early twentieth centuries, the term "negro" was construed to mean a person of mixed blood within three generations, *see* State v. Melton & Byrd, 44 N.C. (Busb.) 49, 51 (1852); a person having one-fourth or more of African blood, *see* Gentry v. McMinnis, 3 Dana (Ky.) 382, 385 (1835); Jones v. Commission, 80 Va. 538, 542 (1885); a person having one-sixteenth or more of African blood, *see* State v. Chavers, 50 N.C. 11, 14–15 (1857); State v. Watters, 25 N.C. (3 Ired.) 455, 457 (1843); a person having one-eighth or more of African blood, *see* Rice v. Gong Lum, 139 Miss. 760, 779 (1925); Marre v. Marre, 184 Mo. App. 198, 211 (1914); anyone with any trace of Negro blood, *see* State v. Montgomery County School Dist. No. 16, 242 S.W. 545, 546 (1922). The term "colored" too had a range of legal meanings. *See* 11 C.J. *Colored* 1224 (1917). For a review of court decisions and statutes of the nineteenth and early twentieth centuries delineating who is a "Negro" or who is colored, see MANGUM, *supra* note 30, at 1–17.

An example of the complexity of defining these terms is revealed in State v. Treadway, 52 So. 500 (La. 1910), in which the Louisiana state supreme court exhaustively reviewed the various meanings of the words "negro" and "colored" in considering whether an "octoroon"—a person of one-eighth Black blood—was a

This legal assumption of race as blood-borne was predicated on the pseudo-sciences of eugenics and craniology that saw their major development during the eighteenth and nineteenth centuries.[72] The legal definition of race was the "objective" test propounded by racist theorists of the day who described race to be immutable, scientific, biologically determined—an unsullied fact of the blood rather than a volatile and violently imposed regime of racial hierarchy.

In adjudicating who was "white," courts sometimes noted that, by physical characteristics, the individual whose racial identity was at issue appeared to be white and, in fact, had been regarded as white in the community. Yet if an individual's blood was tainted, she could not claim to be "white" as the law understood, regardless of the fact that phenotypically

---

Negro within the meaning of a statute barring cohabitation between a person of the "white" race and a person of the "negro or black" race. *See id.* at 501–10. In examining the definitions propounded in various dictionaries, court decisions, and statutory law that used either term, the court concluded that "colored" denoted a person of mixed white and Black blood in any degree, and a "negro" was a "person of the African race, or possessing the black color and other characteristics of the African." *Id.* at 531. Because "there are no negroes who are not persons of color; but there are persons of color who are not negroes," *id.*, the court concluded that the statute did not include octoroons because they were not commonly considered "negroes," although they were persons of color, *see id.* at 537. The response of the Louisiana legislature was to reenact the statute with the identical language, except it substituted the word "colored" for the word "Negro." *See* MANGUM, *supra* note 30, at 5–6.

[72] For example, Samuel Morton, one of the principal architects of these theories, ascribed the basis of Black and non-white racial inferiority to differences in cranial capacity, which purportedly revealed that whites had larger heads. Notwithstanding the gross breaches of scientific method and manipulation of data evident in Morton's theory, *see* GOSSETT, *supra* note 20, at 73–74, his 1839 book, *Crania Americana*, was widely accepted as the scientific explanation of Blacks' inability to mature beyond childhood, *see* Gossett, *supra* note 20, at 58–59 (citing the remarks of Oliver Wendell Holmes, Sr., extolling Morton as a "leader" whose "severe and cautious . . . researches" would provide "permanent data for all future students of Ethology"); TAKAKI, *supra* note 16, at 113 (citing the remarks of an Indiana senator in 1850 who spoke of the diminished brain capacity of Blacks). These and other widely disseminated theories of Black inferiority provided the rationale for the political and popular discourse of the time that argued that Black equality and participation in the polity were impossible because Blacks lacked the capacity to develop rational decisionmaking. *See* REGINALD HORSMAN, RACE AND MANIFEST DESTINY 116–57 (describing the permeation of "scientific" bases for racial inferiority into every aspect of American thought).

she may have been completely indistinguishable from a white person, may have lived as a white person, and have descended from a family that lived as whites. Although socially accepted as white, she could not legally be white.[73] Blood as "objective fact" dominated over appearance and social acceptance, which were socially fluid and subjective measures.

But, in fact, "blood" was no more objective than that which the law dismissed as subjective and unreliable. The acceptance of the fiction that the racial ancestry could be determined with the degree of precision called for by the relevant standards or definitions rested on false assumptions that racial categories of prior ancestors had been accurately reported, that those reporting in the past shared the definitions currently in use, and that racial purity actually existed in the United States.[74] Ignoring these considerations, the law established rules that extended equal treatment to those of the "same blood," albeit of different complexions, because it

---

[73] *See, e.g.,* Sunseri v. Cassagne, 185 So. 1, 4–5 (La. 1938). The case involved a suit by Sunseri to annul his marriage to Cassagne on the grounds that she had a trace of "negro blood." He contended that his wife's great-grea-grandmother was a "full-blooded negress," and Cassagne herself asserted that she was Indian. *See id.* at 2. It was not disputed that all of Cassagne's paternal ancestors from her father to her great-great-grandfather were white men. *See id.* Moreover, Cassagne had been regarded as white in the community, as she and her mother had been christened in a white church, had attended white schools, were registered as white voters, were accepted as white in public facilities, and had exclusively associated with whites. *See id.* at 4–5. Nevertheless, because certificates and official records designated Cassagne and some of her relatives as "colored," the court concluded that she was not white and that thus there were sufficient grounds to annul the marriage. *See* Sunseri v. Cassagne, 196 So. 7, 10 (La. 1940); *see also* Johnson v. Board of Educ. of Wilson County, 82 S.E. 832, 833–35 (1914) (refusing to allow the children of a "pure white" husband and a wife who was less than "one-eighth negro" to be admitted to white schools because of the presence of "negro blood in some degree," even assuming that the marriage was valid and not violative of the miscegenation statute).

[74] It is not at all clear that even the slaves imported from abroad represented "pure Negro races." As Gunner Myrdal noted, many of the tribes imported from Africa had intermingled with peoples of the Mediterranean, among them Portuguese slave traders. Other slaves brought to the United States came via the West Indies, where some Africans had been brought directly, but still others had been brought via Spain and Portugal, countries in which extensive interracial sexual relations had occurred. By the mid-nineteenth century it was, therefore, a virtual fiction to speak of "pure blood" as it relates to racial identification in the United States. *See* MYRDAL, *supra* note 4, at 123.

was acknowledged that, "[t]here are white men as dark as mulattoes, and there are pureblooded albino Africans as white as the whitest Saxons."[75]

The standards were designed to accomplish what mere observation could not: "That even Blacks who did not look Black were kept in their place."[76] Although the line of demarcation between Black and white varied from rules that classified as Black a person containing "any drop of Black blood,"[77] to more liberal rules that defined persons with a preponderance of white blood to be white,[78] the courts universally accepted the notion that white status was something of value that could be accorded only to those persons whose proofs established their whiteness as defined by the law.[79] Because legal recognition of a person as white carried material benefits, "false" or inadequately supported claims were denied like any other unsubstantiated claim to a property interest. Only those who could lay "legitimate" claims to whiteness could be legally recognized as "white," because allowing physical attributes, social acceptance, or self-identification to determine whiteness would diminish its

---

[75] People v. Dean, 14, Mich. 406, 422 (1866).

[76] Diamond & Cottrol, *supra* note 20, at 281.

[77] For a history of the "one-drop" rule, see DAVIS, cited above in note 128 [omitted], at 5. According to Davis:

The nation's answer to the question "Who is black?" has long been that a black is any person with any known African black ancestry. This definition reflects the long experience with slavery and later with Jim Crow segregation. In the South it became known as the "one-drop rule," meaning that a single drop of "black blood" makes a person black. It is also known as the . . . "traceable amount rule," and anthropologists call it the "hypo-descent rule," meaning that racially mixed persons are assigned the status of the subordinate group. This definition emerged from the American South to become the nation's definition, generally accepted by whites and blacks alike. Blacks had no other choice.

Id. (citations omitted).

[78] *See, e.g.*, Gray v. Ohio, 4 Ohio 353, 355 (1831).

[79] The courts adopted this standard even as they critiqued the legitimacy of such rules and definitions. For example, in People v. Dean, 14 Mich. 406 (1886), the court, in interpreting the meaning of the word "white" for the purpose of determining whether the defendant had voted illegally, criticized as "absurd" the notion that "a preponderance of mixed blood, on one side or the other of any given standard, has the remotest bearing upon personal fitness or unfitness to possess political privileges," *id.* at 417, but held that the electorate that had voted for racial exclusion had the right to determine voting privileges, *see id.* at 416.

value and destroy the underlying presumption of exclusivity. In effect, the courts erected legal "No Trespassing" signs.

In the realm of *social* relations, racial recognition in the United States is thus an act of race subordination. In the realm of legal relations, judicial definition of racial identity based on white supremacy reproduced that race subordination at the institutional level. In transforming white to whiteness, the law masked the ideological content of racial definition and the exercise of power required to maintain it: "It convert[ed] [an] abstract concept into [an] entity."[80]

1. *Whiteness as Racialized Privilege.*—The material benefits of racial exclusion and subjugation functioned, in the labor context, to stifle class tensions among whites. White workers perceived that they had more in common with the bourgeoisie than with fellow workers who were Black. Thus, W.E.B. Du Bois's classic historical study of race and class, *Black Reconstruction*,[81] noted that, for the evolving white working class, race identification became crucial to the ways that it thought of itself and conceived its interests. There were, he suggested, obvious material benefits, at least in the short term, to the decision of white workers to define themselves by their whiteness: their wages far exceeded those of Blacks and were high even in comparison with world standards.[82] Moreover, even when the white working class did not collect increased pay as part of white privilege, there were real advantages not paid in direct income: whiteness still yielded what Du Bois termed a "public and psychological wage" vital to white workers.[83] Thus, Du Bois noted:

> They [whites] were given public deference . . . because they were white. They were admitted freely with all classes of white people, to public functions, to public parks. . . . The police were drawn from their ranks, and the courts, dependent on their votes, treated them with . . . leniency. . . . Their vote selected public officials, and while this had small effect upon the economic situation, it had great effect on their personal treatment. . . . White schoolhouses were the best in the community, and conspicuously placed, and

---

[80] STEPHEN J. GOULD, THE MISMEASURE OF MAN 24 (1981).
[81] W.E.B. DU BOIS, BLACK RECONSTRUCTION (photo. reprint 1976) (1935).
[82] *See id.* at 634.
[83] *Id.* at 700.

they cost anywhere from twice to ten times as much per capita as the colored schools.[84]

The central feature of the convergence of "white" and "worker" lay in the fact that racial status and privilege could ameliorate and assist in "evad[ing] rather than confront[ing] [class] exploitation."[85] Although not accorded the privileges of the ruling class, in both the North and South, white workers could accept their lower-class position in the hierarchy "by fashioning identities as 'not slaves' and as 'not Blacks.'"[86] Whiteness produced—and was reproduced by—the social advantage that accompanied it.

Whiteness was also central to national identity and to the republican project. The amalgamation of various European strains into an American identity was facilitated by an oppositional definition of Black as "other."[87] As Hacker suggests, fundamentally, the question was not

---

[84] *Id.* at 700–01.

[85] ROEDIGER, *supra* note 19, at 13. One of Roediger's principal themes is that whiteness was constructed both from the top down and from the bottom up. *See id.* at 8–11. His vigorous analysis of the role of racism in the construction of working class consciousness leads him to conclude that "the pleasures of whiteness could function as a [wage] for white workers. . . . [S]tatus and privilege conferred by race could be used to make up for alienating and exploitive class relationships." *Id.* at 13. Roediger further argues that the conjunction of "white" and "worker" came about in the nineteenth century at a time when the non-slave labor force came increasingly to depend on wage labor. The independence of this sector was then measured in relation to the dependency of Blacks as a subordinated people and class. *See id.* at 20. The involvement of all sectors, including the white working class, in the construction of whiteness aids in explaining the persistence of whiteness in the modern period.

[86] ROEDIGER, *supra* note 19, at 13.

[87] "One of the surest ways to confirm an identity, for communities and individuals, is to find some way of measuring what one is *not*." KAI ERICKSON, WAYWARD PURITANS: A STUDY IN THE SOCIOLOGY OF DEVIANCE 64 (1966). Toni Morrison's study of the Africanist presence in U.S. literature echoes the same theme of the reflexive construction of "American" identity:

It is no accident and no mistake that immigrant populations (and much immigrant literature) understood their Americanness as an opposition to the resident black population. Race in fact now functions as a metaphor so necessary to the construction of Americanness that it rivals the old pseudo-scientific and class-informed racisms whose dynamics we are more used to deciphering. . . . Deep within the word "American" is its association with race. To identify someone as South African is to say very little; we need the

so much "who is white," but "who may be considered white," as the historical pattern was that various immigrant groups of different ethnic origins were accepted into a white identity shaped around Anglo-American norms.[88] Current members then "ponder[ed] whether they want[ed] or need[ed] new members as well as the proper pace of new admissions into this exclusive club."[89] Through minstrel shows in which white actors masquerading in blackface played out racist stereotypes, the popular culture put the Black at "'solo spot centerstage, providing a relational model in contrast to which masses of Americans could establish a positive and superior sense of identity[,]' . . . [an identity] . . . established by an infinitely manipulable negation comparing whites with a construct of a socially defenseless group."[90]

It is important to note the effect of this hypervaluation of whiteness. Owning white identity as property affirmed the self-identity and liberty[91] of whites and, conversely, denied the self-identity and liberty of Blacks.[92] The attempts to lay claim to whiteness through "passing" painfully

adjective "'white" or "black" or "colored" to make our meaning clear. In this country, it is quite the reverse. American means white. . . .
TONI MORRISON, PLAYING IN THE DARK: WHITENESS AND THE LITERARY IMAGINA-TION 46–47 (1992).

[88] Andrew Hacker says that white became a "common front" established across ethnic origins, social class, and language. ANDREW HACKER, TWO NATIONS 12 (1992).

[89] *Id.* at 9.

[90] ROEDIGER, *supra* note 19, at 118 (quoting Alan W.C. Green, *"Jim Crow," "Zip Coon": The Northern Origin of Negro Minstrelsy*, 11 Mass. Rev. 385, 395 (1970)).

[91] I do not attempt here to review or state a position with regard to the profusion of theories that describe the relationship between liberty and property; that is beyond the scope of this inquiry. Rather, I use liberty in the Hohfeldian sense as a privilege, "a legal liberty or freedom," not involving "a correlative duty but the absence of a right on someone else's part to interfere." MUNZER, *supra* note 58, at 18 (1990).

[92] In this respect, whiteness as property followed a familiar paradigm. Although the state can create new forms of property other than those existing at common law, "in each case that it creates new property rights, the state necessarily limits the common law liberty or property rights of other citizens, for conduct which was once legal now becomes an invasion or an infringement of the new set of rights that are established." Epstein, *No New Property, supra* note 68, at 754 [omitted from excerpt]; *see* HIGGINBOTHAM, *supra* note 20, at 13 (noting that, when the law establishes a right for a person, group, or institution, it simultaneously constrains those whose "preferences impinge on the right established").

illustrate the effects of the law's recognition of whiteness. The embrace of a lie, undertaken by my grandmother and the thousands like her, could occur only when oppression makes self-denial and the obliteration of identity rational and, in significant measure, beneficial.[93] The economic coercion of white supremacy on self-definition nullifies any suggestion that passing is a logical exercise of liberty or self-identity. The decision to pass as white was not a choice, if by that word one means voluntariness or lack of compulsion. The fact of race subordination was coercive and circumscribed the liberty to self-define. Self-determination of identity was not a right for all people, but a privilege accorded on the basis of race. The effect of protecting whiteness at law was to devalue those who were not white by coercing them to deny their identity in order to survive.[94]

2. *Whiteness, Rights, and National Identity.*—The concept of whiteness was carefully protected because so much was contingent upon it. Whiteness conferred on its owners aspects of citizenship that were all the more valued because they were denied to others. Indeed, the very fact of citizenship itself was linked to white racial identity. The Naturalization Act of 1790 restricted citizenship to persons who resided in the United States for two years, who could establish their good character in court, and who were "white."[95] Moreover, the trajectory of expanding

---

[93] This problem is at the center of one of the early classics of Black literature, *The Autobiography of an Ex-Coloured Man*, by James Weldon Johnson, the story of a Black man who "passes" for white, crossing between Black and white racial identities four times. *See* Henry L. Gates, Jr., *Introduction* to JAMES W. JOHNSON, THE AUTOBIOGRAPHY OF AN EX-COLOURED MAN vi (Vintage 1989) (1912).

[94] I am indebted to Lisa Ikemoto for the insight regarding how whiteness as property interacts with liberty and self-identity.

[95] *See* Naturalization Act of 1790, ch. 3, § 1, 1 Stat. 103, 103 (1790) (repealed 1795). As Takaki explains, this law "specified a complexion for the members of the new nation" and reflected the explicit merger of white national identity and republicanism. TAKAKI, *supra* note 16, at 15. It was also another arena in which the law promulgated racial definitions as part of its task of allocating rights of citizenship. These decisions further reinforced white hegemony by naturalizing white identity as objective when in fact it was a constructed and moving barrier. As noted in *Corpus Juris*, a white person

> constitutes a very indefinite description of a class of persons, where none can be said to be literally white; and it has been said that a construction of the term to mean Europeans and persons of European descent is ambiguous. "White person" has been held to include an Armenian born in Asiatic

democratic rights for whites was accompanied by the contraction of the rights of Blacks in an ever deepening cycle of oppression.[96] The franchise, for example, was broadened to extend voting rights to unpropertied white men at the same time that Black voters were specifically disenfranchised, arguably shifting the property required for voting from land to whiteness.[97] This racialized version of republicanism—this Herrenvolk[98] republicanism—constrained any vision of democracy from addressing the class hierarchies adverse to many who considered themselves white.

The inherent contradiction between the bondage of Blacks and republican rhetoric that championed the freedom of all men was resolved by positing that Blacks were different.[99] The laws did not mandate that Blacks be accorded equality under the law because nature—not man, not power, not violence—had determined their degraded status. Rights were for those who had the capacity to exercise them, a capacity denoted by racial identity. This conception of rights was contingent on race—on whether one could claim whiteness—a form of property. This articulation of rights that were contingent on property ownership was a familiar paradigm, as similar requirements had been imposed on the

---

Turkey, a person of but one-sixteenth Indian blood, and a Syrian, but not to include Afghans, American Indians, Chinese, Filipinos, Hawaiians, Hindus, Japanese, Koreans, negroes; nor does white person include a person having one fourth of African blood, a person in whom Malay blood predominates, a person whose father was a German and whose mother was a Japanese, a person whose father was a white Canadian and whose mother was an Indian woman, or a person whose mother was a Chinese and whose father was the son of a Portuguese father and a Chinese mother.
C.J. *White* 258 (1934) (citations omitted).

[96] *See* Diamond & Cottrol, *supra* note 20, at 262.

[97] For an account of the linkage between expanding white voting rights and increased constraints on rights for Blacks, see ROEDIGER, *supra* note 19, in which he describes the experience in Pennsylvania, *see id.* at 59; *see also* Diamond & Cottrol, *supra* note 20, at 260–61 n.26 (summarizing the fate of free, enfranchised Blacks who were later disenfranchised in the face of rising racism at the same time that property requirements were abolished for white voters).

[98] Pierre van der Berghe uses this term to describe those societies in which dominant groups operate within democratic and egalitarian rules, and subordinate groups are subjected to un-democratic and tyrannical regulation. The classic contemporary example of this model is South Africa. *See* PIERRE VAN DER BERGHE, RACE AND RACISM: A COMPARATIVE PERSPECTIVE 17–18 (1967).

[99] *See* Diamond & Cottrol, *supra* note 20, at 262.

franchise in the early part of the republic.[100] For the first two hundred years of the country's existence, the system of racialized privilege in both the public and private spheres carried through this linkage of rights and inequality, and rights and property. Whiteness as property was the critical core of a system that affirmed the hierarchical relations between white and Black. . . .

. . . .

IV. THE PERSISTENCE OF WHITENESS AS PROPERTY

In the modern period, neither the problems attendant to assigning racial identities nor those accompanying the recognition of whiteness have disappeared.[101] Nor has whiteness as property. Whiteness as property

---

[100] The organizing principle of the Federalist vision of the republic was that government must protect the rights of persons and the rights of property. *See* JENNIFER NEDELSKY, PRIVATE PROPERTY AND THE LIMITS OF AMERICAN CONSTITUTIONALISM 17 (1991). But if, as Madison stated, "the first object of government is the protection of different and unequal faculties of acquiring property," *id.* at 17 (citation omitted), then an extension of the rights of suffrage to all would subject those with material property, always a minority, to the control of the propertyless, *see id.* at 18. The solution adopted by Madisonian republicanism limited the franchise and installed a system of freehold suffrage. *See id.* at 19. The result, according to Nedelsky, was a distortion of the republican vision as inequality was presumed and protected. *See id.* at 1. *But see* Book Note, *Private Property, Civic Republicanism and the Madisonian Constitution*, 104 HARV. L. REV. 961, 963–64 (1991) (arguing that Nedelsky mischaracterizes the Madisonian vision of property to be referring only to material property when in fact Madison's concept of property included everything to which one could claim a right).

[101] Doe v. State, 479 So.2d 369 (La. App. 4th Cir. 1985), is a prime example. Before this decision, the *Doe* plaintiffs had sued to change the racial classification of their parents on their birth certificate from "colored" to white. *See id.* at 371. Although by upbringing, experience, and appearance they were white, the court noted that, if the plaintiffs had standing, relief would be denied because of the plaintiffs' failure to establish that their grandparents had been incorrectly classified. A subsequent Fourteenth Amendment challenge to the 1970 Louisiana racial classification law was rejected by both the trial and appellate courts on the ground that the statute had been held constitutional in a prior decision of the Louisiana Supreme Court. *See* State *ex. rel.* Plaia v. Louisiana State Bd. of Health, 296 So.2d 809, 810 (La. 1974). The statute was repealed in 1983, and the *Doe* plaintiffs again brought a mandamus action that was again rejected by the trial court. *See Doe*, 479 So.2d at 371. On appeal, the state appellate court concluded that "the very concept of the racial classification of individuals, as opposed to that of a group, is scientifically insupportable . . . [because] [i]ndividual racial designations are purely social

continues to perpetuate racial subordination through the courts' definitions of group identity and through the courts' discourse and doctrine
on affirmative action. The exclusion of subordinated "others" was and
remains a central part of the property interest in whiteness and, indeed,
is part of the protection that the court extends to whites' settled expectations of continued privilege.

The essential character of whiteness as property remains manifest in
two critical areas of the law and, as in the past, operates to oppress Native
Americans and Blacks in similar ways, although in different arenas. This
Part first examines the persistence of whiteness as valued social identity;
then exposes whiteness as property in the law's treatment of the question
of group identity, as the case of the Mashpee Indians illustrates; and finally,
exposes the presence of whiteness as property in affirmative action doctrine.

A. *The Persistence of Whiteness as Valued Social Identity*

Even as the capacity of whiteness to deliver is arguably diminished by
the elimination of rigid racial stratifications, whiteness continues to be
perceived as materially significant. Because real power and wealth never
have been accessible to more than a narrowly defined ruling elite, for
many whites the benefits of whiteness as property, in the absence of leg-
islated privilege, may have been reduced to a claim of relative privilege
only in comparison to people of color.[102] Nevertheless, whiteness retains
its value as a "consolation prize": it does not mean that all whites will
win, but simply that they will not lose,[103] if losing is defined as being

---

and cultural perceptions." *Id.* Louisiana's racial classification system was vigorously
critiqued on constitutional grounds. *See* Diamond & Cottrol, *supra* note 20, at
278–85.

[102] *See* Letter from Leland Ware, Professor of Law, St. Louis University School of
Law, to Cheryl I. Harris, Assistant Professor of Law, Chicago-Kent College of Law
4 (Mar. 23, 1992) (on file at the Harvard Law School Library) [hereinafter Ware,
Letter].

[103] HACKER, *supra* note 155 [88 in this excerpt], at 29. Andrew Hacker says that
given the fierceness of competition in American society, white America

> cannot guarantee full security to every member of its own race. Still, while
> some of its members may fail, there is a limit to how far they can fall. . . . [N]o
> matter to what depths one descends, no white person can ever become black.
> As James Baldwin has pointed out, white people need the presence of black
> people as a reminder of what providence has spared them from becoming.

Id. at 29–30.

on the bottom of the social and economic hierarchy—the position to which Blacks have been consigned.

Andrew Hacker, in his 1992 book *Two Nations*,[104] recounts the results of a recent exercise that probed the value of whiteness according to the perceptions of whites. The study asked a group of white students how much money they would seek if they were changed from white to Black. "Most seemed to feel that it would not be out of place to ask for $50 million, or $1 million for each coming black year."[105] Whether this figure represents an accurate amortization of the societal cost of being Black in the United States, it is clear that whiteness is still perceived to

---

[104] HACKER, *supra* note 155.

[105] *Id.* at 32. Hacker reports these results from white students who were presented with the following parable:

THE VISIT

You will be visited tonight by an official you have never met. He begins by telling you that he is extremely embarrassed. The organization he represents has made a mistake, something that hardly ever happens.

According to their records . . . you were to have been born black: to another set of parents, far from where you were raised.

However, the rules being what they are, this error must be rectified, and as soon as possible. So at midnight tonight, you will become black. And this will mean not simply a darker skin, but the bodily and facial features associated with African ancestry. However, inside you will be the person you always were. Your knowledge and ideas will remain intact. But outwardly you will not be recognizable to anyone you now know.

Your visitor emphasizes that being born to the wrong parents was in no way your fault.

Consequently, his organization is prepared to offer you some reasonable recompense. Would you, he asks, care to name a sum of money you might consider appropriate? . . . [The] records show you are scheduled to live another fifty years—as a black man or woman in America.

How much financial recompense would you request?

Id. at 31–32. Hacker further argues that evidence of the continued value of whiteness is manifested in the fact that no white person would be willing to trade places with an even more successful black person:

All white Americans realize that their skin comprises an inestimable asset. . . .
Its value persists not because a white appearance automatically brings success
and status. . . . What it does ensure is that you will not be regarded as *black*, a
security which is worth so much that no one who has it has ever given it away.
Id. at 60.

be valuable. The wages of whiteness are available to all whites regardless of class position, even to those whites who are without power, money, or influence. Whiteness, the characteristic that distinguishes them from Blacks, serves as compensation even to those who lack material wealth. It is the relative political advantages extended to whites, rather than actual economic gains, that are crucial to white workers. Thus, as Kimberlé Crenshaw points out, whites have an actual stake in racism.[106] Because Blacks are held to be inferior, although no longer on the basis of science as antecedent determinant, but by virtue of their position at the bottom, it allows whites—all whites—to "include themselves in the dominant circle. [Although most whites] hold no real power, [all can claim] their privileged racial identity."[107]

White workers often identify primarily as white rather than as workers because it is through their whiteness that they are afforded access to a host of public, private, and psychological benefits.[108] It is through the

---

[106] *See* Crenshaw, *supra* note 3, at 1381.

[107] *Id.*; *see* ROEDIGER, *supra* note 19, at 5 (describing the significance of whiteness to white workers).

    This argument is not to suggest that poverty does not exist among whites. It is evident, however, that poverty is not proportionately represented across all racial groups. Blacks are and have been disproportionately affected by poverty and all its attendant social ills, such as inadequate housing, health care, and education. The relative advantage accorded to whites because of white supremacy is what I am identifying as a core component of "whiteness." This advantage does not mean that no whites will be poor, but that the poor will be disproportionately Black. *See* BUREAU OF THE CENSUS, U.S. DEP'T OF COMMERCE, SERIES P-60, No. 181, POVERTY IN THE UNITED STATES: 1991, at x (1992) [hereinafter CENSUS] (reporting that the poverty rate of whites, Blacks, Asians, and Hispanics is 11.3%, 32.7%, 13.8%, and 28.7%, respectively).

[108] These benefits may be difficult to discern, yet they often remain crucial. Albert Memmi's classic indictment of French colonialism in pre-independence Algeria offers invaluable insight into the benefits of racism to the working or lower class, notwithstanding the nearly equivalent positions of need of lower class whites and Blacks. He suggests that the problem is not merely gullibility or illusion:

    If the small colonizer defends the colonial system so vigorously, it is because he benefits from it to some extent. His gullibility lies in the fact that to protect his very limited interests, he protects other infinitely more important ones, of which he is, incidentally, the victim. But, though dupe and victim, he also gets his share.

concept of whiteness that class consciousness among white workers is subordinated and attention is diverted from class oppression.[109]

Although dominant societal norms have embraced the idea of fairness and nondiscrimination, removal of privilege and antisubordination principles are actively rejected or at best ambiguously received because expectations of white privilege are bound up with what is considered essential for self-realization. Among whites, the idea persists that their whiteness is meaningful.[110] Whiteness is an aspect of racial identity[111] surely, but it is much more; it remains a concept based on relations of power, a social construct predicated on white dominance and Black subordination. . . .

. . . .

    [P]rivilege is something relative. To different degrees every colonizer is privileged, at least comparatively so, ultimately to the detriment of the colonized. If the privileges of the master of colonization are striking, the lesser privileges of the small colonizer, even the smallest, are very numerous. Every act of his daily life places him in a relationship with the colonized, and with each act his fundamental advantage is demonstrated.

    . . . From the time of his birth, he possesses a qualification independent of his personal merits or his actual class.

ALBERT MEMMI, THE COLONIZER AND THE COLONIZED 11–12 (Howard Greenfield trans., 1965).

[109] Social scientists have noted this phenomenon as part of the social dynamic of the white working class for some time:

    It is through differential access to social institutions and political power that the bourgeoisie binds white workers to it in "whiteness."

    . . .

    . . . [T]o the extent that white workers identify with "whiteness," "a central component of *Anglo-American bourgeois consciousness* . . . ," and not with their proletarian status as workers, they will remain supporters and defenders of relative privileges for whites as extended by capital.

Hermon George, Jr., *Black America, the "Underclass" and the Subordination Process*, BLACK SCHOLAR, May/June 1988, at 44, 49–50 (quoting ROXANNE MITCHELL & FRANK WEISS, A HOUSE DIVIDED: LABOR AND WHITE SUPREMACY 84 (1981)).

[110] Roediger describes this phenomenon as the "white problem." ROEDIGER, *supra* note 19, at 6.

[111] "Racial identities are not only black, Latino, Asian, Native American, and so on; they are also white. To ignore white ethnicity is to redouble its hegemony by naturalizing it." bell hooks, "Representing Whiteness: Seeing Wings of Desire," in *Yearning: Race, Gender, and Cultural Politics* (Toronto: BTL Books, 1990).

VI. CONCLUSION

Whiteness as property has carried and produced a heavy legacy. It is a ghost that has haunted the political and legal domains in which claims for justice have been inadequately addressed for far too long. Only rarely declaring its presence, it has warped efforts to remediate racial exploitation. It has blinded society to the systems of domination that work against so many by retaining an unvarying focus on vestiges of systemic racialized privilege that subordinates those perceived as a particularized few—the "others." It has thwarted not only conceptions of racial justice but also conceptions of property that embrace more equitable possibilities. In protecting the property interest in whiteness, property is assumed to be no more than the right to prohibit infringement on settled expectations, ignoring countervailing equitable claims that are predicated on a right to inclusion. It is long past time to put the property interest in whiteness to rest. Affirmative action can assist in that task. Affirmative action, if properly conceived and implemented, is not only consistent with norms of equality, but is essential to shedding the legacy of oppression.

"The Souls of White Folk"

W. E. B. Du Bois

High in the tower, where I sit above the loud complaining of the human sea, I know many souls that toss and whirl and pass, but none there are that intrigue me more than the Souls of White Folk.

Of them I am singularly clairvoyant. I see in and through them. I view them from unusual points of vantage. Not as a foreigner do I come, for I am native, not foreign, bone of their thought and flesh of their language. Mine is not the knowledge of the traveler or the colonial composite of dear memories, words and wonder. Nor yet is my knowledge that which servants have of masters, or mass of class, or capitalist of artisan. Rather I see these souls undressed and from the back and side. I see the working of their entrails. I know their thoughts and they know that I know. This knowledge makes them now embarrassed, now furious! They deny my right to live and be and call me misbirth! My word is to them mere bitterness and my soul, pessimism. And yet as they preach and strut and shout and threaten, crouching as they clutch at rags of facts and fancies to hide their nakedness, they go twisting, flying by my tired eyes and I see them ever stripped—ugly, human.

The discovery of personal whiteness among the world's peoples is a very modern thing—a nineteenth and twentieth century matter, indeed. The ancient world would have laughed at such a distinction. The Middle Ages regarded skin color with mild curiosity, and even up into the eighteenth century, we were hammering our national manikins into one, great, Universal Man, with fine frenzy which ignored color and race even more than birth. Today we have changed all that, and the world in a sudden, emotional conversion has discovered that it is white and by that token, wonderful!

This essay was originally published in *The Independent*, August 10, 1910, and revised for the collection *Darkwater: Voices from within the Veil* (1920).

This assumption that of all the hues of God whiteness alone is inherently and obviously better than brownness or tan leads to curious acts; even the sweeter souls of the dominant world as they discourse with me on weather, weal, and woe are continually playing above their actual words an obbligato tune and tone, saying:

"My poor, un-white thing! Weep not nor rage. I know, too well, that the curse of God lies heavy on you. Why? That is not for me to say, but be brave! Do your work in your lowly sphere, praying the good Lord that into heaven above, where all is love, you may, one day, be born—white!"

I do not laugh. I am quite straight-faced as I ask soberly:

"But what on earth is whiteness that one should so desire it?" Then always, somehow, some way, silently but clearly, I am given to understand that whiteness is the ownership of the earth forever and ever, Amen!

Now what is the effect on a man or a nation when it comes passionately to believe such an extraordinary dictum as this? That nations are coming to believe it is manifest daily. Wave on wave, each with increasing virulence, is dashing this new religion of whiteness on the shores of our time. Its first effects are funny: the strut of the Southerner, the arrogance of the Englishman amuck, the whoop of the hoodlum who vicariously leads your mob. Next it appears dampening generous enthusiasm in what we once counted glorious; to free the slave is discovered to be tolerable on in so far as it freed his master! Do we sense somnolent writings in black Africa or angry groans in India or triumphant banzais in Japan? "To your tents, O Israel!" These nations are not white!

After the more comic manifestations and the chilling of generous enthusiasm come subtler, darked deeds. Everything considered, the title to the universe claimed by White Folk is faulty. It ought, at least, to look plausible. How easy, then, by emphasis and omission to make children believe that every great soul the world ever saw was a white man's soul; that every great deed the world ever did was a white man's deed; that every great dream the world ever sang was a white man's dream. In fine, that if from the world were dropped everything that could not fairly be attributed to White Folk, the world would, if anything, be even greater, truer, better than now. And if all this be a lie, is it not a lie in a great cause?

Here it is that the comedy verges to tragedy. The first minor note is struck, all unconsciously, by those worthy souls in whom consciousness of high descent brings burning desire to spread the gift abroad—the obligation of nobility to the ignoble. Such sense of duty assumes two things: a real possession of the heritage and its frank appreciation by the humble-born. So long, then, as humble black folk, voluble with thanks, receive barrels of old clothes from lordly and generous whites, there is much mental peace and moral satisfaction. But when the black man begins to dispute the white man's title to certain alleged bequests of the Fathers in wage and position, authority and training, and when his attitude toward charity is sullen anger rather than humble jollity; when he insists on his human right to swagger and swear and waste—then the spell is suddenly broken and the philanthropist is ready to believe that Negroes are impudent, that the South is right, and that Japan wants to fight America.

After this the descent to Hell is easy. On the pale, white faces which the great billows whirl upward to my tower I see again and again, often and still more often, a writing of human hatred, a deep and passionate hatred, vast by the very vagueness of its expressions. Down through the green waters, on the bottom of the world, where men move to and from, I have seen a man—an educated gentleman—grow livid with anger because a little, silent, black woman was sitting by herself in a Pullman car. He was a white man. I have seen a great, grown man curse a little child, who had wandered into the wrong waiting-room, searching for its mother: "Here, you damned black—" He was white. In Central Park I have seen the upper lip of a quiet, peaceful man curl back in a tigerish snarl of rage because black folk rode by in a motor car. He was a white man. We have seen, you and I, city after city drunk and furious with ungovernable lust of blood; mad with murder, destroying, killing, and cursing; torturing human victims because somebody accused of crime happened to be of the same color as the mob's innocent victims and because that color was not white! We have seen—Merciful God! in these wild days and in the name of Civilization, Justice, and Motherhood—what have we not seen, right here in America, of orgy, cruelty, barbarism, and murder done to men and women of Negro descent.

Up through the foam of green and weltering waters wells this great mass of hatred, in wilder, fiercer violence, until I look down and know that today to the millions of my people no misfortune could happen— of death and pestilence, failure and defeat—that would not make the hearts of millions of their fellows beat with fierce, vindictive joy! Do you doubt it? Ask your own soul what it would say if the next census were to report that half of the black America was dead and the other half dying.

Unfortunate? Unfortunate. But where is the misfortune? Mine? Am I, in my blackness, the sole sufferer? I suffer. And yet, somehow, above the suffering, above the shackled anger that beats the bars, above the hurt that crazes there surges in me a vast pity—pity for a people imprisoned and enthralled, hampered and made miserable for such a cause, for such a phantasy!

Conceive this nation, of all human people, engaged in a crusade to make the "World Safe for Democracy"! Can you imagine the United States protesting against Turkish atrocities in Armenia, while the Turks are silent about mobs in Chicago and St. Louis, what is Louvain compared with Memphis, Waco, Washington, Dyersburg, and Estill Springs? In short, what is the black man but America's Belgium, and how could America condemn in Germany what she commits, just as brutally, within her own borders?

A true and worthy ideal frees and uplifts a people; a false ideal imprisons and lowers. Say to men, earnestly and repeatedly: "Honesty is best, knowledge is power; do unto others as you would be done by." Say this and act it and the nation must move toward it, if not to it. But say to people: "The one virtue is to be white," and the people rush to the inevitably conclusion, "Kill the 'nigger'!"

Is not this the record of present America? Is not this its headlong progress? Are we not coming more and more, day by day, to making the statement "I am white," the one fundamental tenet of our practical morality? Only when this basic, iron rule is involved is our defense of right nation-wide and prompt. Murder may swagger, theft may rule and prostitution may flourish and the nation gives by spasmodic, intermittent and lukewarm attention. But let the murderer be black or the thief brown or the violator of womanhood have a drop of Negro blood, and the righteousness of the indignation sweeps the world. Nor would this fact make the indignation less justifiable did not we all know that it was blackness that was condemned and not crime.

In the awful cataclysm of World War, where from beating, slandering, and murdering us the white world turned temporarily aside to kill each other, we of the Darker Peoples looked on in mild amaze.

Among some of us, I doubt not, this sudden descent of Europe into hell brought unbounded surprise, to others, over wide area, it brought the *Schaden Freude* of the bitterly hurt; but most of us, I judge, looked on silently and sorrowfully, in sober though, seeing sadly the prophecy of our own souls.

Here is a civilization that has boasted much. Neither Roman nor Arab, Greek nor Egyptian, Persian nor Mongol ever took himself and his own perfectness with such disconcerting seriousness as the modern white man. We whose shame, humiliation, and deep insult his aggrandizement so often involved were never deceived. We looked at him clearly, with world-old eyes, and saw simply a human thing, weak and pitiable and cruel, even as we are and were.

These super-men and world-mastering demi-gods listened, however, to no low tongues of ours, even when we pointed silently to their feet of clay. Perhaps we, as folk of simpler soul and more primitive type, have been most struck in the welter of recent years by the utter failure of white religion. We have curled our lips in something like contempt as we have witnessed glib apology and weary explanation. Nothing of the sort deceived us. A nation's religion is its life, and as such white Christianity is a miserable failure.

Nor would we be unfair in this criticism: We know that we, too, have failed, as you have, and have rejected many a Buddha, even as you have denied Christ; but we acknowledge our human frailty, while you, claiming super-humanity, scoff endlessly at our shortcomings.

The number of white individuals who are practicing with even reasonable approximation the democracy and unselfishness of Jesus Christ is so small and unimportant as to be fit subject for jest in Sunday supplements and in *Punch, Life, Le Rire*, and *Fliegende Blätter*. In her foreign mission work the extraordinary self-deception of white religion is epitomized: solemnly the white world sends five million dollars worth of missionary propaganda to Africa each year and in the same twelve months adds twenty-five million dollars worth of the vilest gin manufactured. Peace to the augurs of Rome!

We may, however, grant without argument that religious ideals have always far outrun their very human devotees. Let us, then, turn to more mundane matters of honor and fairness. The world today is trade. The world has turned shopkeeper; history is economic history; living is earning a living. Is it necessary to ask how much of high emprise and honorable conduct has been found here? Something, to be sure. The establishment of world credit systems is built on splendid and realizable faith in fellow-men. But it is, after all, so low and elementary a step that somethings it looks merely like honor among thieves, for the revelations of highway robbery and low cheating in the business world and in all its great modern centers have raised in the hearts of all true men in our day an exceeding great cry for revolution in our basic methods and conceptions of industry and commerce.

We do not, for a moment, forget the robbery of other times and races when trade was a most uncertain gamble, but was there not a certain honesty and frankness in the evil that argued a saner morality? There are more merchants today, surer deliveries, and wider well-being; but are those not, also, bigger thieves, deeper injustice, and more calloused selfishness in well-being. Be that as it may—certainly the nicer sense of honor that has risen ever and again in groups of forward-thinking men has been curiously and broadly blunted. Consider our chiefest industry—fighting. Laboriously the Middle Ages built its rules of fairness—equal armament, equal notice, equal conditions. What do we see today? Machine-guns against assegais; conquest sugared with religion; mutilation and rape masquerading as culture—all this, with vast applause at the superiority of white over black soldiers!

War is horrible! This the dark world knows to its awful cost. But has it just become horrible, in these last days, when under essentially equal conditions, equal armament, and equal waste of wealth white men are fighting white men, with surgeons and nurses hovering near?

Think of the wars through which we have lived in the last decade: in German Africa, in British Nigeria, in French and Spanish Morocco, in China, in Persia, in the Balkans, in Tripoli, in Mexico, and in a dozen lesser places—were not these horrible, too? Mind you, there were for most of these wars no Red Cross funds.

Behold little Belgium and her pitiable plight, but has the world forgotten Congo? What Belgium now suffers is not half, not even a tenth, of what she has done to black Congo since Stanley's great dream of 1880. Down the dark forests of inmost Africa sailed this modern Sir Galahad, in the name of "the noble-minded men of several nations," to introduce commerce and civilization. What came of it? "Rubber and murder, slavery in its worst form," wrote Glave in 1895.

Harris declares that King Leopold's regime meant the death of twelve million natives, "but what we who were behind the scenes felt most keenly was the fact that the real catastrophe in the Congo was desolation and murder in the larger sense. The invasion of family life, the ruthless destruction of every social barrier, the shattering of every tribal law, the introduction of criminal practices which struck the chiefs of the people dumb with horror—in a word, a veritable avalanche of filth and immorality overwhelmed the Congo tribes."

Yet the fields of Belgium laughed, the cities were gay, art and science flourished; the groans that helped to nourish civilization fell on deaf ears because the world round about was doing the same sort of thing elsewhere on its own account.

As we saw the dead dimly through rifts of battle-smoke and heart faintly the cursings and accusations of blood brothers, we darker men said: This is not Europe gone mad; this is not aberration nor insanity; this is Europe; this seeming Terrible is the real soul of white culture—back of all culture—stripped and visible today. This is where the world has arrived—these dark and awful depths and not the shining and ineffable heights of which it boasted. Here is whither the might and energy of modern humanity have really gone.

But may not the world cry back at us and ask "What better thing have you to who? What have you done or would do better than this if you had today the world rule? Paint with all riot of hateful colors the thin skin of European culture—is it not better than any culture that arose in Africa or Asia?"

It is. Of this there is no doubt and never has been; but why is it better? Is it better because Europeans are better, nobler, greater, and more gifted than other folk? It is not. Europe has never produced and never will in our day bring forth a single human soul who cannot be matched and over-matched in every line of human endeavor by Asia and Africa. Run the gamut, if you will, and let us have the Europeans who in sober truth over-match Nefartari, Mohammed, Rameses and Askia, Confucius, Buddha, and Jesus Christ. If we could scan the calendar of thousands of lesser men, in like comparison, the result would be the same; but we cannot do this because of the deliberately educated ignorance of white schools by which they remember Napoleon and forget Sonni Ali.

The greatness of Europe has lain in the width of the stage on which she has played her part, the strength of the foundations on which she has builded, and a natural, human ability no whit greater (if as great) than that of other days and races. In other words, the deeper reasons for the triumph of European civilization lie quite outside and beyond Europe—back in the universal struggles of all mankind.

Why, then, in Europe great? Because of the foundations which the mighty past have furnished her to build upon: the iron trade of ancient, black Africa, the religion and empire-building of yellow Asia, the art and science of the "dago" Mediterranean shore, east, south, and west, as well as north. And where she has builded securely upon this great past and learned from it she has gone forward to greater and more splendid human triumph; but where she has ignored this past and forgotten and sneered at it, she has shown the cloven hoof of poor, crucified humanity—she has played, like other empires gone, the world fool!

If, then, European triumphs in culture have been greater, so, too, may her failures have been greater. How great a failure and a failure in what does the World War betoken? Was it national jealousy of the sort of the seventeenth century? But Europe has done more to break down national barriers than any preceding culture. Was it fear of the balance of power in Europe? Hardly, save in the half-Asiatic problems of the Balkans. What, then, does Hauptmann mean when he says: "Our jealous enemies forged an iron ring about our breasts and we knew our breasts had to expand—that we had to split asunder this ring or else we had to cease breathing. But Germany will not cease to breathe and so it came to pass that the iron ring was forced apart."

Whither is this expansion? What is that breath of life, thought to be so indispensable to a great European nation? Manifestly it is expansion overseas, it is colonial aggrandizement which explains, and along adequately explains, the World War. How many of us today fully realize the current theory of colonial expansion, of the relation of Europe which is white, to the world which is black and brown and yellow? Bluntly put, that theory is this: It is the duty of white Europe to divide up the darker world and administer it for Europe's good.

This Europe has largely done. The European world is using black and brown men for all the uses which men know. Slowly but surely white culture is evolving the theory that "darkies" are born beasts of burden for white folk. It were silly to think otherwise, cries the cultured world, with stronger and shrilled accord. The supporting arguments grow and twist themselves in the mouths of merchant, scientist, soldier, traveler, writer, and missionary. Darker peoples are dark in mind as well as in body; of dark, uncertain, and imperfect descent, of frailer, cheaper stuff;

they are cowards in the face of mausers and maxims; they have no feelings, aspirations, and loves; they are fools, illogical idiots—"half-devil and half-child."

Such as they are civilization must, naturally, raise them, but soberly and in limited ways. They are not simply dark white men. They are not "men" in the sense that Europeans are men. To the very limited extent of their shallow capacities lift them to be useful to whites, to raise cotton, gather rubber, fetch ivory, dig diamonds—and let them be paid what men think they are worth—white men who know them to be well-nigh worthless.

Such degrading of men by men is as old as mankind and the invention of no one race or people. Ever have men striven to conceive of their victims as different from the victors, endlessly different, in soul and blood, strength and cunning, race and lineage. It has been left, however, to Europe and to modern days to discover the eternal world-wide mark of meanness—color!

Such is the silent revolution that has gripped modern European culture in the later nineteenth and twentieth centuries. Its zenith came in Boxer times: White supremacy was all but world-wide; Africa was dead, India conquered, Japan isolated, and China prostrate, while white America whetted her sword for mongrel Mexico and mulatto South America, lynching her own Negroes the while. Temporary halt in this program was made by little Japan and the white world immediately sense the peril of such "yellow" presumption! What sort of world would this be if yellow men must be treated "white"? Immediately the eventual overthrow of Japan became a subject of deep thought and intrigue, from St. Petersburg to San Francisco, from the Key of Heaven to the Little Brother of the Poor.

The using of men for the benefit of masters is no new invention of modern Europe. It is quite as old as the world. But Europe proposed to apply it on a scale and with an elaborateness of detail of which no former world ever dreamed. The imperial width of the thing—the heaven-defying audacity—makes its modern newness.

The scheme of Europe was no sudden invention, but a way out of long-pressing difficulties. It is plain to modern white civilization that the subjection of the white working classes cannot much longer be maintained. Education, political power, and increased knowledge of the technique and meaning of the industrial process are destined to make a more and more equitable distribution of wealth in the near future. The day of the very rich is drawing to a close, so far as individual white nations are concerned. But there is a loophole. There is a chance for exploitation on an immense scale for inordinate profit; not simply to the very rich, but to the middle class and to the laborers. This chance lies in the exploitation of darker peoples. It is here that the golden hand beckons. Here are no labor unions or votes or questioning onlookers or inconvenient consciences. These men may be used down to the very bone, and shot and maimed in "punitive" expeditions when they revolt. In these dark lands "industrial development" may repeat in exaggerated form every horror of the industrial history of Europe, from slavery and rape to disease and maiming; with only one test of success—dividends!

This theory of human culture and its aims has worked itself through warp and woof of our daily thought with a thoroughness that few realize. Everything great, good, efficient, fair, and honorable is "white"; every-thing mean, bad, blundering, cheating, and dishonorable is "yellow"; a bad taste is "brown"; and the devil is "black." The changes of this theme are continually rung in picture and story, in newspaper heading and moving-picture, in sermon and school book, until, of course, the King can do no wrong—a White Man is always right and a Black Man has no rights which a white man is bound to respect.

There must come the necessary despisings and hatreds of these savage half-men, this unclean *canaille* of the world—these dogs of men. All through the world this gospel is preaching. It has its literature, it has its priests, it has its secret propaganda and above all—it pays!

There's the rub—it pays. Rubber, ivory, and palm-oil; tea, coffee, and cocoa; bananas, oranges, and other fruit; cotton, gold, and copper—they, and a hundred other things which dark and sweating bodies hand up to the white world from their pits of slime, pay and pay well, but of all that the world gets the black world gets only the pittance that the white world throws it disdainfully.

Small wonder, then, that in the practical world of things-that-be there is jealousy and strife for the possession of the labor of dark millions, for the right to bleed and exploit the colonies of the world where this golden stream may be had, not always for the asking, but surely for the whipping and shooting. It was this competition for the labor of yellow, brown, and black folks that was the cause of the World War. Other causes have been glibly given and other contributing causes there doubtless were, but they were subsidiary and subordinate to this vast quest of the dark world's wealth and toil.

Colonies, we call them, these places where "niggers" are cheap and the earth is rich; they are those outlands where like a swarm of hungry locusts white masters may settle to be served as kings, wield the lash of the slave-drivers, rape girls and wives, grow as rich as Croesus and send homeward a golden stream. They belt the earth, these places, but they cluster in the tropics, with its darkened peoples: in Hong Kong and Anam, in Borneo and Rhodesia, in Sierra Leone and Nigeria, in Panama and Havana—these are El Dorados toward which the world powers stretch itching palms.

Germany, at last one and united and secure on land, looked across the seas and seeing England with sources of wealth insuring a luxury and power which Germany could not hope to rival by the slower processes of exploiting her own peasants and workingmen, especially with these workers half in revolt, immediately built her navy and entered into a desperate competition for possession of colonies of darker peoples. To South America, to China, to Africa, to Asia Minor, she turned like a hound quivering on the leash, impatient, suspicious, irritable, with blood-shot eyes and dripping fangs, ready for the awful word. England and France crouched watchfully over their bones, growling and wary, but gnawing industriously, while the blood of the dark world whetted their greedy appetites. In the background, shut out from the highway to the seven seas, sat Russia and Austria, snarling and snapping at each other and at the last Mediterranean gate to the El Dorado, where the Sick Man enjoyed bad health, and where millions of serfs in the Balkans, Russia, and Asia offered a feast to greed well-nigh as great as Africa.

The fateful day came. It had to come. The cause of war is preparation for war, and of all that Europe has done in a century there is nothing has equaled in energy, though, and time her preparation for wholesale murder. The only adequate cause of this preparation was conquest and conquest, not in Europe, but primarily among the darker peoples of Asia and Africa; conquest, not for assimilation and uplift, but for commerce and degradation. For this, and this mainly, did Europe gird herself at frightful cost for war.

The red day dawned when the tinder was lighted in the Balkans and Austro-Hungary seized a bit which brought her a step nearer to the world's highway; she seized one bit and poised herself for another. Then came that curious chorus of challenges, those leaping suspicions, taking all causes for distrust and rivalry and hatred, but saying little of the real and greatest cause.

Each nation felt its deep interest involved. But how? Not, surely, in the death of Ferdinand the Warlike; not, surely, in the old, half-forgotten *revanche* for Alsace-Lorraine; not even in the neutrality of Belgium. No! But in the possession of land overseas; in the right to colonies, the chance to levy endless tribute on the darker world—on coolies in China, on starving peasants in India, on black savages in Africa, on dying South Sea Islanders, on Indians of the Amazon—all this and nothing more.

Even the broken reed on which we had rested high hopes of eternal peace—the guild of the laborers—the front of that very important movement for human justice on which we had builded most, even this flew like a straw before the breath of king and Kaiser. Indeed, the flying had been foreshadowed when in Germany and America "international" Socialists had all but read yellow and black men out of the kingdom of industrial justice. Subtly had they been bribed, but effectively: Were they not lordly whites and should they not share in the spoils of rape? High wages in the United States and England might be the skillfully manipulated result of slavery in Africa and of peonage in Asia.

With the dog-in-the-manger theory of trade, with the determination to reap inordinate profits and to exploit the weakest to the utmost there came a new imperialism—the rage for one's own nation to own the earth or, at least, a large enough portion of it to insure as big profits as the next nation. Where sections could not be owned by one dominant nation there came a policy of "open door," but the "door" was open to "white people only." As to the darkest and weakest of peoples there was but one unanimity in Europe—that which Herr Dernberg of the German Colonial Office called the agreement with England to maintain white "prestige" in Africa—the doctrine of the divine right of white people to steal.

Thus the world market most wildly and desperately sought today is the market where labor is cheapest and most helpless and profit is most abundant. This labor is kept cheap and helpless because the white world despises "darkies." If one has the temerity to suggest that these workingmen may walk the way of white workingmen and climb by votes and self-assertion and education to the rank of men, he is howled out of court. They cannot do it and if they could, they shall not, for they are the enemies of the white race and the whites shall rule forever and forever and everywhere. Thus the hatred and despising of human beings from whom Europe wishes to extort her luxuries have led to such jealousy and bickering between European nations that they have fallen afoul of each other and have fought like crazed beasts. Such is the fruit of human hatred.

But what of the darker world that watches? Most men belong to this world. With Negro and Negroid, East Indian, Chinese, and Japanese they form two-thirds of the population of the world. A belief in humanity is a belief in colored men. If the uplift of mankind must be done by men, then the destinies of this world rest ultimately in the hands of darker nations.

What, then, is this dark world thinking? It is thinking that as wild and awful as this shameful war was, *it is nothing to compare to that fight for freedom which black and brown and yellow men must and will make unless their oppression and humiliation and insult at the hands of the White World cease. The Dark World is going to submit to its present treatment just as long as it must and not one moment longer.*

Let me say this again and emphasize it and leave no room for mistaken meaning: The World War was primarily the jealous and avaricious struggle for the largest share in exploiting darker races. As such it is and must be but the prelude to the armed and indignant protest of these despised and raped peoples. Today Japan is hammering on the door of justice, China is raising her half-manacled hands to knock next, India is writhing for the freedom to knock, Egypt is sullenly muttering, the Negroes of South and West Africa, of the West Indies, and of the United States are just awakening to their shameful slavery. Is, then, this war the end of wars? Can it be the end, so long as sits enthroned, even in the souls of those who cry peace, the despising and robbing of darker peoples? If Europe hugs this delusion, then this is not the end of world war—it is but the beginning!

We see Europe's greatest sin precisely where we found Africa's and Asia's—in human hatred, the despising of men, with this difference, however. Europe has the awful lesson of the past before her, has the splendid results of widened areas of tolerance, sympathy, and love among men, and she faces a greater, an infinitely greater, world of men than any preceding civilization ever faced.

It is curious to see America, the United States, looking on herself, first, as a sort of natural peacemaker, then as a moral protagonist in this terrible time. No nation is less fitted for this role. For two or more centuries America has marched proudly in the van of human hatred—making bonfires of human flesh and laughing at them hideously, and making the insulting of millions more than a matter of dislike—rather a great religion, a world war-cry: Up white, down black, to your tents, O while folk, and world war with black and parti-colored mongrel beasts!

Instead of standing as a great example of the success of democracy and the possibility of human brotherhood America has taken her place as an awful example of its pitfalls and failures, so far as black and brown and yellow peoples are concerned. And this, too, in spite of the fact that there has been no actual failure; the Indian is not dying out, the Japanese and Chinese have not menaced the land, and the experiment of Negro suffrage has resulted in the uplift of twelve million people at a rate probably unparalleled in history. But what of this? America, Land of Democracy, wanted to believe in the failure of democracy so far as darker peoples were concerned. Absolutely without excuse she established a caste system, rushed into preparation for war, and conquered tropical colonies. She stands today shoulder to shoulder with Europe in Europe's worst sin against civilization. She aspires to sit among the great nations who arbitrate the fate of "lesser breeds with the law" and she is at time heartily ashamed even of the large number of "new" white people whom her democracy has admitted to place and power. Against this surging forward of Irish and German, of Russian Jew, Slav, and "dago" her social bars have not availed, but against Negroes she can and does take her unflinching and immovable stand, backed by this new public policy of Europe. She trains her immigrants to this despising of "niggers" from the day of their landing, and they carry and send the news back to the submerged classes in the fatherlands.

All this I see and hear up in my tower, above the thunder of the seven seas. From my narrowed windows I stare into the night that looms beneath the cloud-swept stars. Eastward and westward storms are breaking—great, ugly whirlwinds of hatred and blood and cruelty. I will not believe them inevitable. I will not believe that all that was must be, that all the shameful drama of the past must be done again today before the sunlight sweeps the silver seas.

If I cry amid this roar of elemental forces, must my cry be in vain, because it is but a cry—a small and human cry amid Promethean gloom?

Back beyond the world and swept by these wild, white faces of the awful dead, why will this Soul of White Folk—this modern Prometheus—hang bound by his own binding, tethered by a fable of the past? I hear his mighty cry reverberating through the world, "I am white!" Well and good, O Prometheus, divine thief! Is not the world wide enough for two colors, for many little shinings of the sun? Why, then, devour your own vitals if I answer even as proudly, "I am black!"

4

Whiteness as Evil

Woe unto them that call evil good, and good evil; that put darkness for light, and light for darkness, those who put bitter for sweet and sweet for bitter!

—Isaiah 5:20

Let love be genuine; hate what is evil, hold fast to what is good. . . . Do not be overcome by evil, but overcome evil with good.

—Romans 12:9, 21

It was as this in those last minutes he was summing up the lesson that this long course in human wickedness had taught us—the lesson on the fearsome, word-and-thought-defying banality of evil.

—Hannah Arendt, *Eichmann in Jerusalem*

For evil has no positive nature; but the loss of good has received the name "evil."

—Saint Augustine, *The City of God*

PREPARATION FOR SESSION 4

In *The Gulag Archipelago 1918–1956*, Russian novelist Aleksandr Solzhenitsyn writes: "If only there were evil people somewhere insidiously committing evil deeds, and it were necessary only to separate them from the rest of us and destroy them. But the line dividing good and evil cuts through the heart of every human being. And who is willing to destroy a piece of his own heart?"[1] Very few of us are willing to destroy a piece of our own hearts, which is why everyone believes in evil, yet no one seems to believe that he or she is evil. We speak with certainty about the existence of evil in other people and the world around us, but we rarely apply the word *evil* to ourselves or the people and things we love. As a result, the word is tossed about casually in conversation as if we all know what we are talking about and have a commonly shared universal understanding of the concept. All decent people can agree that Hitler and the Holocaust were evil, but when we turn the concept of evil toward our own history and ask if settler-colonialism, indigenous genocide, chattel slavery, segregation, red-lining, or mass incarceration are evil there is far less agreement.

Due to the rise of radical individualism, many Americans have become so overly focused on personal evil that we now have trouble recognizing the corporate and systemic evil that arises from ideologies, structures, and institutions in our society that are immoral, unjust, or oppressive. As a result, discussions of evil in our world today are often highly subjective and fruitless. What do we mean when we pray those famous words Jesus taught us to pray in the Lord's Prayer, "Deliver us from evil"? What is evil? Christian theologians like Augustine of Hippo and Thomas Aquinas argued that evil is difficult to define because it has no positive content. Evil, they contend, is the privation or the absence of what is good. Therefore, describing evil is a lot like describing darkness. Darkness is best described as the absence of light, and likewise evil is best described as the absence of the good. This means, in their estimation, that we cannot truly grasp what is evil until we first come to understand what is good.

There are multiple Greek words that are typically translated as "evil" in the New Testament. The primary word for evil that Jesus used was translated in Greek as *ponēros*, which derives from the Greek word *ponos*, meaning "work" or "labor." Therefore, *ponēros* or *evil* means to be full of harmful labors, hardships, and heavy burdens, or to be pressed, harassed

---

[1] Aleksandr Solzhenitsyn, *The Gulag Archipelago 1918–1956*, part 1 (New York: Harper & Row, 1974), 168.

by labors, or bringing toils, annoyances, and peril upon someone or something. In American history the paradigmatic example of *ponēros* was chattel slavery, which was full of harmful labors, hardship, heavy burdens, toil, and peril. A word in English that more precisely describes what Jesus meant by *ponēros* is *oppression*.

It is no surprise that the people Jesus most frequently described as evil in the Gospel were the chief priests, scribes, and Pharisees who were oppressing the common people with heavy burdens, harmful labors, excessive hardships, daily annoyances, toils, and peril. This understanding helps put a new light on Jesus's famous words, "Come to me all who are weary and burdened" and "Deliver us from evil." Jesus used the word we translate as *evil* quite regularly, which suggests that he understood it as a common, frequent, ordinary, everyday human phenomenon. We are imperfect human beings living in a world of other imperfect human beings, which means that the capacity for evil is within us and around us at the same time. Philosopher Hannah Arendt, who studied the German Nazi architects of the Holocaust, called this "the banality of evil" to shed light on the "normalcy" and "complacency" of evil. In *Eichmann in Jerusalem* Arendt sought to demonstrate that Adolf Eichmann, a Nazi officer who was one of the major organizers of the Holocaust, was not mentally ill, psychopathic, or sociopathic but a normal, average, mundane person who considered himself moral and believed he bore no responsibility for his actions because he was simply doing his duty, following orders, and obeying the law. Eichmann's casual, thoughtless, irresponsible deference to authority, which led to a horrific genocide, is what Arendt described as the "banality of evil."[2]

Whiteness is not a God-given identity, a biological phenomenon, a naturally occurring skin color, an ethnicity, a nationality, or even the opposite of Blackness. Whiteness is an invention—a social construction. There are no White people, only people who imagine they are White. Whiteness is a lie that European Christians created for themselves to justify stealing people, land, labor, money, and power. Whiteness is nothing. It has no positive nature. It is the absence of the good. Whiteness is based on the myth of European Christian superiority, and therefore it is the absence of love, justice, freedom, equality, and peace. Whiteness

---

[2] Hannah Arendt, *Eichmann in Jerusalem: A Report on the Banality of Evil* (New York: Penguin, 2006).

was specifically invented to legitimize the practice of chattel slavery and its legacy of oppression on people of color throughout American history. In sum, Whiteness is evil.

Yet, like the banality Hannah Arendt described, the evil of Whiteness is a thoughtless, common, ordinary, and everyday evil that is latent in our culture and society while exerting tremendous power. Sometimes we use the term *systemic racism* to describe the ways that Whiteness has become hidden and invisible from the very people who benefit most from its power. Many people who are racialized as White do not imagine that we need a carefully articulated definition of evil because when it comes to evil "we know it when we see it." However, this is a trap. It is easy to see evil in someone else, but it is extremely hard to see evil in ourselves. The ideology that might be the most dangerous to us, and other people in the world, is the very one we have the hardest time identifying. We believe Whiteness is our natural, God-given, biological ethnicity. "How could it be evil?" we ask, not realizing we are trapped in the banality of Whiteness.

One of the figures in American history who helped make the evil of Whiteness visible and explicit was civil rights leader Malcolm X. By describing Whiteness as evil, Malcolm X employed the strongest possible words available spiritually and theologically to describe the experience of oppression in the White-dominant American society. His words put a mirror up to White America and offered us the chance to see ourselves as evil oppressors through the eyes of those who were being oppressed. European Americans, and especially White Christians prefer to focus on Martin Luther King Jr. rather than Malcolm X. However, failing to listen to Malcolm X has impoverished White Americans' self-understanding. Many White Americans exploit the contrast between Dr. King's Christian nonviolence and Malcolm X's Islam and self-defense to dismiss Malcolm X's critique of White people. To do so requires a willful misreading of Dr. King or a near total ignorance of both King and Malcolm X, because they had far more in common in their thinking than most are willing to admit. Malcolm X's life, words, and witness have the power to confront the myth of innocence that White people have about themselves and their own history. White people must take seriously his suggested solutions to the problem of racial violence and oppression.

Liberal Christians often imagine that they are "good" or "enlightened" White people who are not openly racist and strive to be inclusive.

However, just like his contemporary Martin Luther King Jr., Malcolm X had strong words of warning for Black America about the White liberal. One of the images Malcolm X regularly conjured to reveal the insidious nature of Whiteness is the metaphor of the White conservative as a wolf and the White liberal as a fox. In his sermon "God's Judgment on White America" (1963), Malcolm X said,

> "The white conservatives aren't friends of the Negro either, but they at least don't try to hide it. They are like wolves; they show their teeth in a snarl that keeps the Negro always aware of where he stands with them. But the white liberals are foxes, who also show their teeth to the Negro but pretend that they are smiling. The white liberals are more dangerous than the conservatives; they lure the Negro, and as the Negro runs from the growling wolf, he flees into the open jaws of the 'smiling' fox."

Malcolm X returned to this metaphor repeatedly in interviews such as the one he provided at UC Berkeley in October 1963, in which he said the following:

> "We see the increase of racial animosity, the increase of racial hostility, and the increase of outright racial hatred. We see masses of Black people who have lost all confidence in the false promises of the hypocritical white politicians. We see masses of Black people who are thoroughly fed up with the deceit of the so-called white liberals, or the white so-called liberals. White liberals who have posed as our friends, white liberals who have been eager to point out what the white man in the South is doing to our people there, while they themselves are doing the same thing to us here in the North.
> "They have been making a great fuss over the South only to blind us to what is happening here in the North. And now that the Honorable Elijah Muhammad has opened the eyes of America's 20 million Blacks, we can easily see that this white fox here in the North is even more cruel and more vicious than the white wolf in the South. The southern wolves always let you know where you stand. But these northern foxes pose as white liberals. They pose as your friend, as your benefactor, as your employer, as your landlord, as your neighborhood merchant, as your lawyer. They use

integration for infiltration. They infiltrate all your organizations, and in this manner, by joining you, they strangle your militant efforts toward true freedom."

We don't want to believe that we are capable of evil, but we all are, regardless of how conservative or liberal we may be. As the apostle Paul said, "For all have sinned, and come short of the glory of God" (Rom. 3:23). There is nothing pleasant or comforting about coming to see ourselves as participating in an evil system of oppression, yet that is the way Malcolm X helps us to confront our Whiteness. Can you imagine what would happen if White people could be strong enough and brave enough to see the way we participate in evil, to confront our Whiteness, renounce it, repent, and turn in another direction? Everything would change. Our lives would change. The church would change. America would change. This week we will read an interview with and a letter by Malcolm X, and we will watch another interview with him and the 1992 movie *Malcolm X*, directed by Spike Lee. As you wrestle with the life and teachings of Malcolm X, do not allow yourself to get caught up in disagreeing with his details, but listen for the truth of what he said. Seek to understand his perspective. May our eyes be open to see the evil of Whiteness for the first time or in new ways, and may we learn how to "overcome evil with good" (Rom. 12:21).

DEEP SOUL WORK

Read and View. *Engage these essays, this video, and this film slowly and carefully, taking time to stop and make notes as you go.*
- Read "A Summing Up: Louis Lomax Interviews Malcolm X, November 1963."[3]
- Read "Letter from Mecca" by Malcolm X.[4]

---

[3] Louis E. Lomax, "A Summing Up: Louis Lomax Interviews Malcolm X," in *When the Word Is Given: A Report on Elijah Muhammad, Malcolm X, and the Black Muslim World* (Westport, CT: Praeger, 1979).

[4] Malcolm X with Alex Haley, *The Autobiography of Malcolm X* (New York: Grove Press, 1965).

- Watch Malcolm X interview by Herman Blake at UC Berkeley, October 11, 1963.[5]
- View *Malcolm X* (1992) by Spike Lee.

Meditate and Reflect. *Spend some time in silent meditation after each of the readings and viewings and then write your answers to these questions:*
1. How did the readings and viewings make you feel?
2. What was most meaningful to you?
3. What are you discovering about Whiteness?
4. Where do you see yourself in the readings and films?

Acknowledge and Confess. *Examine your own life story considering the readings and viewings this week and acknowledge what arises.*
- What stories from your life experience relate to what you read and viewed this week? (Be sure to write them in your racial autobiography.)
- What acknowledgments of Whiteness or personal confessions do you need to make based on this week's readings and viewings?
- Read 1 Timothy 6:10: How is the love of money (greed/avarice) the root of all evil? How is the love of money related to Whiteness?
- Do a search for the word *evil* in the Gospels. How does Jesus talk about evil? Who is he talking to? What does he say?
- Read Romans 2 and reflect on Paul's understanding of evil and the path for overcoming evil. How do we overcome the evil of Whiteness?
- In what ways have you seen or experienced the evil of Whiteness in your life, your community, or the world?

Repent, Turn, and Transform. *Try to imagine a new creation and a new humanity for yourself and for our world:*
- Since the time of the early church, candidates for baptism have been asked one question before all others: "Do you renounce the spiritual forces of wickedness, reject the evil powers of this world, and repent of your sin?" Even if we were baptized as infants and our parents answered this question for us, we are all still called to

---

[5] https://archive.org/details/cabemrc_00001.

live into our baptism and to reaffirm our covenant vows. Therefore, "Do you renounce the spiritual forces of *Whiteness*, reject the evil powers of *Whiteness* in the world, and repent of your *Whiteness?*" What do you imagine a renunciation of Whiteness would look like in your life and your church?

- What are the responsibilities that come with renouncing Whiteness as a human being, a citizen, a follower of Jesus, and/or a person of faith?
- What kind of accountability, habits, or practices do you need in your life to help you take responsibility for confronting the evil of Whiteness?
- What do you think would change if you apply what you've discovered this week about Whiteness in your sphere of power and influence?

"A Summing Up"

Louis Lomax Interviews Malcolm X

(November 1963)

Lomax: Minister Malcolm, we are all by now familiar with your basic philosophy; we have heard you speak, seen you on television, and read your remarks in magazines and newspapers. By now, I think, everybody knows your position that the white man is a devil, a man incapable of doing right; you hold that the black man is of God's divine nature, that he fell from power because of weakness; you hold further that the white man's rule over the earth was scheduled to end in 1914, but that his end has been delayed because of the need to get the American Negro into the fold of the black brotherhood.

Malcolm X: Yes, sir, that is what The Honorable Elijah Muhammad teaches us. The white devil's time is up; it has been up for almost fifty years now. It has taken us that long to get the deaf, dumb, and blind black men in the wilderness of North America to wake up and understand who they are. You see, sir, when a man understands who he is, who God is, who the devil is . . . then he can pick himself up out of the gutter; he can clean himself up and stand up like a man should before his God. This is why we teach that in order for a man to really understand himself he must be part of a nation; he must have some land of his own, a God of his own, a language of his own. Most of all he must have love and devotion for his own kind.

Lomax: Wouldn't you say the Negro has a nation—America?

Malcolm X: Sir, how can a Negro say America is his nation? He was brought here in chains; he was put in slavery and worked like a mule for three hundred years; he was separated from his land, his culture, his God, his language!

The Negro was taught to speak the white man's tongue, worship the white God, and accept the white man as his superior.

This is a white man's country. And the Negro is nothing but an ex-slave who is now trying to get himself integrated into the slave master's house.

And the slave master doesn't want you! You fought and bled and died in every war the white man waged, and he still won't give you justice. You nursed his baby and cleaned behind his wife, and he still won't give you freedom; you turned the other cheek while he lynched you and raped your women, but he still won't give you equality. Now, you integration-minded Negroes are trying to force yourselves on your former slave master, trying to make him accept you in his drawing room; you want to hang out with his women rather than the women of your own kind. . . .

Lomax: I have heard you say that a thousand times, but it always jolts me. Why do you call the white man a devil?

Malcolm X: Because that's what he is. What do you want me to call him, a saint? Anybody who rapes, and plunders, and enslaves, and steals, and drops hell bombs on people . . . anybody who does these things is nothing but a devil. Look, Lomax, history rewards all research. And history fails to record one single instance in which the white man—as a people—did good. They have always been devils; they always will be devils, and they are about to be destroyed. The final proof that they are devils lies in the fact that they are about to destroy themselves. Only a devil—and a stupid devil at that—would destroy himself!

Now why would I want to integrate with somebody marked for destruction?

The Honorable Elijah Muhammad teaches us to get away from the devil as soon and as fast as we can. This is why we are demanding a separate state. Tell the slave master we will no longer beg for crumbs from his table; let him give us some land of our own so we can go for ourselves. If he doesn't give us some land, there is going to be hell to pay. . . .

Lomax: But we have made some gains. . . .

Malcolm X: What gains? All you have gotten is tokenism—one or two Negroes in a job or at a lunch counter so the rest of you will be quiet. It took the United States Army to get one Negro into the University of Mississippi; it took troops to get a few Negroes in the white schools at Little Rock and another dozen places in the South. It has been nine years since the Supreme Court decision outlawing segregated schools, yet less than ten percent of the Negro students in the South are in integrated schools. That isn't integration, that's tokenism! In spite of all the dogs, and fire hoses, and club-swinging policemen, I have yet to read of anybody eating an integrated hamburger in Birmingham.

You Negroes are not willing to admit it yet, but integration will not work. Why, it is against the white man's nature to integrate you into his house. Even if he wanted to, he could no more do it than a Model T can sprout wings and fly. It just isn't in him.

Now The Honorable Elijah Muhammad says it would be the easiest thing in the world for the white man to destroy all Black Muslims. We contend that the white man is a devil. If he is not a devil, let him prove it! He can't do it, Lomax; it isn't in him; it is against his nature. . . .

Lomax: This is strong gospel, Minister Malcolm; many people, Negro and white, say what you preach amounts to hate, that your theology is actually anti-Semitic. What is your comment to that?

Malcolm X: The white people who are guilty of white supremacy are trying to hide their own guilt by accusing The Honorable Elijah Muhammad of teaching black supremacy when he tries to uplift the mentality, the social, mental, and economic condition of the black people in this country. Jews who have been guilty of exploiting the black people in this country, economically, civically, and otherwise, hide behind—hide their guilt by accusing The Honorable Elijah Muhammad of being anti-Semitic, simply because he teaches our people to go into business for ourselves and take over the economic leadership in our own community. And since the white people collectively have practiced the worst form of hatred against Negroes in this country and they know that they are guilty of it, now when The Honorable Elijah Muhammad comes along and begins to list the historic deed—the historic attitude, the historic behavior of the white man in this country toward the black people in this country, again, the white people are so guilty and they can't stop doing these things to make Mr. Muhammad appear to be wrong, so they hide their wrong by saying "he is teaching hatred." History is not hatred. Actually, we are Muslims because we believe in the religion of Islam. We believe in one God. We believe Muhammad is the Apostle of God. We practice the principles of the religion of Islam, which mean prayer, charity, fasting, brotherhood, and The Honorable Elijah Muhammad teaches us that since the Western society is deteriorating, it has become overrun with immorality, that God is going to judge it and destroy it, and the only way the black people who are in this society can be saved is not to integrate into this corrupt society but separate ourselves from it, reform ourselves, lift up our moral standards and try and be godly—try to integrate with God—instead of trying to integrate with the white man, or try and imitate God instead of trying to imitate the white man.

Lomax: It is suggested also that your movement preaches violence.

Malcolm X: No, sir. The black people of this country have been victims of violence at the hands of the white men for four hundred years, and following the ignorant Negro preachers, we have thought that it was godlike to turn the other cheek to the brute that was brutalizing us. Today The Honorable Elijah Muhammad is showing black people in this country that, just as the white man and every other person on this earth has God-given rights, natural rights, civil rights, any kind of rights that you can think of, when it comes to defending himself, black people—we should have the right to defend ourselves also. And, because The Honorable Elijah Muhammad makes black people brave enough, men enough to defend ourselves no matter what the odds are, the white man runs around here with a doctrine that Mr. Muhammad is advocating the violence when he is actually telling Negroes to defend themselves against violent people.

Lomax: Reverend Martin Luther King teaches a doctrine of nonviolence. What is your attitude toward this philosophy?

Malcolm X: The white man supports Reverend Martin Luther King, subsidizes Reverend Martin Luther King, so that Reverend Martin Luther King can continue to teach the Negroes to be defenseless—that's what you mean by nonviolent—be defenseless in the face of one of the most cruel beasts that has ever taken people into captivity—that's this American white man, and they have proved it throughout the country by the police dogs and the police clubs. A hundred years ago they used to put on a white sheet and use a bloodhound against Negroes. Today they have taken off the white sheet and put on police uniforms and traded in the bloodhounds for police dogs, and they're still doing the same thing. Just as Uncle Tom, back during slavery, used to keep the Negroes from resisting the bloodhound or resisting the Ku Klux Klan by teaching them to love their enemies or pray for those who use them despitefully, today Martin Luther King is just a twentieth-century or modern Uncle Tom or religious Uncle Tom, who is doing the same thing today to keep Negroes defenseless in the face of attack that Uncle Tom did on the plantation to keep those Negroes defenseless in the face of the attack of the Klan in that day.

Now the goal of Dr. Martin Luther King is to give Negroes a chance to sit in a segregated restaurant beside the same white man who has brutalized them for four hundred years. The goal of Martin Luther King is to get the Negroes to forgive the people, the people who have brutalized them for four hundred years, by lulling them to sleep and making them forget what those whites have done to them, but the masses of black people today don't go for what Martin Luther King is putting down. . . .

Lomax: Then your movement does not share the integration goals of the NAACP, CORE, Martin Luther King's movement, and the Student Nonviolent movement.

Malcolm X: You don't integrate with a sinking ship. You don't do anything to further your stay aboard a ship that you see is going to go down to the bottom of the ocean. Moses tried to separate his people from Pharaoh, and when he tried, the magicians tried to fool the people into staying with the Pharaoh, and we look upon these other organizations that are trying to get Negroes to integrate with this doomed white man as nothing but modern-day magicians, and The Honorable Elijah Muhammad is a modern-day Moses trying to separate us from the modern-day Pharaoh. . . .

. . . Everybody has a God and believes that his God will deliver him and protect him from his enemies! Why can't the black man have a God? What's so wrong when a black man says his God will protect him from his white foe? If Jehovah can slay Philistines for the Jews, why can't Allah slay crackers for the so-called Negro?

Lomax: Is that the reasoning behind your remark after the assassination of President Kennedy? You are reported to have said that Kennedy's death was an instance of "chickens coming home to roost."

Malcolm X: Yes, but let's clear up what I said. I did not say that Kennedy's death was a reason for rejoicing. That is not what I meant at all. Rather I meant that the death of Kennedy was the result of a long line of violent acts, the culmination of hate and suspicion and doubt in this country. You see, Lomax, this country has allowed white people to kill and brutalize those they don't like. The assassination of Kennedy is a result of that way of life and thinking. The chickens came home to roost; that's all there is to it. America—at the death of the President—just reaped what it had been sowing.

Lomax: But you were disciplined for making these remarks; The Honorable Elijah Muhammad has publicly rebuked you and has ordered you not to speak in public until further notice.

Malcolm X: This is true. I was wrong; the Messenger had warned me not to say anything about the death of the President, and I omitted any reference to that tragedy in my main speech. But during a question-and-answer period someone asked about the meaning of the Kennedy assassination, and I said it was a case of chickens coming home to roost. Now about that suspension—it's just as if you have cut off a radio. The radio is still there, but it makes no sound. You can cut it back on when it pleases you.

Lomax: How long do you think this suspension will last?

Malcolm X: Only The Honorable Elijah Muhammad can answer that. I don't think it will be permanent. . . .

Lomax: Are not Negroes American citizens?

Malcolm X: If they were citizens, you wouldn't have a race problem. If the Emancipation Proclamation was authentic, you wouldn't have a race problem. If the 13th, 14th, and 15th Amendments to the Constitution were authentic, you wouldn't have a race problem. If the Supreme Court desegregation decision was authentic, you wouldn't have a race problem. All of this hypocrisy that has been practiced by the so-called white so-called liberal for the past four hundred years compounds the problem, makes it more complicated, instead of eliminating the problem.

Lomax: What, then, do you see as the final result of all these demonstrations?

Malcolm X: Any time you put too many sparks around a powder keg, the thing is going to explode, and if the thing that explodes is still inside the house, then the house will be destroyed. So The Honorable Elijah Muhammad is telling the white man, "Get this powder keg out of your house—let the black people in this country separate from you, while there's still time." If the black man is allowed to separate and go into some land of his own where he can solve his own problems, there won't be any explosion, and the Negroes who want to stay with the white man, let them stay with the white man—but those who want to leave, let them go to The Honorable Elijah Muhammad. . . .

Lomax: According to your own newspaper, one of the things you Muslims may do in the near future is vote.

Malcolm X: Yes. After long and prayerful consideration, The Honorable Elijah Muhammad allowed us to announce the possibility of Muslims voting. The announcement came at our annual Savior's Day Convention in Chicago.

Lomax: What does it mean?

Malcolm X: Mr. Muhammad is the only one who can explain that fully. However, I can say that we may register and be ready to vote. Then we will seek out candidates who represent our interests and support them. They need not be Muslims; what we want are race men who will speak out for our people.

Lomax: There are rumors that you may run against Adam Clayton Powell.

Malcolm X: Why must I run against a Negro? We have had enough of Negroes running against and fighting with each other. The better bet is that we would put a Muslim candidate in the field against a devil, somebody who is against all we stand for.

Lomax: What are the chances of Black Muslims joining us in picket lines for better jobs?

Malcolm X: As I told you, only Mr. Muhammad can answer that. But let me tell you something: Better jobs and housing are only temporary solutions. They are aspects of tokenism and don't go to the heart of the problem.

This is why integration will not work. It assumes that the two races, black and white, are equal and can be made to live as one. This is not true.

The white man is by nature a devil and must be destroyed. The black man will inherit the earth; he will resume control, taking back the position he held centuries ago when the white devil was crawling around the caves of Europe on his all fours. Before the white devil came into our lives we had a civilization, we had a culture, we were living in silks and satins. Then he put us in chains and put us aboard the "Good Ship Jesus," and we have lived in hell ever since.

Now the white man's time is over. Tokenism will not help him, and it will doom us. Complete separation will save us—and who knows, it might make God decide to give the white devil a few more years.

"A Letter from Mecca"

Malcolm X

(April 26, 1964)

Never have I witnessed such sincere hospitality and the overwhelming spirit of true brotherhood as is practiced by people of all colors and races here in this Ancient Holy Land, the home of Abraham, Muhammad, and all the other prophets of the Holy Scriptures. For the past week, I have been utterly speechless and spellbound by the graciousness I see displayed all around me by people *of all colors*.

I have been blessed to visit the Holy City of Mecca. I have made my seven circuits around the Ka'ba, led by a young *Mutawaf* named Muhammad. I drank water from the well of Zem Zem. I ran seven times back and forth between the hills of Mt. Al-Safa and Al-Marwah. I have prayed in the ancient city of Mina, and I have prayed on Mt. Arafat.

There were tens of thousands of pilgrims, from all over the world. They were of all colors, from blue-eyed blonds to black-skinned Africans. But we were all participating in the same ritual, displaying a spirit of unity and brotherhood that my experiences in America had led me to believe never could exist between the white and the non-white.

America needs to understand Islam, because this is the one religion that erases from its society the race problem. Throughout my travels in the Muslim world, I have met, talked to, and even eaten with people who in America would have been considered "white"—but the "white" attitude was removed from their minds by the religion of Islam. I have never before seen *sincere* and *true* brotherhood practiced by all colors together, irrespective of their color.

You may be shocked by these words coming from me. But on this pilgrimage, what I have seen, and experienced, has forced me to *re-arrange* much of my thought-patterns previously held, and to *toss aside* some of

101

my previous conclusions. This was not too difficult for me. Despite my firm convictions, I have been always a man who tries to face facts, and to accept the reality of life as new experience and new knowledge unfolds it. I have always kept an open mind, which is necessary to the flexibility that must go hand in hand with every form of intelligent search for truth.

During the past eleven days here in the Muslim world, I have eaten from the same plate, drunk from the same glass, and slept in the same bed (or on the same rug)—while praying to the *same God*—with fellow Muslims, whose eyes were the bluest of blue, whose hair was the blondest of blond, and whose skin was the whitest of white. And in the *words* and in the *actions* and in the *deeds* of the "white" Muslims, I felt the same sincerity that I felt among the black African Muslims of Nigeria, Sudan, and Ghana.

We were *truly* all the same (brothers)—because their belief in one God had removed the "white" from their *minds*, the "white" from their *behavior*, and the "white" from their *attitude*.

I could see from this, that perhaps if white Americans could accept the Oneness of God, then perhaps, too, they could accept *in reality* the Oneness of Man—and cease to measure, and hinder, and harm others in terms of their "differences" in color.

With racism plaguing America like an incurable cancer, the so-called "Christian" white American heart should be more receptive to a proven solution to such a destructive problem. Perhaps it could be in time to save America from imminent disaster—the same destruction brought upon Germany by racism that eventually destroyed the Germans themselves.

Each hour here in the Holy Land enables me to have greater spiritual insights into what is happening in America between black and white. The American Negro never can be blamed for his racial animosities—he is only reacting to four hundred years of the conscious racism of the American whites. But as racism leads America up the suicide path, I do believe, from the experiences that I have had with them, that the whites of the younger generation, in the colleges and universities, will see the handwriting on the wall and many of them will turn to the *spiritual* path of *truth*—the *only* way left to America to ward off the disaster that racism inevitably must lead to.

Never have I been so highly honored. Never have I been made to feel more humble and unworthy. Who would believe the blessings that have been heaped upon an American Negro? A few nights ago, a man who would be called in America a "white" man, a United Nations diplomat, an ambassador, a companion of kings, gave me his hotel suite, his bed. By this man, His Excellency Prince Faisal who rules this Holy Land, was made aware of my presence here in Jedda. The very next morning, Prince Faisal's son, in person, informed me that by the will and decree of his esteemed father, I was to be a State Guest.

The deputy Chief of Protocol himself took me before the Haff Court. His Holiness Sheikh Muhammad Harkon himself okayed my visit to Mecca. His Holiness gave me two books on Islam, with his personal seal and autograph, and he told me that he prayed that I would be a successful preacher of Islam in America. A car, a driver, and a guide have been placed at my disposal, making it possible for me to travel about this Holy Land almost at will. The government provides air-conditioned quarters and servants in each city that I visit. Never would I have even thought of dreaming that I would ever be a recipient of such honors—honors that in America would be bestowed upon a King—not a Negro.

All praise is due to Allah, the Lord of all the Worlds.

Sincerely,
El-Hajj Malik El-Shabazz
(Malcolm X)

5

Whiteness as Mythology

The American Negro has the great advantage of having never believed that collection of myths to which white Americans cling.

—JAMES BALDWIN, "THE FIRE NEXT TIME"

You were taught to put away your former way of life, your old self, corrupt and deluded by its lusts, and to be renewed in the spirit of your minds, and to clothe yourselves with the new self, created according to the likeness of God in true righteousness and holiness.

—EPHESIANS 4:22–24

Do not lie to one another, seeing that you have stripped off the old self with its practices and have clothed yourselves with the new self, which is being renewed in knowledge according to the image of its creator. In that renewal there is no longer Greek and Jew, circumcised and uncircumcised, barbarian, Scythian, slave and free; but Christ is all and in all!

—COLOSSIANS 3:9–11

PREPARATION FOR SESSION 5

Every nation, culture, and civilization has founding myths, traditional stories, and meta-narratives that explain the early history of a people and

105

typically involve supernatural beings or events. In school we often learn about Egyptian mythology from hieroglyphics, Sumerian mythology from *The Epic of Gilgamesh,* Greek mythology from Homer's *Iliad* and *Odyssey*, Roman mythology from Virgil's *Aeneid*, and English mythology from *Beowulf* and the tales of King Arthur. In many cases the founding myths of a particular civilization become the foundation for a religion with stories as sacred texts; a cosmology and pantheon of gods; as well as rituals and practices of worship, reverence, and veneration.

White America has its own founding myths, beginning with Puritan minister John Winthrop's sermon "A Modell of Christian Charity," delivered from the ship *Arbella* on April 8, 1630. Winthrop envisioned America mythologically as the biblical Promised Land given by God to European settler-colonists who were set apart to create a city on a hill and a perfect society. Later, succeeding generations of preachers, theologians, and settler-colonists twisted Winthrop's ideas to develop the myth of America as a holy nation with a special calling from God, and this unholy theological idea mutated over time into the ideology of Manifest Destiny, or the belief that American settler-colonists possessed a sacred destiny as the "New Israel" to take possession of land across the North American continent, regardless of the fact that there were already approximately six hundred tribes of indigenous people living there.

We also have myths about our founding fathers that are intended to demonstrate their moral virtue, like the story of young George Washington coming clean after chopping down his father's cherry tree because he "could not tell a lie." Throughout American history most of our myths have been fictional stories loosely based on the lives of exceptional people like Christopher Columbus, Daniel Boone, Davy Crockett, Paul Bunyan, Pecos Bill, Johnny Appleseed, and John Henry. These stories have helped to establish the myth of rugged individualism, which enabled settlers to find meaning in the harsh conditions of frontier life and to justify the violence required to colonize indigenous peoples.

However, the ultimate myth of all the founding myths of America is the myth of Whiteness. It is helpful to acknowledge, first and foremost, that there are no White people. As Baldwin notes in our readings this week, there are only people who think they are White, by which he means people who believe in the mythology of Whiteness. The skin of European settler-colonists was not actually white but simply possessed less melanin because their ancestors were from colder climates. The color of European skin is not white but beige, tan, pink, or peach. Therefore, at its most basic level, Whiteness is a lie. The idea of race itself is a lie that was constructed by Europeans to elevate and distinguish themselves from other human beings. Race is not real. It is a mythology our ancestors created.

In 2003, scientists completed the Human Genome Project, making it possible to examine human ancestry with genetics. They were able to map the DNA of human beings from all ethnic backgrounds, and through their research they determined that race is not a biological attribute but a social and political concept. Individuals may be of European or West African descent, but they are not White or Black. While physical differences may appear to be very dramatic, they are only a tiny portion of the human genome. As a species, humans share 99.9 percent of our DNA with one another, and the minuscule differences that exist on the surface (like skin color) simply reflect environmental or external factors, not our core biology.

Why did European settler-colonists create the lie of race or the mythology of Whiteness? In his 1964 essay "The White Problem," James Baldwin explains:

> The people who settled the country had a fatal flaw. They could recognize a man when they saw one . . . but since they were Christian, and since they had already decided that they came here to establish a free country, the only way to justify the role this chattel was playing in one's life was to say that he *was not* a man. For if he wasn't, then no crime had been committed. That lie is the basis of our present trouble.[1]

As Baldwin reveals, the simplest way to define the concept of race is that it is *a lie that is used to steal.* Race is a lie that was used to steal people from their homes, to steal labor, to steal land from the indigenous people, to steal resources, and to steal political power.

The mythology of Whiteness is based on the lie that European settlers and slaveholders are superior to other people because of the color of their skin. This mythology was created to justify the political and

---

[1] James Baldwin, "The White Problem," 1964, republished in *The Cross of Redemption: Uncollected Writings,* ed. Randall Kenan (New York: Pantheon, 2010), 76.

economic system of the plantation, the enslavement of other human beings, as well as the practice of settler-colonialism, which has been described as the genocide of indigenous peoples. Many Americans today identify as White and imagine we are simply participating in a natural, biological, ethnic group, completely unaware that we have not aligned ourselves with a biology or ethnicity but with a lie that has trapped us in a powerful mythology.

The apostle Paul warned the church in Colossae that overly investing our identities in a lie creates a "false self" that places us in opposition to God and neighbor. Therefore, Paul claims, the false self must be stripped away, along with all its practices, and put to death, so that the new, genuine, "true self" can be born and clothed with the virtues and gifts of the Spirit, like compassion, kindness, humility, meekness, patience, forgiveness, and love. Whiteness is a lie that creates a false self, and therefore it must be stripped away and put to death—along with all its practices and habits—so that we can rediscover our true selves and work to realize the beloved community and "kin-dom" of God that Jesus and Paul envisioned and embodied, where there will no longer be Jew and Greek, slave and free, or Black and White.

Howard Thurman said in a baccalaureate address at Spelman College, "You are the only you that has ever lived; your idiom is the only idiom of its kind in all the existences, and if you cannot hear the sound of the genuine in you, you will all of your life spend your days on the ends of strings that somebody else pulls."[2] What is the sound of the genuine in you? What is your true self? If the false White self were stripped away from you, what would you be? Who would you be and what would you be if you weren't White?

This week, we will read two articles James Baldwin wrote about the mythology of Whiteness that are separated by twenty years. We will watch the documentary *I Am Not Your Negro*, which is based on the manuscripts of an unpublished book Baldwin wrote about the lives of civil rights icons Medgar Evers, Malcolm X, and Martin Luther King Jr. As he did in "The Fire Next Time," Baldwin puts a mirror before us

---

[2] Howard Thurman, "The Sound of the Genuine," baccalaureate address at Spelman College, May 4, 1980, as edited by Jo Moore Stewart for *The Spelman Messenger* 96, no. 4 (Summer 1980): 14–15.

so we can see ourselves more clearly and understand the ways we are trapped in the mythology of Whiteness.[3] He shows us the consequences this lie has had for us, America, and our world. May you find the strength to confront the mythology of Whiteness and the courage to begin the process of stripping off the false White self and all its practices as you continue your journey this week.

DEEP SOUL WORK

Read and View. *Engage with these essays and this film slowly and carefully, taking time to stop and make notes as you go.*
- Read "The White Man's Guilt" (1965) by James Baldwin.[4]
- Read "The Price of the Ticket" (1985) by James Baldwin.[5]
- View *I Am Not Your Negro* (2016) by Raoul Peck.[6]

Meditate and Reflect. *Spend some time in silent meditation after each of the readings and the viewing, and then write your answers to these questions.*
1. How did the readings and viewing make you feel?
2. What was most meaningful to you?
3. What are you discovering about Whiteness?
4. Where do you see yourself in the readings and film?

Acknowledge and Confess. *Examine your own life story considering the readings and viewing this week and acknowledge what arises.*
- What stories from your life experience relates to what you read and viewed this week? (Be sure to include them in your racial autobiography.)
- What acknowledgments of Whiteness or personal confessions do you need to make based on this week's readings and viewing?
- Read Colossians 3:9–11; Romans 6:6–8; Ephesians 4:22–24. How do these passages relate to Whiteness?

---

[3] James Baldwin, "The Fire Next Time," in *James Baldwin: Collected Essays*, ed. Toni Morrison (New York: Library of America, 1998).

[4] James Baldwin, "The White Man's Guilt," in Morrison, *James Baldwin: Collected Essays*, 722–27.

[5] Baldwin, 830–42.

[6] Raoul Peck, *I Am Not Your Negro* (United States: Magnolia Pictures, 2016).

Repent, Turn, and Transform. *Try to imagine a new creation and a new humanity for yourself and for our world.*

- Listen for the "sound of the genuine" in you. What is your true self? If the false White self were stripped away from you, what would you be? Who and what would you be if you weren't White?
- What kind of accountability do you need in your life to take responsibility for Whiteness as mythology?
- What do you think could change if you apply what you've discovered this week in your sphere of power and influence?

6

Whiteness as Terror

When Herod saw that he had been tricked by the wise men, he was infuriated, and he sent and killed all the children in and around Bethlehem who were two years old or under, according to the time that he had learned from the wise men. Then was fulfilled what had been spoken through the prophet Jeremiah: "A voice was heard in Ramah, wailing and loud lamentation, Rachel weeping for her children; she refused to be consoled, because they are no more."

—MATTHEW 2:16–18

Meanwhile Saul, still breathing threats and murder against the disciples of the Lord, went to the high priest and asked him for letters to the synagogues at Damascus, so that if he found any who belonged to the Way, men or women, he might bring them bound to Jerusalem.

—ACTS 9:1–2

For, in the generality, as social and moral and political and sexual entities, white Americans are probably the sickest and certainly the most dangerous people, of any color, to be found in the world today.

—JAMES BALDWIN, *NO NAME IN THE STREET*

111

PREPARATION FOR SESSION 6

Anyone in America over the age of thirty who hears the word *terror* immediately remembers the terrorist attacks on 9/11. Most American adults can still remember exactly where they were and what they were doing when they learned that planes had been hijacked by Muslim extremists and flown into the World Trade Center towers and the Pentagon. September 11, 2001, has become our day's Pearl Harbor, and like President Franklin Delano Roosevelt said about that tragic attack, 9/11 will always be "a day that will live in infamy."

Following the attack on 9/11 the United States launched a global War on Terror that led to two of the longest wars in American history in Iraq and Afghanistan, which spawned the birth of ISIL, the Arab Spring, the 2011 Syrian civil war, and the largest refugee crisis in modern history. During that twenty-year period the words *terror* and *terrorist* became synonymous with Islam and Muslim extremism. In the aftermath of 9/11 many Americans wondered why Muslims hated the United States so much that they would attack us in such a horrifying way. The question not only revealed our ignorance of American foreign policy abroad but our pervasive sense of American innocence, righteousness, and exceptionalism.

The US government took the position that terrorists attacked the United States because "they hate us for our freedoms." In a speech to Congress nine days after the attacks, President George W. Bush said, "They hate our freedoms—our freedom of religion, our freedom of speech, our freedom to vote and assemble and disagree with each other."[1] However, the Bush administration's position was a refusal to accept the reasons provided by the attackers themselves. In his 2002 "Letter to America," Osama bin Laden explicitly stated that al-Qaeda's motives for the attacks were the following: Western support for attacking Muslims in Somalia, supporting Russian atrocities against Muslims in Chechnya, supporting the Indian oppression against Muslims in Kashmir, the Jewish aggression against Muslims in Lebanon, the presence of US troops in Saudi Arabia, US support of Israel, and sanctions imposed against Iraq.[2]

---

[1] George W. Bush, "Address to Joint Session of Congress," September 20, 2001.

[2] "Full Text: bin Laden's 'Letter to America,'" *The Guardian* online, November 24, 2002.

At one time bin Laden was trained, armed, and funded by the CIA to fight in the Saudi-backed war against the Russians in Afghanistan. His accusations should have provided Americans with a stunning realization that 9/11 was at least partially a consequence of US foreign policy in the Middle East since 1953, when US forces initiated a coup d'état in Iran to overthrow the democratically elected leader Mohammad Mosaddegh. As a direct result of fifty years of US imperialism in the Middle East, some Muslims came to believe America was the real terrorist. Yet Americans still struggle to see ourselves from their perspective and cannot understand, or take responsibility for, our role in cultivating extremism or inciting attacks on US soil.

Americans struggle to see what other nations around the globe see clearly: American support for terror. Similarly, White Americans struggle to see what people of color here at home see clearly: White American support for White supremacist terror. Whether we are able to see it or willing to admit it, White terrorism has been a constant throughout American history. In the terror of the Middle Passage, chattel slavery, the Ku Klux Klan, lynching, neighborhood massacres, segregation, racist politics, sundown towns, police brutality, red-lining, urban renewal, discrimination, mass incarceration, gerrymandering, and voter suppression, White people have been terrorizing Black people for over four hundred years.

In recent years we have seen horrific displays of White terrorism. The massacre of nine Black people at Emanuel African Methodist Episcopal Church in Charleston, South Carolina, by White supremacist Dylann Roof in 2015 was White terrorism. The Unite the Right Rally in Charlottesville, Virginia, in 2017 and the car attack by White supremacist James Alex Fields that killed thirty-two-year-old Heather Heyer were acts of White terrorism. The mass shooting at Tree of Life synagogue in Pittsburgh, Pennsylvania, in 2018 by White supremacist Robert Gregory Bowers that killed eleven people and wounded six was White terrorism. The mass shooting at a Walmart in El Paso, Texas, in 2019 by White supremacist Patrick Wood Crusius that killed twenty-three people and injured twenty-three more was White terrorism.

Paradigmatically, the January 6, 2021, insurrection and attack on the US Capitol by White supremacist groups Oath Keepers, Proud Boys, Three Percenters, Stop the Steal, American Phoenix Project, Jericho March, and other organized supporters of Donald Trump that sought to overturn the results of a democratic election by infiltrating the Capitol and murdering elected representatives was White terrorism. We must never forget 1/6; it was a day that resulted in the deaths of five people and the injuries of one hundred and forty more. It will live in infamy. Afterward, FBI director Christopher Wray labeled the riot an act of domestic terror, and top law enforcement officials—Attorney General Merrick B. Garland and Director of Homeland Security Alejandro Mayorkas—stated that the greatest internal threat facing the United States is from White domestic terrorists.[3]

Yet White Americans remain in such utter denial about our terrorizing legacy and the current terrorizing reality of Whiteness that we cannot tolerate our own history being taught to our children, as we've seen played out in the fabricated and absurd panic around the manufactured idea that critical race theory is being taught in primary schools. Denial begets denial. Our stubborn refusal as White people to shake off our pathology of denial, face the truth, and learn to live in reality is both the consequence and cause of our inability to see or solve the problem of systemic racism and White supremacy in America.

Denial is a stage of grief, and White people in America are grieving. We should be grieving the ongoing assault on Black life, but what we are really grieving is the loss of our innocence, our righteousness, our exceptionalism, our self-understanding, and (if we are honest) our humanity. Constantly participating in and gaining advantages from the terrorizing dehumanization and oppression of Black people has cost us our sense of reality and our humanity. Waking up to that reality causes White people nothing less than an existential crisis—a crisis we must face.

Grief is the appropriate response to the history and legacy of White terrorism; however, denial is only one stage of grief—there are also anger, bargaining, depression, and acceptance. The inability to lament our participation in White terror has trapped White people in one stage of grief. In the Bible the practice of lament is crucial for people of faith. A significant number of the psalms are laments. The Hebrew prophets, especially Jeremiah, were constantly lamenting and calling the people to engage in lament. When acts of terror took place in the Gospels, like King Herod's genocide of Jewish children living in and around Bethlehem,

---

[3] Eileen Sullivan and Katie Benner, "Top Law Enforcement Officials Say the Biggest Domestic Terror Threat Comes from White Supremacists," *The New York Times* online, May 12, 2021.

the people wailed with loud lamentation. Even Jesus lamented multiple times over the terrorism of those who killed the prophets in Jerusalem: "Jerusalem, Jerusalem, the city that kills the prophets and stones those who are sent to it! How often have I desired to gather your children together as a hen gathers her brood under her wings, and you were not willing!" (Matt. 23:37).

This week we will read and view depictions of Whiteness as terror, including the Kerner Commission Report and bell hooks's essay "Representing Whiteness in the Black Imagination." The Kerner Commission was established by President Lyndon B. Johnson to investigate the causes of the social unrest in American cities during the long, hot summer of 1967 and provide recommendations for the future. Additionally, we will watch the Oscar-nominated psychological thriller *Get Out*, which uses the genre of horror to symbolize the history and ongoing legacy of White terror. Each of these selections offers us the opportunity for deep reflection. May this week's readings and viewing help us see ourselves more clearly and draw us into lament. And may our lamentation lift us out of denial and into the fight for truth and liberation.

DEEP SOUL WORK

Read and View. *Engage with these readings and this film slowly and carefully, taking time to stop and make notes as you go.*
- Read "Representing Whiteness in the Black Imagination" by bell hooks.[4]
- Read "The Kerner Commission Report" summary.[5]
- View *Get Out* by Jordan Peele.[6]

Meditate and Reflect. *Spend some time in silent meditation after each of the readings and viewing, and then write out your answers these questions:*
  1. How did the readings and viewing make you feel?

---

[4] bell hooks, "Representing Whiteness in the Black Imagination," in *Displacin: Essays in Social and Cultural Criticism,* ed. Ruth Frankenberg (Durham, NC: Duke University Press, 1997).

[5] "Report of the National Advisory Commission on Civil Disorders" (New York: Bantam Books, 1968).

[6] Jordan Peele, *Get Out* (United States: Universal Pictures, 2017).

2. What was most meaningful to you?

3. What are you discovering about Whiteness?

4. Where do you see yourself in the readings and films?

Acknowledge and Confess. *Take time to examine your own life story considering the readings and viewing this week and acknowledge what arises.*

- What stories from your life experience relate to what you read and viewed this week? (Be sure to include them in your racial autobiography.)

- What acknowledgments of Whiteness or personal confessions do you need to make based on this week's readings and viewing?

- Read the examples of state terror in Matthew 2:16–18 and Luke 13:1–2. How are we as people of faith called to respond to state terror? The crucifixion of Jesus was also an example of state terror.

- Read the story of Saul's conversion in Acts 9. Saul was a first-century terrorist who terrorized the early church with acts of violence and participated in the stoning of Stephen. Imagine Saul as a White domestic terrorist who was converted to participate in the Black freedom movement. What does his story teach us about our own need for conversion? What was required?

Repent, Turn, and Transform. *Imagine a new creation and a new humanity for yourself and for our world.*

- What does it mean to reckon with our history of violence and terror? How have other people and nations reckoned with theirs? Look into the way Germany responded to the end of the Nazi regime and the Holocaust (Nuremburg trials, reparations for Jewish people, and so on). Look into the way South Africa responded to the end of apartheid (Truth and Reconciliation Commission). What would it take for something like this to take place in America? Why hasn't it happened already?

- What kind of accountability do you need in your life to take responsibility for Whiteness as terror?

- What do you think would change if you apply what you've discovered this week about Whiteness in your sphere of power and influence?

"Representing Whiteness in the Black Imagination"

bell hooks

(1992)

Although there has never been any official body of black people in the United States who have gathered as anthropologists and/or ethnographers whose central critical project is the study of whiteness, black folks have, from slavery on, shared with one another in conversations "special" knowledge of whiteness gleaned from close scrutiny of white people. Deemed special because it was not a way of knowing that has been recorded fully in written material, its purpose was to help black folks cope and survive in a white supremacist society. For years black domestic servants, working in white homes, acted as informants who brought knowledge back to segregated communities details, facts, observations, psychoanalytic readings of the white "Other."

Sharing, in a similar way, the fascination with difference and the different that white people have collectively expressed openly (and at times vulgarly) as they have traveled around the world in pursuit of the other and otherness, black people, especially those living during the historical period of racial apartheid and legal segregation, have maintained steadfast and ongoing curiosity about the "ghosts," "the barbarians," these strange apparitions they were forced to serve. In the chapter on "Wildness" in *Shamanism, Colonialism, and the Wild Man*, Michael Taussig urges a stretching of our imagination and understanding of the Other to include inscriptions "on the edge of official history." Naming his critical project, identifying the passion he brings to the quest to know more deeply *you who are not ourselves*, Taussig explains:

I am trying to reproduce a mode of perception—a way of seeing
through a way of talking—figuring the world through dialogue
that comes alive with sudden transformative force in the crannies
of everyday life's pauses and juxtapositions, as in the kitchens of the
Putumayo or in the streets around the church in the Nina Maria.
It is always a way of representing the world in the roundabout
"speech" of the collage of things. . . . It is a mode of perception
that catches on the debris of history. . . .

I, too, am in search of the debris of history, am wiping the dust from
past conversations, to remember some of what was shared in the old
days, when black folks had little intimate contact with whites, when we
were much more open about the way we connected whiteness with the
mysterious, the strange, the terrible. Of course, everything has changed.
Now many black people live in the "bush of ghosts" and do not know
themselves separate from whiteness, do not know this thing we call
"difference." Though systems of domination, imperialism, colonialism,
racism, actively coerce black folks to internalize negative perceptions of
blackness, to be self-hating, and many of us succumb, blacks who imitate
whites (adopting their values, speech, habits of being, etc.) continue to
regard whiteness with suspicion, fear, and even hatred. This contradictory
longing to possess the reality of the Other, even though that reality is one
that wounds and negates, is expressive of the desire to understand the
mystery, to know intimately through imitation, as though such knowing
worn like an amulet, a mask, will ward away the evil, the terror.

Searching the critical work of postcolonial critics, I found much writing that bespeaks the continued fascination with the way white minds,
particularly the colonial imperialist traveler, perceive blackness, and
very little expressed interest in representations of whiteness in the black
imagination. Black cultural and social critics allude to such representations in their writing, yet only a few have dared to make explicit those
perceptions of whiteness that they think will discomfort or antagonize
readers. James Baldwin's collection of essays *Notes of a Native Son* (1955)
explores these issues with a clarity and frankness that is no longer fash-
ionable in a world where evocations of pluralism and diversity act to
obscure differences arbitrarily imposed and maintained by white racist
domination. Writing about being the first black person to visit a Swiss
village with only white inhabitants, who had a yearly ritual of painting

individuals black who were then positioned as slaves and bought, so that the villagers could celebrate their concern with converting the souls of the "natives," Baldwin responded:

> I thought of white men arriving for the first time in an African vil-
> lage, strangers there, as I am a stranger here, and tried to imagine
> the astounded populace touching their hair and marveling at the
> color of their skin. But there is a great difference between being
> the first white man to be seen by Africans and being the first black
> man to be seen by whites. The white man takes the astonishment
> as tribute, for he arrives to conquer and to convert the natives,
> whose inferiority in relation to himself is not even to be questioned,
> whereas I, without a thought of conquest, find myself among a
> people whose culture controls me, has even in a sense, created me,
> people who have cost me more in anguish and rage than they will
> ever know, who yet do not even know of my existence. The aston-
> ishment with which I might have greeted them, should they have
> stumbled into my African village a few hundred years ago, might
> have rejoiced their hearts. But the astonishment with which they
> greet me today can only poison mine.

My thinking about representations of whiteness in the black imagination has been stimulated by classroom discussions about the way in
which the absence of recognition is a strategy that facilitates making a
group "the Other." In these classrooms there have been heated debates
among students when white students respond with disbelief, shock, and
rage, as they listen to black students talk about whiteness, when they
are compelled to hear observations, stereotypes, etc., that are offered as
"data" gleaned from close scrutiny and study. Usually, white students
respond with naive amazement that black people critically assess white
people from a standpoint where "whiteness" is the privileged signifier.
Their amazement that black people watch white people with a critical
"ethnographic" gaze is itself an expression of racism. Often their rage
erupts because they believe that all ways of looking that highlight difference subvert the liberal conviction that it is the assertion of universal
subjectivity (we are all just people) that will make racism disappear. They
have a deep emotional investment in the myth of "sameness" even as their
actions reflect the primacy of whiteness as a sign informing who they are

and how they think. Many of them are shocked that black people think critically about whiteness because racist thinking perpetuates the fantasy that the Other who is subjugated, who is subhuman, lacks the ability to comprehend, to understand, to see the working of the powerful. Even though the majority of these students politically consider themselves liberals, who are anti-racist, they too unwittingly invest in the sense of whiteness as mystery.

In white supremacist society, white people can "safely" imagine that they are invisible to black people since the power they have historically asserted, and even now collectively assert over black people accorded them the right to control the black gaze. As fantastic as it may seem, racist white people find it easy to imagine that black people cannot see them if within their desire they do not want to be seen by the dark Other. One mark of oppression was that black folks were compelled to assume the mantle of invisibility, to erase all traces of their subjectivity during slavery and the long years of racial apartheid, so that they could be better, less threatening servants. An effective strategy of white supremacist terror and dehumanization during slavery centered around white control of the black gaze. Black slaves, and later manumitted servants, could be brutally punished for looking, for appearing to observe the whites they were serving as only a subject can observe, or see. To be fully an object then was to lack the capacity to see or recognize reality. These looking relations were reinforced as whites cultivated the practice of denying the subjectivity of blacks (the better to dehumanize and oppress), of relegating them to the realm of the invisible. Growing up in a Kentucky household where black servants lived in the same dwelling with her white family who employed them, newspaper heiress Sallie Bingham recalls, in her autobiography *Passion and Prejudice* (1989), "Blacks, I realized, were simply invisible to most white people, except as a pair of hands offering a drink on a silver tray." Reduced to the machinery of bodily physical labor, black people learned to appear before whites as though they were zombies, cultivating the habit of casting the gaze downward so as not to appear uppity. To look directly was an assertion of subjectivity, equality. Safety resided in the pretense of invisibility.

Even though legal racial apartheid no longer is a norm in the United States, the habits of being cultivated to uphold and maintain institutionalized white supremacy linger. Since most white people do not have to "see" black people (constantly appearing on billboards, television, movies, in magazines, etc.) and they do not need to be ever on guard, observing black people, to be "safe," they can live as though black people are invisible and can imagine that they are also invisible to blacks. Some white people may even imagine there is no representation of whiteness in the black imagination, especially one that is based on concrete observation or mythic conjecture; they think they are seen by black folks only as they want to appear. Ideologically, the rhetoric of white supremacy supplies a fantasy of whiteness. Described in Richard Dyer's (1988) essay "White" this fantasy makes whiteness synonymous with goodness:

> Power in contemporary society habitually passes itself off as embodied in the normal as opposed to the superior. This is common to all forms of power, but it works in a peculiarly seductive way with whiteness, because of the way it seems rooted, in common-sense thought, in things other than ethnic difference. . . . Thus it is said (even in liberal textbooks) that there are inevitable associations of white with light and therefore safety, and black with dark and therefore danger, and that this explains racism (whereas one might well argue about the safety of the cover of darkness, and the danger of exposure to the light); again, and with more justice, people point to the Judeo-Christian use of white and black to symbolize good and evil, as carried still in such expressions as "a black mark," "white magic," "to blacken the character" and so on.

Socialized to believe the fantasy, that whiteness represents goodness and all that is benign and non-threatening, many white people assume this is the way black people conceptualize whiteness. They do not imagine that the way whiteness makes its presence felt in black life, most often as terrorizing imposition, a power that wounds, hurts, tortures, is a reality that disrupts the fantasy of whiteness as representing goodness. Collectively, black people remain rather silent about representations of whiteness in the black imagination. As in the old days of racial segregation where black folks learned to "wear the mask," many of us pretend to be comfortable in the face of whiteness only to turn our backs and give expression to intense levels of discomfort. Especially talked about is the representation of whiteness as terrorizing. Without evoking a simplistic, essentialist "us and them" dichotomy that suggests black folks merely invert stereotypical racist interpretations, so that black becomes synonymous with goodness and white with evil, I want to focus on that representation of whiteness that is not formed in reaction to stereotypes but emerges as a response to the traumatic pain and anguish that remains a consequence of white racist domination, a psychic state that informs and shapes the way black folks "see" whiteness. Stereotypes black folks maintain about white folks are not the only representations of whiteness in the black imagination. They emerge primarily as responses to white stereotypes of blackness. Speaking about white stereotypes of blackness as engendering a trickle-down process, where there is the projection onto an Other of all that we deny about ourselves, Lorraine Hansberry in *To Be Young, Gifted, and Black* (1969) identifies particular stereotypes about white people that are commonly cited in black communities and urges us not to "celebrate this madness in any direction":

> Is it not "known" in the ghetto that white people, as an entity, are "dirty" (especially white women—who never seem to do their own cleaning); inherently "cruel" (the cold, fierce roots of Europe; who else could put all those people into ovens *scientifically*); "smart" (you really have to hand it to the m.f.'s); and anything *but* cold and passionless (because look who has had to live with little else than their passions in the guise of love and hatred all these centuries)? And so on.

Stereotypes, however inaccurate, are one form of representation. Like fictions, they are created to serve as substitutions, standing in for what is real. They are there not to tell it like it is but to invite and encourage pretense. They are a fantasy, a projection onto the Other that makes them less threatening. Stereotypes abound when there is distance. They are an invention, a pretense that one knows when the steps that would make real knowing possible cannot be taken—are not allowed.

Looking past stereotypes to consider various representations of whiteness in the black imagination, I appeal to memory, to my earliest recollections of ways these issues were raised in black life. Returning to memories of growing up in the social circumstances created by racial apartheid, to all black spaces on the edges of town, I re-inhabit a location where black folks associated whiteness with the terrible, the terrifying, the terrorizing. White people were regarded as terrorists, especially those who dared to enter that segregated space of blackness. As a child I did not know any white people. They were strangers, rarely seen in our neighborhoods. The "official" white men who came across the tracks were there to sell products, Bibles, insurance. They terrorized by economic exploitation. What did I see in the gazes of those white men who crossed our thresholds that made me afraid, that made black children unable to speak? Did they understand at all how strange their whiteness appeared in our living rooms, how threatening? Did they journey across the tracks with the same "adventurous" spirit that other white men carried to Africa, Asia, to those mysterious places they would one day call the third world? Did they come to our houses to meet the Other face to face and enact the colonizer role, dominating us on our own turf? Their presence terrified *me*. Whatever their mission they looked too much like the unofficial white men who came to enact rituals of terror and torture. As a child, I did not know how to tell them apart, how to ask the "real white people to please stand up." The terror that I felt is one black people have shared. Whites learn about it secondhand. Confessing in *Soul Sister* (1969) that she too began to feel this terror after changing her skin to appear "black" and going to live in the South, Grace Halsell described her altered sense of whiteness:

> Caught in this climate of hate, I am totally terror-stricken, and I search my mind to know why I am fearful of my own people. Yet they no longer seem my people, but rather the "enemy" arrayed in large numbers against me in some hostile territory. . . . My wild heartbeat is a secondhand kind of terror. I know that I cannot possibly experience what *they*, the black people experience. . . .

Black folks raised in the North do not escape this sense of terror. In her autobiography, *Every Good-bye Ain't Gone* (1990), Itabari Njeri begins the narrative of her northern childhood with a memory of southern roots. Traveling south as an adult to investigate the murder of her grandfather by white youth who were drag racing and ran him down in the streets, killing him, Njeri recalls that for many years "the distant and accidental violence that took my grandfather's life could not compete with the psychological terror that begun to engulf my own." Ultimately, she begins to link that terror with the history of black people in the United States, seeing it as an imprint carried from the past to the present:

As I grew older, my grandfather assumed mythic proportions in my imagination. Even in absence, he filled my room like music and watched over me when I was fearful. His fantasized presence diverted thoughts of my father's drunken rages. With age, my fantasizing ceased, the image of my grandfather faded. What lingered was the memory of his caress, the pain of something missing in my life, wrenched away by reckless white youths. I had a growing sense—the beginning of an inevitable comprehension—that this society deals blacks a disproportionate share of pain and denial.

Njeri's journey takes her through the pain and terror of the past, only the memories do not fade. They linger, as does the pain and bitterness: "Against a backdrop of personal loss, against the evidence of history that fills me with a knowledge of the hateful behavior of whites toward blacks, I see the people of Bainbridge. And I cannot trust them. I cannot absolve them." If it is possible to conquer terror through ritual reenactment, that is what Njeri does. She goes back to the scene of the crime, dares to face the enemy. It is this confrontation that forces the terror of history to loosen its grip.

To name that whiteness in the black imagination is often a representation of terror: one must face a palimpsest of written histories that erase and deny, that reinvent the past to make the present vision of racial harmony and pluralism more plausible. To bear the burden of memory one must willingly journey to places long uninhabited, searching the debris of history for traces of the unforgettable, all knowledge of which has been suppressed. Njeri laments in her Prelude that "nobody really knows us"; "So institutionalized is the ignorance of our history, our culture, our everyday existence that, often, we do not even know ourselves." Theorizing black experience, we seek to uncover, restore, as well as to deconstruct, so that new paths, different journeys are possible. Indeed, Edward Said (1983) in "Traveling Theory" argues that theory can "threaten reification, as well as the entire bourgeoisie system on which reification depends, with destruction." The call to theorize black experience is constantly challenged and subverted by conservative voices reluctant to move from fixed locations. Said reminds us:

Theory, in fine, is won as the result of a process that begins when consciousness first experiences its own terrible ossification in the

general reification of all things under capitalism; then when consciousness generalizes (or classes) itself as something opposed to
other objects, and feels itself as contradiction to (or crisis within)
objectification, there emerges a consciousness of change in the status
quo; finally, moving toward freedom and fulfillment, consciousness looks ahead to complete self-realization, which is of course
the revolutionary process stretching forward in time, perceivable
now only as theory or projection.

Traveling, moving into the past, Njeri pieces together fragments.
Who does she see staring into the face of a southern white man who
was said to be the one? Does the terror in his face mirror the look of the
unsuspected black man whose dying history does not name or record?
Baldwin wrote that "people are trapped in history and history is trapped
in them." There is then only the fantasy of escape, or the promise that
what is lost will be found, rediscovered, returned. For black folks, recon-
structing an archaeology of memory makes return possible, the journey
to a place we can never call home even as we reinhabit it to make sense
of present locations. Such journeying cannot be fully encompassed by
conventional notions of travel.

Spinning off from Said's essay, James Clifford in "Notes on Travel and
Theory" celebrates the idea of journeying, asserting that

> this sense of worldly, "mapped" movement is also why it may be
> worth holding on to the term "travel," despite its connotations of
> middle-class "literary," or recreational, journeying, spatial practices
> long associated with male experiences and virtues. "Travel" sug-
> gests, at least, profane activity, following public routes and beaten
> tracks. How do different populations, classes, and genders travel?
> What kinds of knowledges, stories, and theories do they produce?
> A crucial research agenda opens up.

Reading this piece and listening to Clifford talk about theory and travel,
I appreciated his efforts to expand the travel/theoretical frontier so that
it might be more inclusive, even as I considered that to answer the questions he poses is to propose a deconstruction of the conventional sense
of travel, and put alongside it or in its place a theory of the journey
that would expose the extent to which holding on to the concept of

"travel" as we know it is also a way to hold on to imperialism. For some individuals, clinging to the conventional sense of travel allows them to remain fascinated with imperialism, to write about it seductively, evoking what Renato Rosaldo (1988) aptly calls in *Culture and Truth* "imperialist nostalgia." Significantly, he reminds readers that "even politically progressive North American audiences have enjoyed the elegance of manners governing relations of dominance and subordination between the 'races.'" Theories of travel produced outside conventional borders might want the Journey to become the rubric within which travel as a starting point for discourse is associated with different headings—rites of passage, immigration, enforced migration, relocation, enslavement, homelessness. Travel is not a word that can be easily evoked to talk about the Middle Passage, the Trail of Tears, the landing of Chinese immigrants at Ellis Island, the forced relocation of Japanese-Americans, the plight of the homeless. Theorizing diverse journeying is crucial to our understanding of any politics of location. As Clifford asserts at the end of his essay: "Theory is always written from some 'where,' and that 'where' is less a place than itineraries: different, concrete histories of dwelling, immigration, exile, migration. These include the migration of third world intellectuals into the metropolitan universities, to pass through or to remain, changed by their travel but marked by places of origin, by peculiar allegiances and alienations."

Listening to Clifford "playfully" evoke a sense of "travel," I felt such an evocation could always make it difficult for there to be recognition of an experience of travel that is not about play but is an encounter with terrorism. And it is crucial that we recognize that the hegemony of one experience of travel can make it impossible to articulate another experience and be heard. From certain standpoints, to travel is to encounter the terrorizing force of white supremacy. To tell my "travel" stories, I must name the movement from a racially segregated southern community, from a rural black Baptist origin, to prestigious white university settings, etc. I must be able to speak about what it is like to be leaving Italy after I have given a talk on racism and feminism, hosted by the parliament, only to stand for hours while I am interrogated by white officials who do not have to respond when I inquire as to why the questions they ask me are different from those asked the white people in line before me. Thinking only that I must endure this public questioning, the stares of those around me, because my skin is black, I am startled when I am asked if I speak Arabic, when I am told that women like me receive presents from men without knowing what those presents are. Reminded of another time when I was strip-searched by French officials, who were stopping black people to make sure we were not illegal immigrants and/ or terrorists, I think that one fantasy of whiteness is that the threatening Other is always a terrorist. This projection enables many white people to imagine there is no representation of whiteness as terror, as terrorizing. Yet it is this representation of whiteness in the black imagination, first learned in the narrow confines of the poor black rural community, that is sustained by my travels to many different locations.

To travel, I must always move through fear, confront terror. It helps to be able to link this individual experience to the collective journeying of black people, to the Middle Passage, to the mass migration of southern black folks to northern cities in the early part of the twentieth century. Michel Foucault posits memory as a site of resistance suggesting (as Jonathan Arac puts it in his introduction to *Postmodernism and Politics*) that the process of remembering can be a practice which "transforms history from a judgment on the past in the name of a present truth to a 'counter-memory' that combats our current modes of truth and justice, helping us to understand and change the present by placing it in a new relation to the past." It is useful when theorizing black experience to examine the way the concept of "terror" is linked to representations of whiteness.

In the absence of the reality of whiteness, I learned as a child that to be "safe" it was important to recognize the power of whiteness, even to fear it, and to avoid encountering it. There was nothing terrifying about the sharing of this knowledge as survival strategy; the terror was made real only when I journeyed from the black side of town to a predominately white area near my grandmother's house. I had to pass through this area to reach her place. Describing these journeys "across town" in the essay "Homeplace: A Site of Resistance" I remembered:

It was a movement away from the segregated blackness of our community into a poor white neighborhood. I remember the fear, being scared to walk to Baba's, our grandmother's house, because we would have to pass that terrifying whiteness—those white faces on the porches staring us down with hate. Even when empty or vacant those porches seemed to say *danger,* you do not belong here, you are not safe.

Oh! that feeling of safety, of arrival, of homecoming when we finally reached the edges of her yard, when we could see the soot black face of our grandfather, Daddy Gus, sitting in his chair on the porch, smell his cigar, and rest on his lap. Such a contrast, that feeling of arrival, of homecoming—this sweetness and the bitterness of that journey, that constant reminder of white power and control.

Even though it was a long time ago that I made this journey, associations of whiteness with terror and the terrorizing remain. Even though I live and move in spaces where I am surrounded by whiteness, surrounded, there is no comfort that makes the terrorism disappear. All black people in the United States, irrespective of their class status or politics, live with the possibility that they will be terrorized by whiteness.

This terror is most vividly described in fiction writing by black authors, particularly the recent novel by Toni Morrison (1987), *Beloved*. Baby Suggs, the black prophet, who is most vocal about representations of whiteness, dies because she suffers an absence of color. Surrounded by a lack, an empty space, taken over by whiteness, she remembers: "Those white things have taken all I had or dreamed and broke my heartstrings too. There is no bad luck in the world but white folks." If the mask of whiteness, the pretense, represents it as always benign, benevolent, then what this representation obscures is the representation of danger, the sense of threat. During the period of racial apartheid, still known by many folks as Jim Crow, it was more difficult for black people to internalize this pretense, hard for us not to know that the shapes under white sheets had a mission to threaten, to terrorize. That representation of whiteness, and its association with innocence, which engulfed and murdered Emmett Till was a sign; it was meant to torture with the reminder of possible future terror. In Morrison's *Beloved* the memory of terror is so deeply inscribed on the body of Sethe and in her consciousness, and the association of terror with whiteness is so intense, that she kills her young so that they will never know the terror. Explaining her actions to Paul D. she tells him that it is her job "to keep them away from what I know is terrible." Of course Sethe's attempt to end the historical anguish of black people only reproduces it in a different form. She conquers the terror through perverse reenactment, through resistance, using violence as a means of fleeing from a history that is a burden too great to bear. It is the telling of that history that makes possible political self-recovery.

In contemporary society, white and black people alike believe that racism no longer exists. This erasure, however mythic, diffuses the representation of whiteness as terror in the black imagination. It allows for assimilation and forgetfulness. The eagerness with which contemporary society does away with racism, replacing this recognition with evocations of pluralism and diversity that further mask reality, is a response to the terror, but it has also become a way to perpetuate the terror by providing a cover, a hiding place. Black people still feel the terror, still associate it with whiteness, but are rarely able to articulate the varied ways we are terrorized because it is easy to silence by accusations of reverse racism or by suggesting that black folks who talk about the ways we are terrorized by whites are merely evoking victimization to demand special treatment.

Attending a recent conference on cultural studies, I was reminded of the way in which the discourse of race is increasingly divorced from any recognition of the politics of racism. I went there because I was confident that I would be in the company of likeminded, progressive, "aware" intellectuals; instead, I was disturbed when the usual arrangements of white supremacist hierarchy were mirrored both in terms of who was speaking, of how bodies were arranged on the stage, of who was in the audience, of what voices were deemed worthy to speak and be heard. As the conference progressed I began to feel afraid. If progressive people, most of whom were white, could so blindly reproduce a version of the status quo and not "see" it, the thought of how racial politics would be played out "outside" this arena was horrifying. That feeling of terror that I had known so intimately in my childhood surfaced. Without even considering whether the audience was able to shift from the prevailing standpoint and hear another perspective, I talked openly about that sense of terror. Later, I heard stories of white women joking about how ludicrous it was for me (in their eyes I suppose I represent the "bad" tough black woman) to say I felt terrorized. Their inability to conceive that my terror, like that of Sethe's, is a response to the legacy of white domination and the contemporary expressions of white supremacy is an indication of how little this culture really understands the profound psychological impact of white racist domination.

At this same conference I bonded with a progressive black woman and white man who, like me, were troubled by the extent to which folks chose to ignore the way white supremacy was informing the structure of the conference. Talking with the black woman, I asked her: "What do you do, when you are tired of confronting white racism, tired of the day-to-day incidental acts of racial terrorism? I mean, how do you deal with coming home to a white person?" Laughing, she said, "Oh, you mean when I am suffering from White People Fatigue Syndrome. He gets that more than I do." After we finished our laughter, we talked about the way white people who shift locations, as her companion has done, begin to see the world differently. Understanding how racism works, he can see the way in which whiteness acts to terrorize without seeing himself as bad, or all white people as bad, and black people as good. Repudiating "us and them" dichotomies does not mean that we should *never* speak the ways observing the world from the standpoint of "whiteness" may indeed distort perception, impede understanding of the way racism works both in the larger world as well as the world of our intimate interactions. Calling for a shift in locations in "the intervention interview" published with the collection *The Post-Colonial Critic* (1990), Gayatri Spivak clarifies the radical possibilities that surface when positionality is problematized, explaining that "what we are asking for is that the hegemonic discourses, the holders of hegemonic discourse should de-hegemonize their position and themselves learn how to occupy the subject position of the other." Generally, this process of repositioning has the power to deconstruct practices of racism and make possible the disassociation of whiteness with terror in the black imagination. As critical intervention, it allows for the recognition that progressive white people who are anti-racist might be able to understand the way in which their cultural practice reinscribes white supremacy without promoting paralyzing guilt or denial. Without the capacity to inspire terror, whiteness no longer signifies the right to dominate. It truly becomes a benevolent absence. Baldwin ends his essay "Stranger in the Village" with the declaration: "This world is white no longer, and it will never be white again." Critically examining the association of whiteness as terror in the black imagination, deconstructing it, we both name racism's impact and help to break its hold. We decolonize our minds and our imaginations.

Report of the National Advisory Commission on Civil Disorders

Summary of Report[1]

INTRODUCTION

The summer of 1967 again brought racial disorders to American cities, and with them shock, fear and bewilderment to the nation.

The worst came during a two-week period in July, first in Newark and then in Detroit. Each set off a chain reaction in neighboring communities.

On July 28, 1967, the President of the United States established this Commission and directed us to answer three basic questions:

1. What happened?
2. Why did it happen?
3. What can be done to prevent it from happening again?

To respond to these questions, we have undertaken a broad range of studies and investigations. We have visited the riot cities; we have heard many witnesses; we have sought the counsel of experts across the country.

This is our basic conclusion: Our nation is moving toward two societies, one black, one white—separate and unequal.

Reaction to last summer's disorders has quickened the movement and deepened the division. Discrimination and segregation have long permeated much of American life; they now threaten the future of every American.

---

[1] *Report of the National Advisory Commission on Civil Disorders* (New York: Bantam Books, 1968), 1–29.

This deepening racial division is not inevitable. The movement apart can be reversed. Choice is still possible. Our principal task is to define that choice and to press for a national resolution.

To pursue our present course will involve the continuing polarization of the American community and, ultimately, the destruction of basic democratic values.

The alternative is not blind repression or capitulation to lawlessness. It is the realization of common opportunities for all within a single society.

This alternative will require a commitment to national action—compassionate, massive and sustained, backed by the resources of the most powerful and the richest nation on this earth. From every American it will require new attitudes, new understanding, and, above all, new will.

The vital needs of the nation must be met; hard choices must be made, and, if necessary, new taxes enacted.

Violence cannot build a better society. Disruption and disorder nourish repression, not justice. They strike at the freedom of every citizen. The community cannot—it will not—tolerate coercion and mob rule.

Violence and destruction must be ended—in the streets of the ghetto and in the lives of people.

Segregation and poverty have created in the racial ghetto a destructive environment totally unknown to most white Americans.

What white Americans have never fully understood but what the Negro can never forget—is that white society is deeply implicated in the ghetto. White institutions created it, white institutions maintain it, and white society condones it.

It is time now to turn with all the purpose at our command to the major unfinished business of this nation. It is time to adopt strategies for action that will produce quick and visible progress. It is time to make good the promises of American democracy to all citizens—urban and rural, white and black, Spanish-surname, American Indian, and every minority group.

Our recommendations embrace three basic principles:

- To mount programs on a scale equal to the dimension of the problems;
- To aim these programs for high impact in the immediate future in order to close the gap between promise and performance;

- To undertake new initiatives and experiments that can change the system of failure and frustration that now dominates the ghetto and weakens our society.

These programs will require unprecedented levels of funding and performance, but they neither probe deeper nor demand more than the problems which called them forth. There can be no higher priority for national action and no higher claim on the nation's conscience.

We issue this Report now, four months before the date called for by the President. Much remains that can be learned. Continued study is essential.

As Commissioners we have worked together with a sense of the greatest urgency and have sought to compose whatever differences exist among us. Some differences remain. But the gravity of the problem and the pressing need for action are too clear to allow further delay in the issuance of this Report.

PART I—WHAT HAPPENED?

Chapter 1—Profiles of Disorder

The report contains profiles of a selection of the disorders that took place during the summer of 1967. These profiles are designed to indicate how the disorders happened, who participated in them, and how local officials, police forces, and the National Guard responded. Illustrative excerpts follow:

Newark

. . . It was decided to attempt to channel the energies of the people into a nonviolent protest. While Lofton promised the crowd that a full investigation would be made of the Smith incident, the other Negro leaders began urging those on the scene to form a line of march toward the city hall.

Some persons joined the line of march. Others milled about in the narrow street. From the dark grounds of the housing project came a barrage of rocks. Some of them fell among the crowd. Others hit persons in the line of march. Many smashed the windows of the police station. The rock throwing, it was believed, was the work of youngsters; approximately 2,500 children lived in the housing project.

Almost at the same time, an old car was set afire in a parking lot. The line of march began to disintegrate. The police, their heads protected by World War I–type helmets, sallied forth to disperse the crowd. A fire engine, arriving on the scene, was pelted with rocks. As police drove people away from the station, they scattered in all directions.

A few minutes later a nearby liquor store was broken into. Some persons, seeing a caravan of cabs appear at city hall to protest Smith's arrest, interpreted this as evidence that the disturbance had been organized, and generated rumors to that effect. However, only a few stores were looted. Within a short period of time, the disorder appeared to have run its course.

. . . .

. . . On Saturday, July 15, [Director of Police Dominick] Spina received a report of snipers in a housing project. When he arrived he saw approximately 100 National Guardsmen and police officers crouching behind vehicles, hiding in corners and lying on the ground around the edge of the courtyard.

Since everything appeared quiet and it was broad daylight, Spina walked directly down the middle of the street. Nothing happened. As he came to the last building of the complex, he heard a shot. All around him the troopers jumped, believing themselves to be under sniper fire. A moment later a young Guardsman ran from behind a building.

The Director of Police went over and asked him if he had fired the shot. The soldier said yes, he had fired to scare a man away from a window; that his orders were to keep everyone away from windows.

Spina said he told the soldier: "Do you know what you just did? You have now created a state of hysteria. Every Guardsman up and down this street and every state policeman and every city policeman that is present thinks that somebody just fired a shot and that it is probably a sniper."

A short time later more "gunshots" were heard. Investigating, Spina came upon a Puerto Rican sitting on a wall. In reply to a question as to whether he knew "where the firing is coming from?" the man said:

"That's no firing. That's fireworks. If you look up to the fourth floor, you will see the people who are throwing down these cherry bombs."

By this time four truckloads of National Guardsmen had arrived and troopers and policemen were again crouched everywhere looking for a sniper. The Director of Police remained at the scene for three hours, and the only shot fired was the one by the Guardsman.

Nevertheless, at six o'clock that evening two columns of National Guardsmen and state troopers were directing mass fire at the Hayes Housing Project in response to what they believed were snipers. . . .

Detroit

. . . A spirit of carefree nihilism was taking hold. To riot and destroy appeared more and more to become ends in themselves. Late Sunday afternoon it appeared to one observer that the young people were "dancing amidst the flames."

A Negro plainclothes officer was standing at an intersection when a man threw a Molotov cocktail into a business establishment at the corner. . . . In the heat of the afternoon, fanned by the 20 to 25 m.p.h. winds of both Sunday and Monday, the fire reached the home next door within minutes. As residents uselessly sprayed the flames with garden hoses, the fire jumped from roof to roof of adjacent two- and three-story buildings. Within the hour the entire block was in flames. The ninth house in the burning row belonged to the arsonist who had thrown the Molotov cocktail. . . .

. . . .

. . . Employed as a private guard, 55-year-old Julius L. Dorsey, a Negro, was standing in front of a market when accosted by two Negro men and a woman. They demanded he permit them to loot the market. He ignored their demands. They began to berate him. He asked a neighbor to call the police. As the argument grew more heated, Dorsey fired three shots from his pistol into the air.

The police radio reported: "Looters, they have rifles." A patrol car driven by a police officer and carrying three National Guardsmen arrived. As the looters fled, the law enforcement personnel opened fire. When the firing ceased, one person lay dead.

He was Julius L. Dorsey. . .

. . . .

. . . As the riot alternately waxed and waned, one area of the ghetto remained insulated. On the northeast side the residents of some 150 square
blocks inhabited by 21,000 persons had, in 1966, banded together in the
Positive Neighborhood Action Committee (PNAC). With professional
help from the Institute of Urban Dynamics, they had organized block
clubs and made plans for the improvement of the neighborhood. . . .

When the riot broke out, the residents, through the block clubs, were
able to organize quickly. Youngsters, agreeing to stay in the neighborhood, participated in detouring traffic. While many persons reportedly
sympathized with the idea of a rebellion against the "system," only two
small fires were set—one in an empty building.

. . . .

. . . According to Lt. Gen. Throckmorton and Col. Bolling, the city, at
this time, was saturated with fear. The National Guardsmen were afraid,
the residents were afraid, and the police were afraid. Numerous persons,
the majority of them Negroes, were being injured by gunshots of unde-
termined origin. The general and his staff felt that the major task of the
troops was to reduce the fear and restore an air of normalcy.

In order to accomplish this, every effort was made to establish contact
and rapport between the troops and the residents. The soldiers—20
percent of whom were Negro—began helping to clean up the streets,
collect garbage, and trace persons who had disappeared in the confusion.
Residents in the neighborhoods responded with soup and sandwiches for
the troops. In areas where the National Guard tried to establish rapport
with the citizens, there was a smaller response.

New Brunswick

. . . A short time later, elements of the crowd—an older and rougher
one than the night before—appeared in front of the police station. The
participants wanted to see the mayor.

Mayor [Patricia] Sheehan went out onto the steps of the station.
Using a bullhorn, she talked to the people and asked that she be given
an opportunity to correct conditions. The crowd was boisterous. Some
persons challenged the mayor. But, finally, the opinion, "She's new! Give
her a chance!" prevailed.

A demand was issued by people in the crowd that all persons arrested the previous night be released. Told that this already had been done, the people were suspicious. They asked to be allowed to inspect the jail cells.

It was agreed to permit representatives of the people to look in the cells to satisfy themselves that everyone had been released. The crowd dispersed. The New Brunswick riot had failed to materialize.

Chapter 2—Patterns of Disorder

The "typical" riot did not take place. The disorders of 1967 were unusual, irregular, complex and unpredictable social processes. Like most human events, they did not unfold in an orderly sequence. However, an analysis of our survey information leads to some conclusions about the riot process. In general:

- The civil disorders of 1967 involved Negroes acting against local symbols of white American society, authority and property in Negro neighborhoods—rather than against white persons.
- Of 164 disorders reported during the first nine months of 1967, eight (5 percent) were major in terms of violence and damage; 33 (20 percent) were serious but not major; 123 (75 percent) were minor and undoubtedly would not have received national attention as "riots" had the nation not been sensitized by the more serious outbreaks.
- In the 75 disorders studied by a Senate subcommittee, 83 deaths were reported. Eighty-two percent of the deaths and more than half the injuries occurred in Newark and Detroit. About 10 percent of the dead and 38 percent of the injured were public employees, primarily law officers and firemen. The overwhelming majority of the persons killed or injured in all the disorders were Negro civilians.
- Initial damage estimates were greatly exaggerated. In Detroit, newspaper damage estimates at first ranged from $200 million to $500 million; the highest recent estimate is $45 million. In Newark, early estimates ranged from $15 to $25 million. A month later damage was estimated at $10.2 million, over 80 percent in inventory losses.

In the 24 disorders in 23 cities which we surveyed:

- The final incident before the outbreak of disorder, and the initial violence itself, generally took place in the evening or at night at a place in which it was normal for many people to be on the streets.
- Violence usually occurred almost immediately following the occurrence of the final precipitating incident, and then escalated rapidly. With but few exceptions, violence subsided during the day, and flared rapidly again at night. The night-day cycles continued through the early period of the major disorders.
- Disorder generally began with rock and bottle throwing and window breaking. Once store windows were broken, looting usually followed.
- Disorder did not erupt as a result of a single "triggering" or "precipitating" incident. Instead, it was generated out of an increasingly disturbed social atmosphere, in which typically a series of tension-heightening incidents over a period of weeks or months became linked in the minds of many in the Negro community with a reservoir of underlying grievances. At some point in the mounting tension, a further incident—in itself often routine or trivial—became the breaking point and the tension spilled over into violence.
- "Prior" incidents, which increased tensions and ultimately led to violence, were police actions in almost half the cases; police actions were "final" incidents before the outbreak of violence in 12 of the 24 surveyed disorders.
- No particular control tactic was successful in every situation. The varied effectiveness of control techniques emphasizes the need for advance training, planning, adequate intelligence systems, and knowledge of the ghetto community.
- Negotiations between Negroes—including young militants as well as older Negro leaders—and white officials concerning "terms of peace" occurred during virtually all the disorders surveyed. In many cases, these negotiations involved discussion of underlying grievances as well as the handling of the disorder by control authorities.
- The typical rioter was a teenager or young adult, a lifelong resident of the city in which he rioted, a high school dropout; he was, nevertheless, somewhat better educated than his nonrioting Negro neighbor, and was usually underemployed or employed in a menial

job. He was proud of his race, extremely hostile to both whites and middle-class Negroes and, although informed about politics, highly distrustful of the political system.

- A Detroit survey revealed that approximately 11 percent of the total residents of two riot areas admitted participation in the rioting, 20 to 25 percent identified themselves as "bystanders," over 16 percent identified themselves as "counter-rioters" who urged rioters to "cool it," and the remaining 48 to 53 percent said they were at home or elsewhere and did not participate. In a survey of Negro males between the ages of 15 and 35 residing in the disturbance area in Newark, about 45 percent identified themselves as rioters, and about 55 percent as "noninvolved."

- Most rioters were young Negro males. Nearly 53 percent of arrestees were between 15 and 24 years of age; nearly 81 percent between 15 and 35.

- In Detroit and Newark about 74 percent of the rioters were brought up in the North. In contrast, of the noninvolved, 36 percent in Detroit and 52 percent in Newark were brought up in the North.

- What the rioters appeared to be seeking was fuller participation in the social order and the material benefits enjoyed by the majority of American citizens. Rather than rejecting the American system, they were anxious to obtain a place for themselves in it.

- Numerous Negro counter-rioters walked the streets urging rioters to "cool it." The typical counter-rioter was better educated and had higher income than either the rioter or the noninvolved.

- The proportion of Negroes in local government was substantially smaller than the Negro proportion of population. Only three of the 20 cities studied had more than one Negro legislator; none had ever had a Negro mayor or city manager. In only four cities did Negroes hold other important policy-making positions or serve as heads of municipal departments.

- Although almost all cities had some sort of formal grievance mechanism for handling citizen complaints, this typically was regarded by Negroes as ineffective and was generally ignored.

- Although specific grievances varied from city to city, at least 12 deeply held grievances can be identified and ranked into three levels of relative intensity:

First Level of Intensity

1. Police practices
2. Unemployment and underemployment
3. Inadequate housing

Second Level of Intensity

4. Inadequate education
5. Poor recreation facilities and programs
6. Ineffectiveness of the political structure and grievance mechanisms

Third Level of Intensity

7. Disrespectful white attitudes
8. Discriminatory administration of justice
9. Inadequacy of federal programs
10. Inadequacy of municipal services
11. Discriminatory consumer and credit practices
12. Inadequate welfare programs

- The results of a three-city survey of various federal programs—man-power, education, housing, welfare and community action—indicate that, despite substantial expenditures, the number of persons assisted constituted only a fraction of those in need.

The background of disorder is often as complex and difficult to analyze as the disorder itself. But we find that certain general conclusions can be drawn:

- Social and economic conditions in the riot cities constituted a clear pattern of severe disadvantage for Negroes compared with whites, whether the Negroes lived in the area where the riot took place or outside it. Negroes had completed fewer years of education and fewer had attended high school. Negroes were twice as likely to be unemployed and three times as likely to be in unskilled and service jobs. Negroes averaged 70 percent of the income earned by whites and were more than twice as likely to be living in poverty. Although housing cost Negroes relatively more, they had worse housing—three times as likely to be overcrowded and substandard. When compared to white suburbs, the relative disadvantage is even more pronounced.

A study of the aftermath of disorder leads to disturbing conclusions. We find that, despite the institution of some postriot programs:

- Little basic change in the conditions underlying the outbreak of disorder has taken place. Actions to ameliorate Negro grievances have been limited and sporadic; with but few exceptions, they have not significantly reduced tensions.
- In several cities, the principal official response has been to train and equip the police with more sophisticated weapons. In several cities, increasing polarization is evident, with continuing breakdown of inter-racial communication, and growth of white segregationist or black separatist groups.

Chapter 3—Organized Activity

The President directed the Commission to investigate "to what extent, if any, there has been planning or organization in any of the riots."

To carry out this part of the President's charge, the Commission established a special investigative staff supplementing the field teams that made the general examination of the riots in 23 cities. The unit examined data collected by federal agencies and congressional committees, including thousands of documents supplied by the Federal Bureau of Investigation, gathered and evaluated information from local and state law enforcement agencies and officials, and conducted its own field investigation in selected cities.

On the basis of all the information collected, the Commission concludes that:

The urban disorders of the summer of 1967 were not caused by, nor were they the consequence of, any organized plan or "conspiracy."

Specifically, the Commission has found no evidence that all or any of the disorders or the incidents that led to them were planned or directed by any organization or group, international, national or local.

Militant organizations, local and national, and individual agitators, who repeatedly forecast and called for violence, were active in the spring and summer of 1967. We believe that they sought to encourage violence, and that they helped to create an atmosphere that contributed to the outbreak of disorder.

We recognize that the continuation of disorders and the polarization of the races would provide fertile ground for organized exploitation in the future.

Investigations of organized activity are continuing at all levels of government, including committees of Congress. These investigations relate not only to the disorders of 1967 but also to the actions of groups and individuals, particularly in schools and colleges, during this last fall and winter. The Commission has cooperated in these investigations. They should continue.

PART II—WHY DID IT HAPPEN?

Chapter 4—The Basic Causes

In addressing the question "Why did it happen?" we shift our focus from the local to the national scene, from the particular events of the summer of 1967 to the factors within the society at large that created a mood of violence among many urban Negroes.

These factors are complex and interacting; they vary significantly in their effect from city to city and from year to year; and the consequences of one disorder, generating new grievances and new demands, become the causes of the next. Thus was created the "thicket of tension, conflicting evidence and extreme opinions" cited by the President.

Despite these complexities, certain fundamental matters are clear. Of these, the most fundamental is the racial attitude and behavior of white Americans toward black Americans.

Race prejudice has shaped our history decisively; it now threatens to affect our future.

White racism is essentially responsible for the explosive mixture which has been accumulating in our cities since the end of World War II. Among the ingredients of this mixture are:

- Pervasive discrimination and segregation in employment, education and housing, which have resulted in the continuing exclusion of great numbers of Negroes from the benefits of economic progress.
- Black in-migration and white exodus, which have produced the massive and growing concentrations of impoverished Negroes in our major cities, creating a growing crisis of deteriorating facilities and services and unmet human needs.

- The black ghettos where segregation and poverty converge on the young to destroy opportunity and enforce failure. Crime, drug addiction, dependency on welfare, and bitterness and resentment against society in general and white society in particular are the result.

At the same time, most whites and some Negroes outside the ghetto have prospered to a degree unparalleled in the history of civilization. Through television and other media, this affluence has been flaunted before the eyes of the Negro poor and the jobless ghetto youth.

Yet these facts alone cannot be said to have caused the disorders. Recently, other powerful ingredients have begun to catalyze the mixture:

- Frustrated hopes are the residue of the unfulfilled expectations aroused by the great judicial and legislative victories of the Civil Rights Movement and the dramatic struggle for equal rights in the South.

- A climate that tends toward approval and encouragement of violence as a form of protest has been created by white terrorism directed against nonviolent protest; by the open defiance of law and federal authority by state and local officials resisting desegregation; and by some protest groups engaging in civil disobedience who turn their backs on nonviolence, go beyond the constitutionally protected rights of petition and free assembly, and resort to violence to attempt to compel alteration of laws and policies with which they disagree.

- The frustrations of powerlessness have led some Negroes to the conviction that there is no effective alternative to violence as a means of achieving redress of grievances, and of "moving the system." These frustrations are reflected in alienation and hostility toward the institutions of law and government and the white society which controls them, and in the reach toward racial consciousness and solidarity reflected in the slogan "Black Power."

- A new mood has sprung up among Negroes, particularly among the young, in which self-esteem and enhanced racial pride are replacing apathy and submission to "the system."

- The police are not merely a "spark" factor. To some Negroes police have come to symbolize white power, white racism and white repression. And the fact is that many police do reflect and express these white attitudes. The atmosphere of hostility and cynicism is

reinforced by a widespread belief among Negroes in the existence
of police brutality and in a "double standard" of justice and protection—one for Negroes and one for whites.

To this point, we have attempted to identify the prime components
of the "explosive mixture." In the chapters that follow we seek to analyze
them in the perspective of history. Their meaning, however, is clear:

In the summer of 1967, we have seen in our cities a chain reaction
of racial violence. If we are heedless, none of us shall escape the consequences.

Chapter 5—Rejection and Protest: An Historical Sketch

The causes of recent racial disorders are embedded in a tangle of issues
and circumstances—social, economic, political and psychological which
arise out of the historic pattern of Negro-white relations in America.

In this chapter we trace the pattern, identify the recurrent themes
of Negro protest and, most importantly, provide a perspective on the
protest activities of the present era.

We describe the Negro's experience in America and the development
of slavery as an institution. We show his persistent striving for equality
in the face of rigidly maintained social, economic and educational barriers, and repeated mob violence. We portray the ebb and flow of the
doctrinal tides—accommodation, separatism, and self-help—and their
relationship to the current theme of Black Power. We conclude:

> The Black Power advocates of today consciously feel that they
> are the most militant group in the Negro protest movement. Yet
> they have retreated from a direct confrontation with American
> society on the issue of integration and, by preaching separatism,
> unconsciously function as an accommodation to white racism.
> Much of their economic program, as well as their interest in Negro
> history, self-help, racial solidarity and separation, is reminiscent of
> Booker T. Washington. The rhetoric is different, but the ideas are
> remarkably similar.

Chapter 6—The Formation of the Racial Ghettos[2]

Throughout the 20th century the Negro population of the United States has been moving steadily from rural areas to urban and from South to North and West. In 1910, 91 percent of the nation's 9.8 million Negroes lived in the South and only 27 percent of American Negroes lived in cities of 2,500 persons or more. Between 1910 and 1966 the total Negro population more than doubled, reaching 21.5 million, and the number living in metropolitan areas rose more than fivefold (from 2.6 million to 14.8 million). The number outside the South rose eleven-fold (from 880,000 to 9.7 million).

Negro migration from the South has resulted from the expectation of thousands of new and highly paid jobs for unskilled workers in the North and the shift to mechanized farming in the South. However, the Negro migration is small when compared to earlier waves of European immigrants. Even between 1960 and 1966, there were 1.8 million immigrants from abroad compared to the 613,000 Negroes who arrived in the North and West from the South.

As a result of the growing number of Negroes in urban areas, natural increase has replaced migration as the primary source of Negro population increase in the cities. Nevertheless, Negro migration from the South will continue unless economic conditions there change dramatically.

Basic data concerning Negro urbanization trends indicate that:

- Almost all Negro population growth (98 percent from 1950 to 1966) is occurring within metropolitan areas, primarily within central cities.[3]
- The vast majority of white population growth (78 percent from 1960 to 1966) is occurring in suburban portions of metropolitan areas. Since 1960, white central-city population has declined by 1.3 million.
- As a result, central cities are becoming more heavily Negro while the suburban fringes around them remain almost entirely white.

---

[2] The term "ghetto" as used in this report refers to an area within a city characterized by poverty and acute social disorganization, and inhabited by members of a racial or ethnic group under conditions of involuntary segregation.

[3] A "central city" is the largest city of a standard metropolitan statistical area, that is, a metropolitan area containing at least one city of 50,000 or more inhabitants.

- The twelve largest central cities now contain over two-thirds of the Negro population outside the South, and one-third of the Negro total in the United States.

Within the cities, Negroes have been excluded from white residential areas through discriminatory practices. Just as significant is the withdrawal of white families from, or their refusal to enter, neighborhoods where Negroes are moving or already residing. About 20 percent of the urban population of the United States changes residence every year. The refusal of whites to move into "changing" areas when vacancies occur means that most vacancies eventually are occupied by Negroes.

The result, according to a recent study, is that in 1960 the average segregation index for 207 of the largest United States cities was 86.2. In other words, to create an unsegregated population distribution, an average of over 86 percent of all Negroes would have to change their place of residence within the city.

Chapter 7—Unemployment, Family Structure, and Social Disorganization

Although there have been gains in Negro income nationally, and a decline in the number of Negroes below the "poverty level," the condition of Negroes in the central city remains in a state of crisis. Between 2 and 2.5 million Negroes—16 to 20 percent of the total Negro population of all central cities—live in squalor and deprivation in ghetto neighborhoods.

Employment is a key problem. It not only controls the present for the Negro American but, in a most profound way, it is creating the future as well. Yet, despite continuing economic growth and declining national unemployment rates, the unemployment rate for Negroes in 1967 was more than double that for whites.

Equally important is the undesirable nature of many jobs open to Negroes and other minorities. Negro men are more than three times as likely as white men to be in low paying, unskilled or service jobs. This concentration of male Negro employment at the lowest end of the occupational scale is the single most important cause of poverty among Negroes.

In one study of low-income neighborhoods, the "subemployment rate," including both unemployment and underemployment, was about

33 percent, or 8.8 times greater than the overall unemployment rate for all United States workers.

Employment problems, aggravated by the constant arrival of new unemployed migrants, many of them from depressed rural areas, create persistent poverty in the ghetto. In 1966, about 11.9 percent of the nation's whites and 40.6 percent of its nonwhites were below the "poverty level" defined by the Social Security Administration (currently $3,335 per year for an urban family of four). Over 40 percent of the nonwhites below the poverty level live in the central cities.

Employment problems have drastic social impact in the ghetto. Men who are chronically unemployed or employed in the lowest status jobs are often unable or unwilling to remain with their families. The handicap imposed on children growing up without fathers in an atmosphere of poverty and deprivation is increased as mothers are forced to work to provide support.

The culture of poverty that results from unemployment and family breakup generates a system of ruthless, exploitative relationships within the ghetto. Prostitution, dope addiction, and crime create an environmental "jungle" characterized by personal insecurity and tension. Children growing up under such conditions are likely participants in civil disorder.

Chapter 8—Conditions of Life in the Racial Ghetto

A striking difference in environment from that of white, middle-class Americans profoundly influences the lives of residents of the ghetto.

Crime rates, consistently higher than in other areas, create a pronounced sense of insecurity. For example, in one city one low-income Negro district had 35 times as many serious crimes against persons as a high-income white district. Unless drastic steps are taken, the crime problems in poverty areas are likely to continue to multiply as the growing youth and rapid urbanization of the population outstrip police resources.

Poor health and sanitation conditions in the ghetto result in higher mortality rates, a higher incidence of major diseases, and lower availability and utilization of medical services. The infant mortality rate for nonwhite babies under the age of one month is 58 percent higher than for whites; for one to 12 months it is almost three times as high. The level of sanitation in the ghetto is far below that in high income areas. Garbage collection is often inadequate. Of an estimated 14,000 cases of rat bite in the United States in 1965, most were in ghetto neighborhoods.

Ghetto residents believe they are "exploited" by local merchants, and evidence substantiates some of these beliefs. A study conducted in one city by the Federal Trade Commission showed that distinctly higher prices were charged for goods sold in ghetto stores than in other areas.

Lack of knowledge regarding credit purchasing creates special pitfalls for the disadvantaged. In many states garnishment practices compound these difficulties by allowing creditors to deprive individuals of their wages without hearing or trial.

Chapter 9—Comparing the Immigrant and Negro Experience

In this chapter, we address ourselves to a fundamental question that many white Americans are asking: why have so many Negroes, unlike the European immigrants, been unable to escape from the ghetto and from poverty? We believe the following factors play a part:

- The Maturing Economy: When the European immigrants arrived, they gained an economic foothold by providing the unskilled labor needed by industry. Unlike the immigrant, the Negro migrant found little opportunity in the city. The economy, by then matured, had little use for the unskilled labor he had to offer.

- The Disability of Race: The structure of discrimination has stringently narrowed opportunities for the Negro and restricted his prospects. European immigrants suffered from discrimination, but never so pervasively.

- Entry into the Political System: The immigrants usually settled in rapidly growing cities with powerful and expanding political machines, which traded economic advantages for political support. Ward-level grievance machinery, as well as personal representation, enabled the immigrant to make his voice heard and his power felt. By the time the Negro arrived, these political machines were no longer so powerful or so well equipped to provide jobs or other favors, and in many cases were unwilling to share their influence with Negroes.

- Cultural Factors: Coming from societies with a low standard of living and at a time when job aspirations were low, the immigrants sensed little deprivation in being forced to take the less desirable and poorer-paying jobs. Their large and cohesive families contributed to total income. Their vision of the future—one that led to a life outside of the ghetto—provided the incentive necessary to endure the present.

Although Negro men worked as hard as the immigrants, they were unable to support their families. The entrepreneurial opportunities had vanished. As a result of slavery and long periods of unemployment, the Negro family structure had become matriarchal; the males played a secondary and marginal family role—one which offered little compensation for their hard and unrewarding labor. Above all, segregation denied Negroes access to good jobs and the opportunity to leave the ghetto. For them, the future seemed to lead only to a dead end.

Today, whites tend to exaggerate how well and quickly they escaped from poverty. The fact is that immigrants who came from rural backgrounds, as many Negroes do, are only now, after three generations, finally beginning to move into the middle class.

By contrast, Negroes began concentrating in the city less than two generations ago, and under much less favorable conditions. Although some Negroes have escaped poverty, few have been able to escape the urban ghetto.

PART III—WHAT CAN BE DONE?

Chapter 10—The Community Response

Our investigation of the 1967 riot cities establishes that virtually every major episode of violence was foreshadowed by an accumulation of unresolved grievances and by widespread dissatisfaction among Negroes with the unwillingness or inability of local government to respond.

Overcoming these conditions is essential for community support of law enforcement and civil order. City governments need new and more vital channels of communication to the residents of the ghetto; they need to improve their capacity to respond effectively to community needs before they become community grievances; and they need to provide opportunity for meaningful involvement of ghetto residents in shaping policies and programs which affect the community.

The Commission recommends that local governments:

- Develop Neighborhood Action Task Forces as joint community government efforts through which more effective communication can be achieved, and the delivery of city services to ghetto residents improved.
- Establish comprehensive grievance-response mechanisms in order to bring all public agencies under public scrutiny.
- Bring the institutions of local government closer to the people they serve by establishing neighborhood outlets for local, state and federal administrative and public service agencies.
- Expand opportunities for ghetto residents to participate in the formulation of public policy and the implementation of programs affecting them through improved political representation, creation of institutional channels for community action, expansion of legal services, and legislative hearings on ghetto problems.

In this effort, city governments will require state and federal support. The Commission recommends:

- State and federal financial assistance for mayors and city councils to support the research, consultants, staff and other resources needed to respond effectively to federal program initiatives.
- State cooperation in providing municipalities with the jurisdictional tools needed to deal with their problems; a fuller measure of financial aid to urban areas; and the focusing of the interests of suburban communities on the physical, social and cultural environment of the central city.

Chapter 11—Police and the Community

The abrasive relationship between the police and the minority communities has been a major—and explosive—source of grievance, tension and disorder. The blame must be shared by the total society.

The police are faced with demands for increased protection and service in the ghetto. Yet the aggressive patrol practices thought necessary to meet these demands themselves create tension and hostility. The resulting grievances have been further aggravated by the lack of effective mechanisms for handling complaints against the police. Special programs for bettering police-community relations have been instituted, but these alone are not enough. Police administrators, with the guidance of public officials, and the support of the entire community, must take vigorous action to improve law enforcement and to decrease the potential for disorder.

The Commission recommends that city government and police authorities:

- Review police operations in the ghetto to ensure proper conduct by police officers, and eliminate abrasive practices.
- Provide more adequate police protection to ghetto residents to eliminate their high sense of insecurity, and the belief of many Negro citizens in the existence of a dual standard of law enforcement.
- Establish fair and effective mechanisms for the redress of grievances against the police, and other municipal employees.
- Develop and adopt policy guidelines to assist officers in making critical decisions in areas where police conduct can create tension.
- Develop and use innovative programs to ensure widespread community support for law enforcement.
- Recruit more Negroes into the regular police force, and review promotion policies to ensure fair promotion for Negro officers.
- Establish a "Community Service Officer" program to attract ghetto youths between the ages of 17 and 21 to police work. These junior officers would perform duties in ghetto neighborhoods, but would not have full police authority. The federal government should provide support equal to 90 percent of the costs of employing CSOs on the basis of one for every ten regular officers.

Chapter 12—Control of Disorder

Preserving civil peace is the first responsibility of government. Unless the rule of law prevails, our society will lack not only order but also the environment essential to social and economic progress.

The maintenance of civil order cannot be left to the police alone. The police need guidance, as well as support, from mayors and other public officials. It is the responsibility of public officials to determine proper police policies, support adequate police standards for personnel and performance, and participate in planning for the control of disorders.

To maintain control of incidents which could lead to disorders, the Commission recommends that local officials:

- Assign seasoned, well-trained policemen and supervisory officers to patrol ghetto areas, and to respond to disturbances.
- Develop plans which will quickly muster maximum police manpower and highly qualified senior commanders at the outbreak of disorders.
- Provide special training in the prevention of disorders, and prepare police for riot control and for operation in units, with adequate command and control and field communication for proper discipline and effectiveness.
- Develop guidelines governing the use of control equipment and provide alternatives to the use of lethal weapons. Federal support for research in this area is needed.
- Establish an intelligence system to provide police and other public officials with reliable information that may help to prevent the outbreak of a disorder and to institute effective control measures in the event a riot erupts.
- Develop continuing contacts with ghetto residents to make use of the forces for order which exist within the community.
- Establish machinery for neutralizing rumors, and enabling Negro leaders and residents to obtain the facts. Create special rumor details to collect, evaluate, and dispel rumors that may lead to a civil disorder.

The Commission believes there is a grave danger that some communities may resort to the indiscriminate and excessive use of force. The harmful effects of overreaction are incalculable. The Commission condemns moves to equip police departments with mass destruction weapons, such as automatic rifles, machine guns and tanks. Weapons which are designed to destroy, not to control, have no place in densely populated urban communities.

The Commission recognizes the sound principle of local authority and responsibility in law enforcement, but recommends that the federal government share, in the financing of programs for improvement of police forces, both in their normal law enforcement activities as well as in their response to civil disorders.

To assist government authorities in planning their response to civil disorder, this report contains a Supplement on Control of Disorder. It deals with specific problems encountered during riot-control operations, and includes:

- Assessment of the present capabilities of police, National Guard and Army forces to control major riots, and recommendations for improvement;
- Recommended means by which the control operations of those forces may be coordinated with the response of other agencies, such as fire departments, and with the community at large;
- Recommendations for review and revision of federal, state and local laws needed to provide the framework for control efforts and for the call-up and interrelated action of public safety forces.

Chapter 13—*The Administration of Justice Under Emergency Conditions*

In many of the cities which experienced disorders last summer, there were recurring breakdowns in the mechanisms for processing, prosecuting and protecting arrested persons. These resulted mainly from long-standing structural deficiencies in criminal court systems, and from the failure of communities to anticipate and plan for the emergency demands of civil disorders.

In part, because of this, there were few successful prosecutions for serious crimes committed during the riots. In those cities where mass arrests occurred many arrestees were deprived of basic legal rights.

The Commission recommends that the cities and states:

- Undertake reform of the lower courts so as to improve the quality of justice rendered under normal conditions.
- Plan comprehensive measures by which the criminal justice system may be supplemented during civil disorders so that its deliberative functions are protected, and the quality of justice is maintained.

Such emergency plans require broad community participation and dedicated leadership by the bench and bar. They should include:

- Laws sufficient to deter and punish riot conduct.
- Additional judges, bail and probation officers, and clerical staff.

- Arrangements for volunteer lawyers to help prosecutors and to represent riot defendants at every stage of proceedings.
- Policies to ensure proper and individual bail, arraignment, pre-trial, trial and sentencing proceedings.
- Procedures for processing arrested persons, such as summons and release, and release on personal recognizance, which permit separation of minor offenders from those dangerous to the community, in order that serious offenders may be detained and prosecuted effectively.
- Adequate emergency processing and detention facilities.

Chapter 14—Damages: Repair and Compensation

The Commission recommends that the federal government:
- Amend the Federal Disaster Act—which now applies only to natural disasters—to permit federal emergency food and medical assistance to cities during major civil disorders, and provide long-term economic assistance afterwards.
- With the cooperation of the states, create incentives for the private insurance industry to provide more adequate property-insurance coverage in inner-city areas.

The Commission endorses the report of the National Advisory Panel on Insurance in Riot-Affected Areas: "Meeting the Insurance Crisis of Our Cities."

Chapter 15—The News Media and the Disorders

In his charge to the Commission, the President asked: "What effect do the mass media have on the riots?"

The Commission determined that the answer to the President's question did not lie solely in the performance of the press and broadcasters in reporting the riots. Our analysis had to consider also the overall treatment by the media of the Negro ghettos, community relations, racial attitudes, and poverty—day by day and month by month, year in and year out. A wide range of interviews with government officials, law enforcement authorities, media personnel and other citizens, including ghetto residents, as well as a quantitative analysis of riot coverage and a special conference with industry representatives, leads us to conclude that:

- Despite instances of sensationalism, inaccuracy and distortion, newspapers, radio and television tried on the whole to give a balanced, factual account of the 1967 disorders.
- Elements of the news media failed to portray accurately the scale and character of the violence that occurred last summer. The overall effect was, we believe, an exaggeration of both mood and event.
- Important segments of the media failed to report adequately on the causes and consequences of civil disorders and on the underlying problems of race relations. They have not communicated to the majority of their audience—which is white—a sense of the degradation, misery and hopelessness of life in the ghetto.

These failings must be corrected, and the improvement must come from within the industry. Freedom of the press is not the issue. Any effort to impose governmental restrictions would be inconsistent with fundamental constitutional precepts.

We have seen evidence that the news media are becoming aware of and concerned about their performance in this field. As that concern grows, coverage will improve. But much more must be done, and it must be done soon.

The Commission recommends that the media:

- Expand coverage of the Negro community and of race problems through permanent assignment of reporters familiar with urban and racial affairs, and through establishment of more and better links with the Negro community.
- Integrate Negroes and Negro activities into all aspects of coverage and content, including newspaper articles and television programming. The news media must publish newspapers and produce programs that recognize the existence and activities of Negroes as a group within the community and as a part of the larger community.
- Recruit more Negroes into journalism and broadcasting and promote those who are qualified to positions of significant responsibility. Recruitment should begin in high schools and continue through college; where necessary, aid for training should be provided.
- Improve coordination with police in reporting riot news through advance planning, and cooperate with the police in the designation of police information officers, establishment of information

centers, and development of mutually acceptable guidelines for riot reporting and the conduct of media personnel.

- Accelerate efforts to ensure accurate and responsible reporting of riot and racial news, through adoption by all news gathering organizations of stringent internal staff guidelines.
- Cooperate in the establishment of a privately organized and funded Institute of Urban Communications to train and educate journalists in urban affairs, recruit and train more Negro journalists, develop methods for improving police-press relations, review coverage of riots and racial issues, and support continuing research in the urban field.

Chapter 16—The Future of the Cities

By 1985, the Negro population in central cities is expected to increase by 72 percent to approximately 20.8 million. Coupled with the continued exodus of white families to the suburbs, this growth will produce majority Negro populations in many of the nation's largest cities.

The future of these cities, and of their burgeoning Negro populations, is grim. Most new employment opportunities are being created in suburbs and outlying areas. This trend will continue unless important changes in public policy are made.

In prospect, therefore, is further deterioration of already inadequate municipal tax bases in the face of increasing demands for public services, and continuing unemployment and poverty among the urban Negro population:

Three choices are open to the nation:

- We can maintain present policies, continuing both the proportion of the nation's resources now allocated to programs for the unemployed and the disadvantaged, and the inadequate and failing effort to achieve an integrated society.
- We can adopt a policy of "enrichment" aimed at improving dramatically the quality of ghetto life while abandoning integration as a goal.
- We can pursue integration by combining ghetto "enrichment" with policies which will encourage Negro movement out of central city areas.

The first choice, continuance of present policies, has ominous consequences for our society. The share of the nation's resources now allocated to programs for the disadvantaged is insufficient to arrest the deterioration of life in central city ghettos. Under such conditions, a rising proportion of Negroes may come to see in the deprivation and segregation they experience, a justification for violent protest, or for extending support to now isolated extremists who advocate civil disruption. Large-scale and continuing violence could result, followed by white retaliation, and, ultimately, the separation of the two communities in a garrison state.

Even if violence does not occur, the consequences are unacceptable. Development of a racially integrated society, extraordinarily difficult today, will be virtually impossible when the present black ghetto population of 12.5 million has grown to almost 21 million.

To continue present policies is to make permanent the division of our country into two societies; one, largely Negro and poor, located in the central cities; the other, predominantly white and affluent, located in the suburbs and in outlying areas.

The second choice, ghetto enrichment coupled with abandonment of integration, is also unacceptable. It is another way of choosing a permanently divided country. Moreover, equality cannot be achieved under conditions of nearly complete separation. In a country where the economy, and particularly the resources of employment, are predominantly white, a policy of separation can only relegate Negroes to a permanently inferior economic status.

We believe that the only possible choice for America is the third-a policy which combines ghetto enrichment with programs designed to encourage integration of substantial numbers of Negroes into the society outside the ghetto.

Enrichment must be an important adjunct to integration, for no matter how ambitious or energetic the program, few Negroes now living in central cities can be quickly integrated.

In the meantime, large-scale improvement in the quality of ghetto life is essential.

But this can be no more than an interim strategy. Programs must be developed which will permit substantial Negro movement out of the ghettos. The primary goal must be a single society, in which every citizen will be free to live and work according to his capabilities and desires, not his color.

Chapter 17—Recommendations for National Action

INTRODUCTION

No American—white or black—can escape the consequences of the continuing social and economic decay of our major cities.

Only a commitment to national action on an unprecedented scale can shape a future compatible with the historic ideals of American society.

The great productivity of our economy, and a federal revenue system which is highly responsive to economic growth, can provide the resources.

The major need is to generate new will—the will to tax ourselves to the extent necessary, to meet the vital needs of the nation.

We have set forth goals and proposed strategies to reach those goals. We discuss and recommend programs not to commit each of us to specific parts of such programs but to illustrate the type and dimension of action needed.

The major goal is the creation of a true union—a single society and a single American identity. Toward that goal, we propose the following objectives for national action:

- Opening up opportunities to those who are restricted by racial segregation and discrimination, and eliminating all barriers to their choice of jobs, education and housing.
- Removing the frustration of powerlessness among the disadvantaged by providing the means for them to deal with the problems that affect their own lives and by increasing the capacity of our public and private institutions to respond to these problems.
- Increasing communication across racial lines to destroy stereotypes, to halt polarization, end distrust and hostility, and create common ground for efforts toward public order and social justice.

We propose these aims to fulfill our pledge of equality and to meet the fundamental needs of a democratic and civilized society—domestic peace and social justice.

EMPLOYMENT

Pervasive unemployment and underemployment are the most persistent and serious grievances in minority areas. They are inextricably linked to the problem of civil disorder.

Despite growing federal expenditures for manpower development and training programs, and sustained general economic prosperity and increasing demands for skilled workers, about two million—white and nonwhite—are permanently unemployed. About ten million are underemployed, of whom 6.5 million work full time for wages below the poverty line.

The 500,000 "hard-core" unemployed in the central cities who lack a basic education and are unable to hold a steady job are made up in large part of Negro males between the ages of 18 and 25. In the riot cities which we surveyed, Negroes were three times as likely as whites to hold unskilled jobs, which are often part time, seasonal, low-paying and "dead end."

Negro males between the ages of 15 and 25 predominated among the rioters. More than 20 percent of the rioters were unemployed, and many who were employed held intermittent, low status, unskilled jobs which they regarded as below their education and ability.

The Commission recommends that the federal government:

- Undertake joint efforts with cities and states to consolidate existing manpower programs to avoid fragmentation and duplication.
- Take immediate action to create 2,000,000 new jobs over the next three years—one million in the public sector and one million in the private sector—to absorb the hard-core unemployed and materially reduce the level of underemployment for all workers, black and white. We propose 250,000 public sector and 300,000 private sector jobs in the first year.
- Provide on-the-job training by both public and private employers with reimbursement to private employers for the extra costs of training the hard-core unemployed, by contract or by tax credits.
- Provide tax and other incentives to investment in rural as well as urban poverty areas in order to offer to the rural poor an alternative to migration to urban centers.
- Take new and vigorous action to remove artificial barriers to employment and promotion, including not only racial discrimination

but, in certain cases, arrest records or lack of a high school diploma. Strengthen those agencies such as the Equal Employment Opportunity Commission, charged with eliminating discriminatory practices, and provide full support for Title VI of the 1964 Civil Rights Act allowing federal grant-in-aid funds to be withheld from activities which discriminate on grounds of color or race.

The Commission commends the recent public commitment of the National Council of the Building and Construction Trades Unions, AFL-CIO, to encourage and recruit Negro membership in apprenticeship programs. This commitment should be intensified and implemented.

EDUCATION

Education in a democratic society must equip children to develop their potential and to participate fully in American life. For the community at large, the schools have discharged this responsibility well. But for many minorities, and particularly for the children of the ghetto, the schools have failed to provide the educational experience which could overcome the effects of discrimination and deprivation.

This failure is one of the persistent sources of grievance and resentment within the Negro community. The hostility of Negro parents and students toward the school system is generating increasing conflict and causing disruption within many city school districts. But the most dramatic evidence of the relationship between educational practices and civil disorders lies in the high incidence of riot participation by ghetto youth who have not completed high school.

The bleak record of public education for ghetto children is growing worse. In the critical skills—verbal and reading ability—Negro students are falling further behind whites with each year of school completed. The high unemployment and underemployment rate for Negro youth is evidence, in part, of the growing educational crisis.

We support integration as the priority education strategy; it is essential to the future of American society. In this last summer's disorders we have seen the consequences of racial isolation at all levels, and of attitudes toward race, on both sides, produced by three centuries of myth, ignorance and bias. It is indispensable that opportunities for interaction between the races be expanded.

We recognize that the growing dominance of pupils from disadvantaged minorities in city school populations will not soon be reversed. No matter how great the effort toward desegregation, many children of the ghetto will not, within their school careers, attend integrated schools.

If existing disadvantages are not to be perpetuated, we must drastically improve the quality of ghetto education. Equality of results with all-white schools must be the goal.

To implement these strategies, the Commission recommends:

- Sharply increased efforts to eliminate de facto segregation in our schools through substantial federal aid to school systems seeking to desegregate either within the system or in cooperation with neighboring school systems.
- Elimination of racial discrimination in Northern as well as Southern schools by vigorous application of Title VI of the Civil Rights Act of 1964.
- Extension of quality early childhood education to every disadvantaged child in the country.
- Efforts to improve dramatically schools serving disadvantaged children through substantial federal funding of year-round compensatory education programs, improved teaching, and expanded experimentation and research.
- Elimination of illiteracy through greater federal support for adult basic education.
- Enlarged opportunities for parent and community participation in the public schools.
- Reoriented vocational education emphasizing work-experience training and the involvement of business and industry.
- Expanded opportunities for higher education through increased federal assistance to disadvantaged students.
- Revision of state aid formulas to assure more per student aid to districts having a high proportion of disadvantaged school-age children.

THE WELFARE SYSTEM

Our present system of public welfare is designed to save money instead of people, and, tragically, ends up doing neither. This system has two critical deficiencies:

First, it excludes large numbers of persons who are in great need, and who, if provided a decent level of support, might be able to become more productive and self-sufficient. No federal funds are available for millions of men and women who are needy but neither aged, handicapped nor the parents of minor children.

Second, for those included, the system provides assistance well below the minimum necessary for a decent level of existence, and imposes restrictions that encourage continued dependency on welfare and undermine self-respect.

A welter of statutory requirements and administrative practices and regulations operate to remind recipients that they are considered untrustworthy, promiscuous and lazy. Residence requirements prevent assistance to people in need who are newly arrived in the state. Regular searches of recipients' homes violate privacy. Inadequate social services compound the problems.

The Commission recommends that the federal government, acting with state and local governments where necessary, reform the existing welfare system to:

- Establish uniform national standards of assistance at least as high as the annual "poverty level" of income, now set by the Social Security Administration at $3,335 per year for an urban family of four.
- Require that all states receiving federal welfare contributions participate in the Aid to Families with Dependent Children Unemployed Parents program (AFDC-UP) that permits assistance to families with both father and mother in the home, thus aiding the family while it is still intact.
- Bear a substantially greater portion of all welfare costs—at least 90 percent of total payments.
- Increase incentives for seeking employment and job training, but remove restrictions recently enacted by the Congress that would compel mothers of young children to work.
- Provide more adequate social services through neighborhood centers and family-planning programs.
- Remove the freeze placed by the 1967 welfare amendments on the percentage of children in a state that can be covered by federal assistance.
- Eliminate residence requirements.

As a long-range goal, the Commission recommends that the federal government seek to develop a national system of income supplementation based strictly on need with two broad and basic purposes:

- To provide, for those who can work or who do work, any necessary supplements in such a way as to develop incentives for fuller employment;
- To provide, for those who cannot work and for mothers who decide to remain with their children, a minimum standard of decent living, and to aid in the saving of children from the prison of poverty that has held their parents.

A broad system of implementation would involve substantially greater federal expenditures than anything now contemplated. The cost will range widely depending on the standard of need accepted as the "basic allowance" to individuals and families, and on the rate at which additional income above this level is taxed. Yet if the deepening cycle of poverty and dependence on welfare can be broken, if the children of the poor can be given the opportunity to scale the wall that now separates them from the rest of society, the return on this investment will be great indeed.

HOUSING

After more than three decades of fragmented and grossly underfunded federal housing programs, nearly six million substandard housing units remain occupied in the United States.

The housing problem is particularly acute in the minority ghettos. Nearly two-thirds of all non-white families living in the central cities today live in neighborhoods marked with substandard housing and general urban blight. Two major factors are responsible.

First: Many ghetto residents simply cannot pay the rent necessary to support decent housing. In Detroit, for example, over 40 percent of the non-white occupied units in 1960 required rent of over 35 percent of the tenants' income.

Second: Discrimination prevents access to many non-slum areas, particularly the suburbs, where good housing exists. In addition, by creating a "back pressure" in the racial ghettos, it makes it possible for landlords to break up apartments for denser occupancy, and keeps prices and rents of deteriorated ghetto housing higher than they would be in a truly free market.

To date, federal programs have been able to do comparatively little to provide housing for the disadvantaged. In the 31-year history of subsidized federal housing, only about 800,000 units have been constructed, with recent production averaging about 50,000 units a year. By comparison, over a period only three years longer, FHA insurance guarantees have made possible the construction of over ten million middle- and upper-income units.

Two points are fundamental to the Commission's recommendations:

First: Federal housing programs must be given a new thrust aimed at overcoming the prevailing patterns of racial segregation. If this is not done, those programs will continue to concentrate the most impoverished and dependent segments of the population into the central-city ghettos where there is already a critical gap between the needs of the population and the public resources to deal with them.

Second: The private sector must be brought into the production and financing of low and moderate rental housing to supply the capabilities and capital necessary to meet the housing needs of the nation.

The Commission recommends that the federal government:
- Enact a comprehensive and enforceable federal open housing law to cover the sale or rental of all housing, including single family homes.
- Reorient federal housing programs to place more low and moderate income housing outside of ghetto areas.
- Bring within the reach of low and moderate income families within the next five years six million new and existing units of decent housing, beginning with 600,000 units in the next year.

To reach this goal we recommend:
- Expansion and modification of the rent supplement program to permit use of supplements for existing housing, thus greatly increasing the reach of the program.
- Expansion and modification of the below-market interest rate program to enlarge the interest subsidy to all sponsors and provide interest-free loans to nonprofit sponsors to cover pre-construction costs, and permit sale of projects to nonprofit corporations, cooperatives, or condominiums.

- Creation of an ownership supplement program similar to present rent supplements, to make home ownership possible for low-income families.
- Federal writedown of interest rates on loans to private builders constructing moderate-rent housing.
- Expansion of the public housing program, with emphasis on small units on scattered sites, and leasing and "turnkey" programs.
- Expansion of the Model Cities program.
- Expansion and reorientation of the urban renewal program to give priority to projects directly assisting low-income households to obtain adequate housing.

CONCLUSION

One of the first witnesses to be invited to appear before this Commission was Dr. Kenneth B. Clark, a distinguished and perceptive scholar. Referring to the reports of earlier riot commissions, he said:

> I read that report . . . of the 1919 riot in Chicago, and it is as if I were reading the report of the investigating committee on the Harlem riot of '35, the report of the investigating committee on the Harlem riot of '43, the report of the McCone Commission on the Watts riot.
>
> I must again in candor say to you members of this Commission—it is a kind of Alice in Wonderland—with the same moving picture re-shown over and over again, the same analysis, the same recommendations, and the same inaction.

These words come to our minds as we conclude this report.

We have provided an honest beginning. We have learned much. But we have uncovered no startling truths, no unique insights, no simple solutions. The destruction and the bitterness of racial disorder, the harsh polemics of black revolt and white repression have been seen and heard before in this country.

It is time now to end the destruction and the violence, not only in the streets of the ghetto but in the lives of people.

7

Whiteness as Principality

Put on the whole armor of God, so that you may be able to stand against the wiles of the devil. For our struggle is not against enemies of blood and flesh, but against the rulers, against the authorities, against the cosmic powers of this present darkness, against the spiritual forces of evil in the heavenly places.

—EPHESIANS 6:11–12

Insofar as this country is seeking to make whiteness the dominating power throughout the world, whiteness is the symbol of the Antichrist.

—JAMES CONE, *A BLACK THEOLOGY OF LIBERATION*

Whiteness, alone, is mute, meaningless, unfathomable, pointless, frozen, veiled, curtained, dreaded, senseless, implacable. Or so our writers seem to say.

—TONI MORRISON, *PLAYING IN THE DARK*

PREPARATION FOR SESSION 7

During my senior year of high school our family began attending an evangelical Methodist church in Concord, North Carolina. It was the first place that I heard the term *spiritual warfare*. The church and its leaders introduced our family to the novels of Frank E. Peretti and a burgeoning

167

field of spiritual-warfare literature that has become so large it now has its own distinct category on Amazon. Practitioners of spiritual warfare believe there is an invisible war being waged by angels, evil spirits, and demonic forces for the control of our lives and the world. These angels, evil spirits, and demonic forces are believed to be constantly intervening in human affairs in various ways, and the followers of Jesus are called to join with God in fighting a spiritual war against what Paul called "cosmic powers of this present darkness" (Eph. 6:12). However, in my childhood church it was clear that the primary goal of spiritual warfare in the minds of our leaders was to protect our sexual purity and the virtue of the family. All the so-called demons who possessed people seemed to drive them toward what evangelicals at the time believed were the worst of all evils—sexual sins and lusts of the flesh like premarital sex, adultery, homosexuality, and abortion. Racism was never mentioned. Spiritual warfare, it seemed, was nothing more than an unhealthy way for evangelical Christians to combat our deepest anxieties and fears through social control.

In the Gospels spiritual warfare can be seen as beginning with Jesus, who was tempted by the devil in the wilderness, engaged in ministry as a first-century Galilean exorcist, cast out demons, liberated people possessed by unclean spirits, and regularly commissioned his followers to do the same. Consequently, throughout history many Christians have practiced some form of spiritual warfare. The desert mothers and fathers often described demonic encounters as a normal and commonly occurring part of the monastic life. In the Middle Ages demonology became an important and respected field of Christian theology. Most early Christian demonologists believed that the mission of demons was to induce human beings to sin and embrace evil. It was also commonly held that demons could torment people through possession, terrorizing them, and provoking fantastic visions.

The desert mothers and fathers believed that the Roman Empire was a demonic principality and fled out into the desert to escape, thus giving birth to the monastic tradition. However, by 381 CE Christianity had become the official religion of the Roman Empire, which led demonology to become a more individualized discipline, and spiritual warfare took an ugly turn. As with the problem of evil, people are rarely able to see themselves as beset by demonic forces or to view their own institutions or society as filled with principalities. Instead, people in power often use the language of spiritual warfare to scapegoat outsiders and enemies. It is not surprising that the biblical demand to confront evil quickly became deranged when Christians gained some level of power. As the church merged with the empire, Christians started imagining themselves as tasked by God to build a Christian world and set out to be liberators and protectors of purity and virtue. Yet we became the dominators and oppressors of many other peoples, which is the definition of a principality.

Frightening social and political consequences of demonology creep into the practice of spiritual warfare when the church is operating with political or imperial power. For instance, from the first century to the present, the development of Christian demonology has intertwined with the development of anti-Semitism. Theologians and early church leaders believed the primary historical figures who were possessed by demons were the Jewish people. Therefore, in much of Europe during the Middle Ages, Jews were denied citizenship and civil rights, barred from holding positions in the government or military, and excluded from membership in guilds and other professions. In 1096, the First Crusade unleashed a wave of anti-Semitic violence in France and what is now Germany. In addition, the superstitious accusation of "blood libel," or the horrifying belief that Jews ritually sacrifice Christian children at Passover to obtain blood for unleavened bread, first emerged in Europe in the twelfth century, leading to further Christian terror and violence against the Jewish people.

During the Protestant Reformation, Martin Luther and other prominent figures in the movement wrote expansive treatises on the devil and demons. However, they also associated the Jewish people with demonic possession. Luther's obscene anti-Semitic treatise "On the Jews and Their Lies" argued that Jews were filled with the devil and that their synagogues and schools should be set on fire, their prayer books destroyed, their homes burned, their rabbis forbidden to preach, and their property and money confiscated.[1] He claimed Jewish people should be shown no mercy or kindness, afforded no legal protection, and should be drafted into forced labor or expelled from society for a time. If Luther's recommendations sound familiar, it is because they were explicitly used by German Nazi leaders as propaganda during the rise of the Third

---

[1] Martin Luther, "On the Jews and Their Lies," (1543), in *Luther's Works*, trans. Martin H. Bertram (Philadelphia: Fortress Press, 1971).

Reich and became the blueprint for the so-called Final Solution, which culminated in the Holocaust.

Throughout history spiritual warfare has been wildly anti-Semitic and has consistently devolved into social oppression and political violence against Jews and other marginalized groups. For instance, colonial America's most notorious case of mass hysteria, the Salem witch trials, was another appalling example of the way demonology has been misused by Christians as a tool for social control, group oppression, and political violence—in this case especially toward women. Indigenous peoples, Africans, Asians, Latinx, Middle Easterners, immigrants, foreigners, and people of color have been demonized throughout American history, which has often led to marginalization, oppression, and violence. Yet despite this violent history, since the 1980s a growing number of American evangelicals have taken up the practice of spiritual warfare and given this fight against demons a key role in their spirituality and their politics, viewing demons as central actors in geopolitics and everyday life.

Unfortunately, the current fascination with spiritual warfare mimics the way it has been traditionally misused in Christian history. The demons are not the ideologies and systems of power and domination in our world, but rather symbolic bogeymen for all our fears. The temptations they supposedly provoke are desires for the same sexual sins that evangelicals have already groundlessly predetermined are the highest evils (premarital sex, adultery, homosexuality, and abortion). Again, the problem is that when spiritual warfare is in the hands of those in power, it is never applied self-referentially but always ends up as a tool for oppression and social control. This is exactly the reason why most practitioners of spiritual warfare who are racialized as White could not imagine waging a spiritual war against systemic racism or Whiteness. When we are a part of the dominant culture, it is extremely difficult to see the ways we have become the principality.

Growing up in the evangelical church, I did not realize that our focus on spiritual warfare was connected to a long history of Christian violence or that it was part of a larger sociopolitical movement in America. I simply thought that my friends and fellow church members were trying to protect me from temptation. Once I discovered that their application of this historic practice was wildly misguided, I was tempted to dismiss, disregard, and demythologize every instance of demonic possession, unclean spirits, exorcism, principalities and powers, or spiritual forces of evil in the New Testament. Thankfully, I encountered the work of Walter Wink, which provides a definitive scholarly examination of the "principalities and powers" and describes them as "the powers that be" and "systems of domination" in our world. Wink contends:

> The expression "the Powers" should no longer be reserved for the special category of spiritual forces, but should rather be used generically for all manifestations of power, seen under the dual aspect of their physical or institutional concretion on the one hand, and their inner essence or spirituality on the other. Popular speech, often more accurate in unconscious matters than it is given credit for being, has quite properly referred to the whole range of phenomena as "The Powers That Be."[2]

Like demonologists and practitioners of spiritual warfare throughout church history, Wink claims that scripture describes a fundamental conflict between the forces of evil and the reign of God. However, for Wink the principalities and powers, demons, unclean spirits, and the forces of evil are synonymous with what he calls the "domination system," and he states that this overarching network of powers is "characterized by unjust economic relations, oppressive political relations, biased race relations, patriarchal gender relations, hierarchical power relations, and the use of violence to maintain them all."[3] In another essay Wink elaborates as follows: "Jesus denounced the Domination System of his day and proclaimed the advent of the reign of God, which *would transform every aspect of reality, even the social framework of existence.* . . . And it set in motion a permanent revolution against the Power System whose consequences we are still only beginning to grasp to this day."[4]

If the systems of domination in our world can be identified with the principalities and powers that Paul described in his letters, as Wink suggests, then that means the church has often been a demonic force throughout history. Instead of empowering the followers of Jesus to

---

[2] Walter Wink, *Naming the Powers: The Language of Power in the New Testament* (Philadelphia: Fortress Press, 1984), 107.

[3] Walter Wink, *The Powers That Be: Theology for a New Millennium* (New York: Doubleday, 1998), 39.

[4] Walter Wink, *Walter Wink: Collected Readings*, ed. Henry French (Minneapolis: Fortress Press, 2013), 185.

confront the spiritual forces of evil in our world, the church has regularly encouraged anti-Semitism and patriarchy, thereby aligning itself with the demonic-spirit domination systems. This reality should cause us to reassess the groups the church has traditionally demonized and ask ourselves if we are standing against the domination system or have become it. As it turns out, the problem is not the idea of spiritual warfare itself or that Jesus exorcised demons. The problem is that the church has often been unable to see the real demonic forces in the world.

The church has often been the most powerful system of domination in the Western world. The church could not see the real demonic forces in the world because the church itself was the chief principality in history. Tragically, the church often found itself on the wrong side of the war and ended up fighting against God.

I sometimes wonder what it would have been like for the ministers and members of the evangelical church I grew up in to have seen race as a demonic force or principality against which we were called to wage spiritual warfare. What if they had opposed racism as seriously as they opposed premarital sex, adultery, homosexuality, and abortion? Most of those church folks believed that racism was a sin, but they were trapped in a history they could not understand and were blind to the fact that they were living in the lie of Whiteness. We were all benefitting from Whiteness, so we never saw racism as an urgent problem, a demonic power that possessed us, or a principality waging war on our souls. The leaders in the evangelical church of my youth were not mistaken about the need for spiritual warfare; they were simply on a lesser battlefield fighting a misguided war. If only we had been able to see what we were truly up against, perhaps our efforts at spiritual warfare would have put us on a path toward becoming anti-racist followers of the one who exorcised the demons of ethnic and religious domination and oppression to embody the beloved community of God.

Whiteness is a system of domination that often operates invisibly like the powers and principalities, and it is one of the most pervasive spiritual forces of evil in our world. This week the work of two distinguished theologians, Willie James Jennings and Kelly Brown Douglas, will focus our attention on the ways that Whiteness entangled itself with Christianity in America. Jennings clearly describes Whiteness as a principality, while Douglas claims that Whiteness is a "crucifying reality." In addition, we will view Ava DuVernay's docu-drama *When They See Us,* which reenacts the story of the Central Park Five from the perspective of the victims and their families. May the words of these theologians and story of the Central Park Five enable us to see the domination system of Whiteness as a truly demonic force of evil in our world. Let's roll up our sleeves and get ready for some real spiritual warfare.

DEEP SOUL WORK

Read and View. *Engage with these essays and the film slowly and carefully, taking time to stop and make notes as you go.*
- Read "Can White People Be Saved?" by Willie James Jennings Jr.[5]
- Read "To Be a Christian Intellectual" by Willie James Jennings Jr.[6]
- Read "What Does Jesus Have to Do with Whiteness?" by Kelly Brown Douglas.[7]
- View *When They See Us* by Ava DuVernay.[8]

Meditate and Reflect. *Spend some time in silent meditation after each of the readings and viewing, and then write your answers to these questions:*
1. How did the readings and viewing make you feel?
2. What was most meaningful to you?
3. What are you discovering about Whiteness?
4. Where do you see yourself in the readings and film?

Acknowledge and Confess. *Examine your own life story considering the readings and viewing this week and acknowledge what arises.*
- What stories from your life experience relate to what you read/viewed this week? (Be sure to include them in your racial autobiography.)

---

[5] Willie James Jennings, "Can White People Be Saved?: Reflections on the Relationship of Missions and Whiteness," in *Can "White" People Be Saved: Triangulating Race, Theology, and Mission,* ed. Love L. Sechrest, Johnny Ramirez-Johnson, and Amos Young (Downers Grove, IL: IVP Academic, 2018).

[6] Willie James Jennings, "To Be a Christian Intellectual," *Yale Divinity School News,* October 30, 2015.

[7] Kelly Brown Douglas, "What Does Jesus Have to Do with Whiteness?" *Feminism and Religion,* December 20, 2013.

[8] Ava DuVernay, *When They See Us* (United States: Netflix, 2019).

- What acknowledgments of Whiteness or personal confessions do you need to make based on this week's readings and viewing?
- Read Ephesians 6:10–18 and imagine that the rulers, authorities, cosmic powers of this present darkness, and spiritual forces of evil are synonyms for Whiteness. What does the author challenge us to do?
- Considering what you read in Jennings and Douglas, meditate on this quotation from Walter Wink: "Any attempt to transform a social system without addressing both its spirituality and its outer forms is doomed to failure. Only by confronting the spirituality of an institution and its concretions can the total entity be transformed, and that requires a kind of spiritual discernment and praxis that the materialistic ethos in which we live knows nothing about."[9]

Repent, Turn, and Transform. *Imagine a new creation and a new humanity for yourself and for our world.*
- What can we do today to begin disentangling Whiteness from Christianity, our personal faith, and the church?
- What would it look like to engage in spiritual warfare against Whiteness? What rituals and practices would be required? How would our prayer and devotional life change? What sacraments would need to be adjusted? What alterations or additions are needed in our worship?
- Develop your own strategy for spiritual warfare against Whiteness. Look at every aspect of your life—home, family, work, friends, church, hobbies, organizations, entertainment—and determine what needs to change.
- What kind of accountability do you need in your life to take responsibility for Whiteness as a principality?
- What do you think would change if you apply what you've discovered this week in your sphere of power and influence?

---

[9] Walter Wink, *Engaging the Powers: 25th Anniversary Edition* (Philadelphia: Fortress Press, 2017), 8.

"Can White People Be Saved?"

Willie James Jennings

(2018)

Can White people be saved? For some, the question that titles this essay is deeply offensive. It suggests that there is a category of people whose existence raises the question of the efficacy of salvation. The efficacy of salvation is a very complicated theological idea, involving not just one's status in eternity (as many great evangelists have put it) but also the quality and character of one's Christian commitment—and not only these matters but also the nature of the redemptive dynamic of a life, that is, the level or depth of one's deliverance from captivity or bondage. At this moment, I am less concerned about the efficacy of salvation with this question and more interested in the status of two keywords in the question: salvation and whiteness. These terms point to a history that we yet live within, a history where whiteness as a way of being in the world has been parasitically joined to a Christianity that is also a way of being in the world. It was the fusion of these two realities that gave tragic shape to Christian faith in the New World at the dawn of what we now call the modern colonialist era, or colonial modernity.[1]

It is precisely this fusing together of Christianity with whiteness that constitutes the ground of many of our struggles today. The struggle

---

[1] I am not sure who first coined the term *colonial modernity*, but a good definition of it can be found in Walter Mignolo's *The Darker Side of Western Modernity: Global Futures, Decolonial Options* (Durham, NC: Duke University Press, 2011). Colonial modernity is the moment of ascendency (from the 1500s forward) when those who inhabited the geographic and cultural sites designated the West and the Global North gained dominant control over the peoples who inhabited places of colonial conquest and forced them into temporal and spatial schemas that defined and determined every aspect of their existence.

against aggressive nationalism is the struggle against the fusion of Christianity and whiteness. The struggle against racism and white supremacy and some aspects of sexism and patriarchy is the struggle against this fusion. The struggle against the exploitation of the planet is bound up in the struggle against this joining. So many people today see these problems—of planetary exploitation, of racism, of sexism, of nationalism and so forth but they do not see the deeper problem of this fusion, which means they have not yet grasped the energy that drives many of our problems.

We have always had difficulty in seeing the deeper problem of this fusion. On the one hand, many people have not been able to see this as a fusion, a joining that should never have happened. Many people collapse Christianity and whiteness into one thing, loved or hated. They cannot see two things, two mutual interpenetrating realities, the one always performing itself inside the other. On the other hand, there are just as many people who do not see this as a deep problem or even as a problem. They have made whiteness an irreversible accident of history or even an attribute of creation. That whiteness is a problem remains an elusive point to get across because too many people have no idea what to do with such a concept. Beside bewilderment, the typical response I get to the idea that whiteness is a problem is a mixture of guilt and anger, and of course the inevitable pushback. (I will return to these important emotional responses later.)

It is an ironic truth of Christian life that most people perform a faith, embody a faith, far more complex than they articulate. There is a vastness to our lives in faith that we cannot adequately capture with our words. The difficulty with racial existence, and with whiteness in particular, is that it has woven itself into that vastness, making seeing the fusion and seeing our way beyond the fusion very difficult work. This essay aims to aid us in the work of ending the fusion of whiteness and Christianity.

To speak of whiteness is not to speak of particular people but of people caught up in a deformed building project aimed at bringing the world to its full maturity. What does maturity look like, maturity of mind and body, land and animal (use), landscape and building, family and government? Whiteness is a horrific answer to this question formed exactly at the site of Christian missions. So in this essay I want to explore whiteness as a deformed formation toward maturity, along the way to consider some of its affective (emotional) dimensions, and finally to suggest how we might begin to separate whiteness from Christianity by forming places that offer a different building project toward maturity. But before we turn to these matters, let me raise a couple of questions that some will want addressed.

Have I already made whiteness too important, made matters of racial identity too decisive? This is a fair question if it is asked from a position where the history and the continuing influence of the West and of Christianity have only been and continue to be tangential at best. But if I am inside the story of modern Christianity, then I am inside the story of racial identity and if I am inside a faith confessed or a social and economic order performed that echoes down the centuries from the colonial shores or homes of the masters of the Old World of Europe, then I am inside the story of whiteness, whether I see it that way or not.

Another related question often asked at this moment is whether a focus on whiteness obscures the voices and visions of all those peoples designated non-White, especially those designated Black?[2] Does focusing on whiteness continue the tragic history of making the minds, actions, and decisions of Europeans and their descendants central to our imaginations and our actions? In short, does this focus continue to undermine non-White agency both historically and existentially? This too is a fair question if it is asked with a view toward the struggle of so many peoples in the world to be heard and taken seriously. But if we want to understand what finding voice and forming life-sustaining vision mean at this moment, then we have to understand how whiteness informs the intellectual, artistic, economic, and geographic stage on which vision and voice are realized and performed.

Moreover, both of these questions have not yet reckoned with the reality of creaturely entanglement. We have always lived in an enmeshed world where lives are intertwined and constantly and continuously interweaving. It was and is a mistake to ever imagine a separate but equal existence. It is one thing to imagine the voice and vision of a people being

---

[2] I am using the term *non-White* rather than *people of Color* to highlight the historical trajectory from which came racial designations as well as the continuing energy that drives forward racial designation. Without the emergence of whiteness, there would be no people of Color, that is, no racial designation in its current forms. Racial designation lives through the originating energy of whiteness as a powerful and attractive form of self-designation that continues to this moment. So by preferring the clunky designation *non-White*, I am pointing not to the people so designated but to the colonial matrix of designation itself.

heard and seen. It is an entirely different matter to imagine voice and vision existing alone, singularly or in competition with other voices. Even if it could be imagined in the past, it certainly cannot and should not be imagined now. Yet even in the past, separate existence was never realized as sequestered existence. We are joined at the site of the dirt, and the dirt is our undeniable kin. Even geographic distance and the difference of strange tongues cannot thwart this truth—we are creatures bound together. It was precisely this recognition and the historic resistance to it that showed itself so powerfully in the emergence of whiteness.

WHITENESS AS A FORMATION TOWARD MATURITY

Imagine people who recognize our creaturely connection and deny it at the exact moment they recognize it. Whiteness as we now know it and experience it emerged at a moment in human history when the world in all its epistemological density was opening up to those we would later call Europeans.[3] It began simply as an impulse. Early Europeans entered worlds overwhelming in every way, not just in majestic beauty but also in stunning landscapes, not just with inexplicable animals in their mind-bending variety but with a vast array of differing languages carried by different peoples. Different peoples—similar but different. These early Europeans in these new places asked themselves the question, who am I in this strange new place? This is the right question, the holy and good question. The newness of place should provoke from us such questions. The question is never the root of selfishness. Selfishness grows from its answer.

---

[3] To speak of Europeans at the emergence of colonial modernity is an anachronism that most scholars working in these matters acknowledge. *European* is a placeholder for peoples, some of whom formed themselves into sovereign states or transatlantic corporations and positioned themselves at the sites of difference in the New World and from those sites formed settler colonialism as a crucial precursor to the formation of a shared imperialist vision of superiority, oversight, authority, and control over indigenous peoples and their lands. In this regard, Indigenous and European share in the same history of geographic struggle over control of lands and the formation of bordered and racial existence. See Anthony Pagden, *The Idea of Europe: From Antiquity to the European Union* (Cambridge, UK: Woodrow Wilson Center Press; Cambridge University Press, 2002); and Brendan Simms, *Europe: The Struggle for Supremacy, from 1453 to the Present* (New York: Basic Books, 2013).

These early Europeans answered the question without the voice or vision of the peoples of the New World.[4] They self-designated. This was bad enough, but the horror continued as they designated vast numbers of remarkably different peoples. As they did this, they quickly began to suture different peoples, clans, and tribes into racial categories. They, the Europeans, were White, and the others were almost White, not quite White, or non-White, or almost Black, not quite Black, or Black. They also created a viral world of designation between White and Black, capable of capturing all people in racial identity. What began, we should say, as harmless designating soon took its place in a matrix of harm. In that matrix of harm, these categories took on an aggressive life of their own. As I have noted elsewhere in print, the work of proto-Europeans naming themselves White and others not White was only one side of what constituted racial identity.[5] The other crucial part of that constitution was the formation of modern private property and the destruction of place-centered identities.

For the first time in human history, peoples (especially in the colonized world) would be forced to think of themselves in disorienting ways, to think of themselves away from land and away from animals and into racial encasement, that is, into races. They were forced to reduce their identities down to their bodies and the activities of the body. Why? Because the land was being taken, the animals were being captured and killed at a monstrous rate, and the plants and the landscape were being altered irreversibly. These Christian settlers understood themselves to be

---

[4] Take, for example, a comment by Pedro de Cieza de León, from his important text, *The Discovery and Conquest of Peru: Chronicles of the New World Encounter*, ed. and trans. Alexandra Parma Cook and Noble David Cook (Durham, NC: Duke University Press, 1998), which offers us an indispensable account of the conquest of Peru and also a window into the logics of a Spanish colonialist. He states, "And that God could have permitted something so great [Peru] would be hidden from the world for so many years and such a long time, and not known by men, yet that it would be found and discovered and won, all in the time of Emperor Charles, who had such need of its help because of the wars that had taken place in Germany against the Lutherans and [because of] other most important expeditions" (Cieza de León, *Discovery and Conquest of Peru*, 37). Cieza de León imagines the New World as a resource for the emperor, a resource with no relevant past but only a useful future.

[5] Willie James Jennings, *The Christian Imagination: Theology and the Origins of Race* (New Haven, CT: Yale University Press, 2010), chap. 1.

present in the new worlds only by the hand of God, only through God's ineffable providence. They were there for one central purpose—to bring the New World into maturity, mature use, mature development, and of course a mature perception of the world.

As the taking of land and animals was being done, European Christians challenged to its core the vision shared by many Native peoples that both their identities and their sense of well-being formed and flourished through constant interaction with specific places and animals. They were not simply in a place and with animals. They were not simply on land. The place was in them, and they were within the animals, sharing life and vision, joined together as family. Such a vision for most missionaries was demonically inspired confusion, later in time to be called by others animism, and still later to be called cultural primitivism. In place of this vision, these Christians installed the conceptual building we live into this day. That is, the vision of a world that revolves around a centered White self, a body that projects meaning onto the world, onto land and animals, through reductive forms of naming, designating, classifying, analyzing, and summarizing the nature of being and the beings of nature. There was a central reason for the emergence of this new self. It was necessary in order to bring nature and human beings to maturity, to the full realization of their purpose and their use.[6]

The pedagogical goal of missionaries and others was not simply to bring New World peoples into the reality of salvation, but it was fundamental to that salvation to change their ways of seeing the world so that they too would see themselves rightly as centered selves who project meaning onto the world and who may bring nature to its full purpose and use. This crucial educational hope was to disabuse Native peoples of any idea that lands and animals, landscapes and seasons carried any communicative or animate density, and therefore any ethical or moral direction in how to live in the world. Instead, they offered peoples a relationship with the world that was basically one dimensional—we interpret and manipulate the world as we see

---

[6] Father Bernabe Cobo in his crucial text, *History of the Inca Empire: An Account of the Indians' Customs and Their Origin Together with a Treatise on Inca Legends, History and Social Institution,* ed. and trans. Roland Hamilton (Austin: University of Texas Press, 1979), 46, gives us an example of someone who offers categorization of the various kinds of Natives in order to help establish the best way to convert them and bring them into a rightly ordered New World.

fit, taking from it what we need, and caring for it within the logics of making it more productive for us; that is, we draw the world to its proper fulfillment. This is crudely put, but it captures the trajectory of how humanity's imperial position as stewards of the creation was most often interpreted in colonial contexts.

The whole world in this way of thinking was framed temporally, always in need of being moved from its potential to its full realization, potentiality to actuality. This way of perceiving the world, as the great Native American religious scholar Vine Deloria Jr. reminds us, drained the spatial realities of life of any real significance. Native peoples, he says, were forced to think of their lives temporally and not spatially.[7] The Western Christianity they received taught them this crucial lesson: where you are (temporally), that is, where you are going, moving, developing toward is far more important than where you are (spatially)—that is, where you live, where you live now or with what people, animals, plants, and landscape you share habitation. In fact, the latter is utterly inconsequential.

The most important thing in the world, in this Christianized way of thinking, is to allow yourself to be moved toward maturity. It is precisely this commitment to a life aimed at maturity that joined visions of salvation to ideas of the transformation of lands and peoples and together formed visions of Christian missions. Whiteness formed at this joining. From the beginning of colonialism, salvation and the transformation of land and peoples have been coupled together, and that coupling turned Christianity's creative powers against itself. Christian faith is about new life in Christ and forming life inside that newness. The new situation of colonial power enfolded the newness that is Christian faith within the newness that was the transformation of land and people, earth and animal.

We need precision here to see the problem. The problem is not that things change. Things do change. We could even say things evolve. Nor is the problem the impulse to transform. Transformation is not inherently evil. The horror here is the colonialist's denial of the voice and vision of

---

[7] Vine Deloria Jr., *God Is Red: A Native View of Religion,* 30th anniv. ed. (Golden, CO: Fulcrum, 2003), 61–76, 113–32. Also see Barbara Alice Mann, *Spirits of Blood, Spirits of Breath: The Twinned Cosmos of Indigenous America* (New York: Oxford University Press, 2016), 15–40.

peoples who inhabit a place, denial that defies the logic of life together in a place as the basic wisdom that should shape change and transformation. The horror here is the emergence of a form of creating that destroys creation. This is not the logic of breaking eggs to make omelets, recognizing that some destruction is always inherent in creation. This logic destroys the life of chickens by distorting their bodies to maximize egg production. This logic drives creation toward death.

Death began with denying the voice of peoples and the voice of the earth, that is, the earth's own semiotic reality, and in doing this rendered inconsequential peoples' identities as bound to places.[8] Death expanded its reach by designating peoples and the earth in reductive categories, isolating lives and life itself into fragments in order to make them useful, turning everything into commodities. We were then taught to project meaning onto our lives and to life itself, which was now formed in fragments. We learned to reassemble life as interchangeable, exchangeable, and connectible bodies, buildings, goods, and services.[9] We have remained on this trajectory, and it set in place the processes of transformation that captured the energy and logic of Christian conversion and placed it inside whiteness as a formation toward maturity.

If you have not followed this, let me state it clearly. No one is born white. There is no white biology, but whiteness is real. Whiteness is a working, a forming toward a maturity that destroys. Whiteness is an invitation to a form of agency and a subjectivity that imagines life progressing toward what is in fact a diseased understanding of maturity, a maturity that invites us to evaluate the entire world by how far along it is toward this goal. Most people have a sense of what agency is—to be the source of one's own actions and decisions and to claim immediate control over one's body. Subjectivity is a more recent addition to our thinking about a self, and in this regard what I mean by subjectivity

---

[8] Eduardo Kohn, *How Forests Think: Toward an Anthropology beyond the Human* (Berkeley: University of California Press, 2013), 27–100. In this groundbreaking book, Kohn articulates a vision of semiotic reality (semiosis) that cannot be reduced to the symbolic as that which is the sole reality of human communicability or representation. He argues that more than humans operate in representation, and thereby more than humans constitute the semiotic nature of the world.

[9] Jason W. Moore, *Capitalism in the Web of Life: Ecology and the Accumulation of Capital* (London: Verso, 2015), 141–92.

is the narrative form one gives to one's life.[10] Subjectivity is the way people imagine their negotiating of the positions and roles they occupy, the circumstances and situations they must traverse, the pleasures they seek, and the pain they wish to avoid. Subjectivity is created both by that which is placed upon us and by the drama we form to make sense of the world we inhabit.

White agency and subjectivity form as people imagine themselves being transformed in three fundamental ways: (1) from being owned to being an owner, (2) from being a stranger to being a citizen, and (3) from being identified with darkness to being seen as White. It should also be clear at this point that anyone can enter White agency and subjectivity. In the limited space of this essay, I will only briefly outline these three ways.

From Owned to Ownership

"You were bought with a price; do not become slaves of human masters." So says 1 Corinthians 7:23. It is the purchase of a life, the taking back of it from enslavement that signals a powerful motif of our salvation. Someone gave what is necessary for us to be freed from slavery. What was necessary for freedom in the new colonial world was labor that led to ownership. There were two questions people had to wrestle with when it came to labor and work in the new colonial world. First, what would you do in order to work in a way that would bring you to ownership? Second, what would you do if you were forced to work as if you were owned? Both questions are really the one question of New World labor—what would you do to survive? What would you do to hold death at bay? "If you don't work, you don't eat, and if you don't eat. . . ." It all comes back to the land. From the sixteenth century forward, as more and more land is seized, enclosed, and turned into private property, labor is fundamentally transformed—people are placed on a trajectory that is inescapable—you must see your own body as raw material just like the land.

The body stood at the center of this powerful commodification of the New World, and no one escaped. Two kinds of workers become paradigmatic for labor, the indentured servant and the slave. Indentured

---

[10] Kelly Oliver, *Colonization of Psychic Space: A Psychoanalytic Social Theory of Oppression* (Minneapolis: University of Minnesota Press, 2004).

servitude is an old practice by which workers offer themselves in service (sometimes edging toward slavery) for a specific length of time in
exchange for something, normally a skill only obtained through apprenticeship or, in the case of the New World, for passage to it and land
on it once the time of indentured servitude ends. In the New World
of colonial modernity, indentured servitude would become more than
just a discrete practice. It pointed to the very character of hired labor in
the New World. Indentured servitude suggested a trajectory of identity
whereby poor Old World people could become like wealthy landed
people, become like the landed class, if they agreed with the work of
transformation, transforming themselves from Old World people to
owners of the New World. There has always been a level of submission
or subservience that has characterized American labor, even with the rise
of unions, protest movements, and labor negotiations. That submission
has been in large measure energized by the imagined fraternity of whiteness and especially of white masculinity.[11]

The second kind of paradigmatic labor was of course the slave. Slavery is also an ancient practice, but in the New World and with colonial
modernity, the slave was most intensely raw material. All bodies in the
New World were captured in narratives of development and processes
of commodification. It is crucial that we hold these things together.
If the slave was property, then the indentured servant was temporary
property, and between them labor and work formed in the New World.
This meant that labor formed in the New World as first a sacrifice of the
body, an offering up of the body. The wellbeing of the body was never a
central part of the calculus of work. Work as survival, yes—work bound
to well-being and to flourishing, no.

Flourishing life was reserved for ownership. Ownership of property
and of one's own labor meant freedom. Advancement from being raw
material to owning property and labor was very serious business. It meant
you would move from vulnerability to invulnerability, from being one
without voice to one with some measure of voice in society. Historically,
owning land not only connected one to the land but also connected

[11] Dana Nelson, *National Manhood: Capitalist Citizenship and the Imagined Fraternity of White Men* (Durham, NC: Duke University Press, 1998). Also see David T. Roediger and Elizabeth D. Esch, *The Production of Difference: Race and the Management of Labor in U.S. History* (New York: Oxford University Press, 2012).

one to the growing nationalist ideologies of land ownership being the prerequisite for freedom, which brings me to the next transformation.

From Stranger to Citizen

"So then you are no longer strangers and aliens, but you are citizens with the saints and also members of the household of God." So says Ephesians 2:19. To be a stranger is to live in vulnerability, subject to isolation and violence, and clothed in suspicion. No immigrant ever wanted to be a stranger. Immigrants transform, not always quickly, almost never uniformly, but all aim at the "no longer" of being never again in the position of stranger. Coming to the New World as an immigrant, especially to the place that would come to be called the United States, meant you were willing to tame the wilderness. Taming the wilderness meant much more than clearing land. It meant that you were willing to place your bodies in the unfolding drama of destroying the Native inhabitants. Participating in the destruction of Indigenous peoples was one of the primary ways immigrants signaled to the world and to themselves that they were part of the American landscape, the formation of a White nation in contrast to the "Indians": Yet taming the wilderness was also an analogy for stripping away their immigrant past—that is, those cultural artifacts that signaled indebtedness to the old country, the old cultural ways, and the primitive mentalities of lower classes of the Old World.[12]

To look like a Native, of the New World or the Old World or of a different world, was to be deemed inappropriate to the new order emerging in America. Barbarians existed, and they were those who by their appearance signaled they were not ready to participate in the formation of this new nation. They showed immaturity. This meant that transformation was the order of the day. To transform requires creation not only out of destruction, the stripping away of the foreign worlds inappropriate to this new national space, but also by the concealment of those worlds. Immigrants conceal, not always quickly, almost never uniformly, but all aim at dismissing that for which they might be dismissed or determined

---

[12] Nell Irvin Painter, *The History of White People* (New York: Norton and Norton, 2010). Also see Matthew Frye Jacobson, *Barbarian Virtues: The United States Encounters Foreign Peoples at Home and Abroad, 1876–1917* (New York: Hill and Wang, 2000).

to be, barbarians inside the gate. Nationalism formed between the twin energies of immigrant angst and the privatization of property where old logics of boundaries and borders transformed inside the new logic of the commodification of space. That is, boundaries and borders matured.

Nationalism was a new way to reassemble life with land. Nationalism was never life inside the land, never life lived in serious reciprocity with plant and animal, sky and season, dirt and water, listening, learning, and finding a way to know oneself as deep partner in the world through a particular place. Nationalism was ownership, property ownership made plural and made the universal right of a people to their space. Yes, there was attachment to the land; yes, there was blood bound to soil; and yes, there were deep sentiment and sensibilities born of living in a land, but this was different. This was owning the land, not being owned by the land. This was speaking for the land as one who controls it, not having land and animal speak through you, as though you extended their lives through your life. Nationalism places people inside borders, and borders inside people; place-centered identity removes the borders between people and the actual world and points to the artificiality of all borders. Yet few people see the artificiality of borders because the transformation toward citizens has distorted our view of the world. It creates a sense of sovereignty that Christian conversion has been forced to serve.[13] Conversion to the faith has been brought inside the cultivating work of turning immigrants into citizens. Christianity indeed makes good citizens. This brings me to the third transformation.

From Darkness to White

"Work out your own salvation with fear and trembling; for it is God who is at work in you, enabling you both to will and to work for his good pleasure": This is the famous passage from Philippians 2:12–13. Salvation is not our work. It is God working on us and in us, enabling us in and through our work to show God's own work. Work transforms and labor ennobles—this is what colonial settlers in many ways imagined for themselves and their Native subjects. They imagined a moral transformation at work in the transformation of the New World. That

---

[13] Reviel Netz, *Barbed Wire: An Ecology of Modernity* (Middletown, CT: Wesleyan University Press, 2004).

moral transformation captured both body and labor, drawing all workers toward an idealized vision of the morality of work.

In order to understand this moral transformation, we have to return to the formation of labor in the New World. Central to that formation was the juxtaposing of two racialized body types energized through the mechanisms of modern slavery and indentured servitude. Between these two body types the entire world of bodies and labor would be judged, gauged, and articulated.[14] There was the White body—the civilized, honorable, and beautiful prototype—and the non-White body, most centrally the Black body—the uncivilized, primitive, dangerous, and ugly body. In the New World of Indigenous peoples, Native bodies were perceived as closer to nature and its raw condition of unproductivity, of potentiality, yet to be realized.

Long before the shadow of colonialism covered the New World, peoples worked, but under its transformational regimes, their work was framed inside a project of morality that meant very different things for racialized bodies. No matter how hard the Black slave worked, her work was read through the prism of a primitive and uncivilized body, one that was inefficient, lazy, and in need of constant supervision. These dark bodies must be drawn through work from their raw condition of potentiality. White workers and their work have always been read differently as the bearers of an inherent moral integrity. This does not mean that White workers were never accused of being lazy or inefficient, but this was never assumed as their natural state, a state out of which they must be disciplined.

The labor of White workers revealed their honor, the honor inherent to the White body. The labor of Black workers (and all whose bodies were associated with the Black body) proved that they were worthy of honor; through working they were moving away from the primitive and uncivilized Black body. That is, Black workers held at bay dishonor by their work. This racial anthropology has always flowed through work and workers in the West, shaping how the energy and efforts of people are read. From factory floors to playing fields, from shops and corner stores

---

[14] David R. Roediger, *The Wages of Whiteness: Race and the Making of the American Working Class* (London: Verso, 2007). Also see George Lipsitz, *The Possessive Investment in Whiteness: How White People Profit from Identity Politics* (Philadelphia: Temple University Press, 2006).

to corporate offices, non-White workers work to prove their honor; the work of White workers simply reveals their honor. So labor has been framed inside a movement toward a morality bound up in whiteness, which means there is a double burden for people without work shaped in this vision, both the burden of a lack of income and the burden of a lack of honor. This is the tormented search for honor—honor that is yet to be revealed for the White worker or honor that is yet to be created for the Black worker. For so many people the latter burden weighs heavier than the former.

The association of honor with work did not begin with colonialism, and the double burden of losing honor with the loss of work is not new. This, however, is a double burden framed inside the racialization of bodies and the long history of racial hierarchies that played with Black and White, dark and light, forming them into signs of the deep connection of appearance and behavior. It is precisely this framing that remains untouched by a Christianity that helped to give it life and continues to breathe life into it. This idealized morality of work has helped to conceal the immorality of the kinds of work we are often pressed to do, work that destroys the earth, animals, and our own bodies. No one disputes the value of work or the importance of being a worker, but not enough of us dispute what work is calibrated to a flourishing life. No one imagined that those slaves working from sunup to sundown and then by candlelight and then late into the night should gain from their labor the fruits of a good life. As far as the master class was concerned, these workers were property. However, the slave masters did imagine that slavery was good for them. And in a tragic way, being formed to be a worker today continues along that same path.

These three imagined transformations, from raw material to owner, from stranger to citizen, and from darkness to whiteness, formed at the site of hope for these Christian settlers who did not simply want to make the New World their world but wished to make them the way the world ought to be. "Do not be conformed to this world, but be transformed by the renewing of your minds, so that you may discern what is the will of God—what is good and acceptable and perfect." So says Romans 12:2. Transforming the world, drawing it toward maturity is exactly what they imagined it meant to not be conformed to a world still in its adolescence or even in its embryonic form. They bequeathed to us whiteness and formed Christian mission inside it. I am certainly not saying that all European Christian settlers in the New World from generation to generation understood that this is what they were doing. They did in fact understand themselves to be doing exactly what was normal and natural, a normal planting and a natural harvesting, a normal tearing down and a natural building up.

THE FEELING OF WHITENESS

The difficulty we face at this moment is the success of that work. Whiteness feels normal and natural. It feels normal and natural because it is woven into how we imagine moving toward maturity. Whiteness feels. It has an affective structure. So, like extremely comfortable clothing that moves with the body, whiteness becomes what Anne Anlin Cheng calls a second skin.[15] Whiteness is being questioned at this moment like never before, and it feels terrible to so many people. We have to talk about whiteness in relation to affect and feeling because how whiteness feels is how whiteness thinks. Agency and subjectivity form in how we feel and think as one single reality of personhood. So the questioning of whiteness feels terrible in two ways to many people. First, it feels as if we are abandoning the goal of progress, and, second, it feels as if we have become obsessed with matters of identity and have lost a sense of common purpose.

It feels as if we are abandoning the goal of progress because we have been led to believe that the way life has formed over the colonial centuries is the only viable way that remains open to us. Some argue strongly that the denial of Indigenous ways summarized as primitivisms; the necessary reductionism inherent in scientific investigation; and the commodification, fragmentation, and reassembling of life into products for exchange necessary for modern economies may have had some bad consequences and collateral damage, but look at all that has been produced and continues to be produced thanks to the transforming of the

---

[15] Anne Anlin Cheng, *Second Skin: Josephine Baker and the Modern Surface* (New York: Oxford University Press, 2011). What I mean by second skin is not a direct application of Cheng's brilliant meditation on Josephine Baker's deployment of a "second skin" to challenge and make productive counteruse of the gaze of whiteness. My use of the idea of second skin refers to the loss of sight of authentic creatureliness beneath or below the formation of whiteness.

new worlds. Ownership and nations and productive labor are all good and necessary things. The way things have formed is a sign of maturity, they contend. Yet what is at stake here for so many people is defense of a maturity that is not maturity at all but defense of a vision that has left them with no other path that can look backward or forward. They are forced to minimize the horrors of the past, maximize the accomplishments of the present, and live with a highly constrained imagination for what is possible. For many Christians the tragedy here is even greater. We have often baptized this progress as a blessing of God. We have too quickly blessed this sick vision of maturity as consistent with faithful growth, and we have failed to remember what was lost, not simply ways of life but the ways of many peoples for living and moving forward in and with the world.

Those who are uncomfortable with the questioning of whiteness also feel as though we have become obsessed with matters of identity and have lost a sense of common purpose. There is a sense in which whiteness is invisible, not because it cannot be seen but because the point was never to see it. Rather, the point was to live life and perform life toward it. It is only when you resist that performance that you can actually start to see it. People have resisted from the very beginning—resisted the loss of life in a place; resisted being designated racially; resisted their lives being commodified; resisted being forced to live inside global systems of exchange, debt, and money; and resisted as long as they could the relentless systems of education and evaluation that supported these things. They sought to perform a different life than the life demanded by whiteness and to suggest for consideration a different path to a common purpose. The issue was never having a common purpose. The issue has always been who gets to define the common purpose and what energies and instruments have been used to force people into a common purpose that destroys life. So, from the beginning of the workings of whiteness, people have used the only weapon consistently at their disposal to challenge that common purpose—their bodies, their stories, their memories, and their hopes, all found in their identities.

For Christians, the struggle for us here has been exquisitely painful because we have been of two minds from the very beginning of colonialism. We have been those who have accepted and sometimes promoted a death-dealing common purpose aimed at eradicating all differences that we imagined would undermine a uniform efficiency in the creation of the good life. But we have also remembered our difference. We remembered from time to time that we were not of this world and of its common purposes. And many who became Christian whose identities were formed in the New World resisted the plans and purposes of Europeans who feverishly wanted to transform their world. Christianity is about identities woven together in Christ to transform the world and not about a common purpose that transforms identities.

FORMING A PLACE TO BE

We need at this moment a Christian faith that can start to break our deep connection to whiteness by resisting its vision of maturity. Suggesting a first step is all I have space for in this essay, but the first step is decisively the most important. The paths that have been formed by whiteness, carved on the earth and in bodies, cannot be undone, but they can be redirected, drawn into new paths that lead away from death and into life. It all begins again with the land, with dirt, air, water, cities, towns, neighborhoods, and homes. It begins with new kinds of intentional communities that challenge where people live and how people live in places. As I close, I am doubling down on what some people know and feel but are afraid to say—it all comes to rest in geography and living spaces. Whiteness comes to rest in space. The maturity whiteness aims at always forms segregated spaces. It forms lives lived in parallel, whether separated by miles or inches. It constructs bordered life, life lived in separate endeavors of wish fulfillment.

Segregated spaces must be turned toward living places where people construct together an everyday that turns life in health-giving directions. Overcoming whiteness begins by reconfiguring life geographically so that all the flows work differently; the flows of money, education, support, and attention move across people who have been separated by the processes that have formed us racially, economically, and nationally. We start with the communities that have been left behind in the movement toward maturity, those no longer imagined through the goals of ownership, citizenship, or productive labor, and we join them, we move to them, or we stay in them, or we form them, or we advocate for them, or we protect them. The we here are we Christians and all those willing to live toward a different formation of places. We fight against the segregation that shapes our worlds, and we work to weave lives together. Remember, this is only the first step; there are many more to follow. But the point not to be missed is that we should feel compelled to form what Gerhard Lohfink many years ago called a contrast society, by forming contrast communities.[16] But that contrast must be formed on the actual ground, in neighborhoods and living spaces.

Indeed, this is what Christian mission at its best was always aiming at—following Jesus into new places to form new life, life together. So am I advocating compelling people to live together across all the lines of formation that divide us and have habituated us to be comfortable with those divides? Yes, because I want to turn us from a formation that is yet compelling people to aim their lives toward a vision of maturity that is bound in death. I want to save us from becoming or being White people.

---

[16] Gerhard Lohfink, *Jesus and Community* (Philadelphia: Fortress Press, 1984).

"To Be a Christian Intellectual"

Willie James Jennings

(2015)

Christian intellectual life is by no means the sole property of those who inhabit the theological academy or those who live their lives from the sight lines of pulpits or the comfort of counselor chairs. Christian intellectual life is the inheritance of every Christian and the calling on every believer to reflect deeply about their faith from the sites in this world that matter—where lives are at stake, and hope hangs in the balance. For me one crucial site has always been where race and Christian faith have enfolded one another. Race and Christian faith have always played together in the Western world, woven inside of each other like strands of braided hair. We know this but we do not like to remember this, because remembering the torturous racial past of the modern world is difficult remembering. That remembering obligates us to give an honest account of ourselves, and giving an honest account of oneself is serious moral work.

It is precisely this serious moral work that continues to escape the attention of many Christians in this America. We have never unbraided the strands of race and Christian faith, and because of this our Christian faith is deeply diseased. That we are Christians is not in dispute; that we understand what it means to perform our faith, to think as Christians— that is contested terrain. What we are in need of at this crucial moment are women and men who know how to think their faith, perform their faith in ways that untangle the racial imagination from the Christian imagination. What we desperately need at this critical moment are indeed Christian intellectuals.

The great literary theorist and philosopher of culture Edward Said asked what it means to be an intellectual today.[1] His answer was famously that an intellectual was one who had the courage to speak truth to power. The intellectual was one who fearlessly challenged the gods of this age and was (even as a person of faith) a secular critic. The intellectual, he said, always stands between loneliness and alignment.[2] Said is pointing in the right direction for us, because to be a Christian intellectual today is to confront those powers, those principalities, if you will, that continue to distort our Christianity. Allow me to name three powers that a Christian intellectual must confront.

1. We must confront the principality of whiteness.
2. We must confront the principalities of greed and violence.
3. We must confront the principality of fear.

We must confront the principality of whiteness. We have now reached a point where we can name what has not been adequately named, and that is whiteness as a principality. For a myriad of historical reasons, we have not had the conceptual ability to name whiteness for what it is—not a particular people, not a particular gender, not a particular nation, but an invitation, a becoming, a transformation, an accomplishment. It was an accomplishment sought after by immigrant group after immigrant group coming to these shores hoping to strip away their ethnic past and claim an American future. Before that it was an accomplishment born of discovery, of European men who discovered their unchecked and unrestrained power over indigenous peoples to claim and rename and alter their worlds. Before that it was an accomplishment born of Christian election and supersessionism that removed Jewish people from the privileged position of being the people of God and replaced them with people who imagined their flesh (white flesh) to be saved and saving flesh.

Whiteness was and is a way of being in the world and a way of seeing the world at the same time. It was nurtured and grew inside of Christianity, its voice mimicking Christianity, saying sweetly, "This is what it means to be Christian." But now we know that whiteness is not a given. It is a choice. Whiteness is not the equal and opposite of blackness. It

---

[1] Edward Said, *Representations of the Intellectual* (New York: Vintage Books, 1994).

[2] Said, 22.

is not one racial flavor next to others. Whiteness is a way of imagining the world moving around you, flowing around your body with you being at the center. Whiteness is a way of imagining the true, the good, and the beautiful configured around white bodies. Whiteness is a way of imagining oneself as the central facilitating reality of the world, the reality that makes sense of the world, that interprets, organizes, and narrates the world, and whiteness is having the power to realize and sustain that imagination.

Whiteness is not a given. It is a goal. Immigrants who come to America now know this. Immigrants who came here in the beginning learned this. But we have forgotten this and have baptized our Christianity in that forgetting. We need Christian intellectuals who will challenge the formed and forming power of whiteness. We need Christian intellectuals who will resist the desire to interpret, organize, and narrate the world around themselves. We need Christian intellectuals who will listen to their sisters and brothers who live beyond the vale of whiteness and allow themselves to be changed through the listening. A Christian intellectual in this first sense is one who understands that whiteness must be exorcised from the intellectual life.

We who work and live in the academy are yet to face our spiritual bondage in this regard. The history of Christian institutions of higher education in this country is not simply the history of Christian striving. It is also the history of immigrant longing, longing for survival, for acceptance, for accomplishment, for making good in America. It is the story of uplift, but it is also the story of racial assimilation and of a reality of formation that constantly reestablishes whiteness. Until Christian educational endeavors in this country face this legacy and its ongoing influence on what we imagine an educated person to look and sound like, we will constantly confuse racial assimilation with Christian formation.

To be a Christian intellectual also requires that *we confront the principalities of greed and violence.* I have stopped ignoring the true history that the men who founded this country were in fact bound by their lust for land, natural resources, black slave labor, and power to control their destiny and that of this world's indigenous peoples. I have also stopped ignoring the history of the gun in this country and its pride of place in guiding men in the performance of their masculinity. We are a country that has never had the power to resist death or its greatest power, violence.

I have stopped ignoring the fact that greed and violence were the mid-wives of this country. But unlike the biblical Shiphrah and Puah, these midwives did not fear God; they acted like God for us.

We must never forget that the church came to life in this country formed between greed and violence—greed and violence playing off of each other, shouting across land and sky, from sea to shining sea, saying to each other, "This is the way it is, this is the way it should be, this is the given." The church in this country has grown up in greed and violence. We have become accustomed to it, comfortable with it all around us. But we have reached a moment of crisis in this country. Greed and violence wish to expand their thrones, and the only substantial question in front of us is whether we will allow for that expansion.

It is a Christian question that is not just for Christians. It is a Christian question because we know principalities. Black people and all people of color in this country have especially felt their power, watched their expansion, and seen them take hold of lives and draw them toward death. But what is necessary at this moment is not to know them but to unmask them. What is necessary at this moment is the unmasking, the exposing, the naming, and the challenging of those who are yielding to the forces of greed and violence.

We are in need of Christian intellectuals who will challenge the economic configurations of this world and challenge those who traffic in the currencies of violence. The very definition of a Christian intellectual is an activist intellectual. Our goal is to change the world we understand, not because Karl Marx suggested we do so, but because we serve a God who has changed this world and invites us to yield our bodies to that changing power. It is about bodies, and we are in need of Christian intellectual formation that takes the body seriously, but not just our bodies, or random bodies, but specific bodies. I suggest to you a new test for the character and quality of Christian intellectual work today: What effect does our work have on the bodies of poor women of color in this world? How is their situation helped or hurt by our work? Are we forming students and are we thinking together in ways that will make a difference for them?

Edward Said also said that "the intellectual always has a choice either to side with the weaker, the less well represented, the forgotten or ignored, or to side with the more powerful."[3] I have found this choice to always be at play in the academy. Despite our endless qualifications, justifications,

---

[3] Said, 32–33.

excuses, and complexities, it always comes down to whether our work presses the concerns of those in power or those at the margins. I am afraid that the recent history of Christian institutions of higher learning is that we are producing graduates who are in significant numbers choosing to side with the more powerful in this world, who have accepted greed and violence as the given. A Christian intellectual in this second sense is one committed to the unmasking of the powers of greed and violence, and who is willing to name people and processes that bind death to the bodies of women of color and their children.

This is a work of discernment, but sadly we have so mystified discernment that we have lost sight of its concrete history. God clearly drew our attention to the widow and the poor, to the stranger, to those who are weak, hungry, or in prison. God even drew our attention to a poor young girl carrying a child and living in danger. The lines of direction for the intellectual life are clearly drawn, and we need Christian intellectuals who never forget where those lines lead.

To be a Christian intellectual today also requires that we confront the principality of fear. In 1961, Martin Luther King Jr. gave a speech at the annual meeting of the Fellowship of the Concerned in which he explained the logic behind civil disobedience. His argument was quite simple but elegant—just people should obey just laws and the processes through which just laws are created, but just people should disobey unjust laws and challenge the processes that create unjust laws. King also answered the question that would naturally arise from this argument: How do you know just from unjust laws? Again his answer was quite simple but profound—unjust laws increase suffering and silence voices, and in this regard such laws are immoral. King marveled at the courage of the women and men (especially the young) who were willing to engage in civil disobedience against unjust laws. He said, "I submit that the individual who disobeys the law, whose conscience tells him it is unjust and who is willing to accept the penalty . . . of jail . . . is expressing at the moment the very highest respect for the law."[4]

If there is anything that the civil rights movement taught us it is that fear normalizes oppression. Fear normalizes the absurd. African

---

[4] James Washington, ed., *Testament of Hope: The Essential Writings and Speeches of Martin Luther King Jr.* (New York: Harper & Row, 1986), 49. Fuller Theological Seminary's David Allan Hubbard Library has a special collection of James Washington's books.

Americans and other people of color have always had to face a choice—do I push against the absurdities of racial oppression and white supremacy or do I accept them as the given? Choosing to challenge the natural order of things is a challenge made for the sake of life. But not everyone chooses life. This is also part of the legacy of life in America that continues to this very moment. It is absurd to accept a society awash in guns. It is absurd to think we are most safe when we are most armed. It is absurd to think that health care should be part of a calculus for profit. It is absurd to think that workers should be reduced to indentured servitude or, worse, slavery. But we have normalized these absurdities.

Christian intellectuals refuse to accept these absurdities because we will not accept the contradictions. We serve a God who did not leave the world trapped in its own contradictions and caught in its own entanglements. It does not take a scholar to see contradictions. It does not take a theologian or an ethicist or a biologist or an academic to see the contradictions. Seeing the contradictions only makes one an observer, but challenging the contradictions places us on the side of life. Challenging the contradictions is a holy calling that places us on the path that follows Jesus.

There is a sacrificial logic at the heart of overcoming the fear to speak up and speak out and press against the absurdities of injustice and oppression. And sacrifice has always joined the political to the theological, the social to the religious. Martin Luther King Jr. called such sacrifice acts of redemptive suffering whereby people are willing to take on the form of the criminal and put themselves in harm's way for the sake of others. We understand what King was saying. We of all people hear the echo of our savior's life in his words. It is that echo that should sound in our words and in our actions. But there is another characteristic of Christian intellectuals that I must note. They find the joy in life. They spy out the joy even in the midst of struggle. We cannot give witness to the life of God if we do not give witness to the love of life and the love of people. Ultimately, a Christian intellectual is one who is convinced by the love of God for this world and is compelled to live out that conviction.

"What Does Jesus Have to Do with Whiteness?"

Kelly Brown Douglas

(2013)

A firestorm has been set off recently concerning the self-assured observations by Fox News anchor Megyn Kelly that Santa Claus is white and so too is Jesus. These comments, which were in defiant response to a Slate article "Santa Claus Should Not Be a White Man Anymore," by Alisha Harris, have been spoofed by late night talk shows and satirized across social media. Scholars and others have also weighed in on the matter. All have pointed out that Santa is not real and that Jesus was not white. The fact of the matter is that Jesus was a Jew born in ancient Israel and St. Nikolaos upon which the make-believe Santa character was based was from ancient Myra. The fact of the matter is that neither Jesus or St. Nikolaos were white; indeed both were likely to have had swarthy complexions. While it is easy to laugh at Kelly's comments or to simply dismiss them as curiously misguided and ill-informed, they point to something even more significant that is worthy of discussion—the meaning of whiteness and its theological implications. And so, I offer some random thoughts for further reflection.

Whiteness does matter. When whiteness emerged as a social, cultural, and racial construct in America, even as it had throughout the Western world at least, it did so as a mark of privilege and power. There was value in whiteness. It became a measure of one's potential, one's worthiness, indeed, one's very humanity. Historically, whiteness—however that was determined—was the ticket to social, political, and economic status. To be non-white was to be considered an inferior being, worthy of being subjugated. To be a non-white body was to be a subjugated or oppressed body. Essentially, symbolically and practically, whiteness has signified privilege if not oppressive power. As James Baldwin once observed, whiteness has "choked many a human to death."

It is important to point out that to be born into a culture of whiteness or to be considered racially white does not mean that one has to claim whiteness or to live into an identity of whiteness. Put simply, all persons whether white or not can choose not to affirm and perpetuate the unjust reality of privileged whiteness. Unfortunately, however, Kelly's passionate defense of Santa and Jesus' whiteness reminds all of us once again that an insidious and troubling narrative of "whiteness" continues to persist in America. Whiteness has meaning. It is considered by many "treasured property" that must be defended culturally as well as socially and politically. So, what does this mean for those of us who are feminist, womanist, and people committed to a world where all bodies are free to experience the fullness of their humanity, even those which do not claim whiteness?

It means that we must recognize the persistence of "whiteness" in our world and society and the implications for "non-white" bodies. In response to the outcry about her comments, Kelly rather dismissively, if not sarcastically, commented that it goes to show you that race still matters. Race does still matter, as revealed by Kelly's very defense of whiteness. That it matters means that our theological, ethical, and religious discourse must engage racial matters, especially if we are to disrupt and dismantle the social/political/cultural systems and structures that threaten the well-being and freedom of far too many communities of people. There is still much work to be done. We do not live in a post-racial society. This matter of race and whiteness must be confronted head-on. We must not run away from it, or avoid the difficult, uncomfortable conversations. We must name the sin of whiteness and repent of our complicity in it if indeed we are ever to live into the reality of freedom that our gods promise us. For inasmuch as race and whiteness is a social/cultural issue it is as well a theological issue.

And so, the question is what does Jesus have to do with whiteness? Not only was Jesus not historically "white" but neither was he existentially white. Given who Christians proclaim Jesus to be, Jesus' existential whiteness becomes a significant theological matter. For Christians, Jesus is more than just a man—he is the incarnate revelation of God. He, as "Son of God," is Christ. It matters, therefore, that Jesus boldly and passionately rejected the conventions and supremacy of social, political, religious, and cultural power in his own day. It matters that he consistently affirmed, empowered, and befriended those who were the outcast, marginalized, oppressed, and rejected of his day—such as Samaritans and women.

His very human particularities further suggest that one does not have to be defined by one's biological/social/cultural realities but can in fact live against them as one lives into freedom. Instead of claiming the privilege that was associated with his ethnicity and maleness, Jesus lived against it and identified with those who did not enjoy such privilege. This brings us to the theological significance of whiteness. As long as whiteness remains a marker of subjugating and of othering power, then Jesus cannot be white—for to suggest such a thing would imply the whiteness of God. Yet as long as God stands for justice, freedom and peace, then whiteness is antithetical to God. It is anti-Christ.

Yes, there is a certain insipid silliness when it comes to Megyn Kelly's comments. Yet, as silly as they are, they are not innocent. It is the task of all of us who believe in the freedom, justice and peace of God to recognize the danger of such comments, to interrogate them, call them out so that we can indeed move beyond a world where "whiteness" matters.

8

Whiteness as Nationalism

Peter began to speak to them: "I truly understand that God shows no partiality, but in every nation anyone who fears him and does what is just is acceptable to him."

—ACTS 10:34

There is no longer Jew or Greek, there is no longer slave or free, there is no longer male and female; for all of you are one in Christ Jesus. And if you belong to Christ, then you are Abraham's offspring, heirs according to the promise.

—GALATIANS 3:28–29

American means white, and Africanist people struggle to make the term applicable to themselves with ethnicity and hyphen after hyphen after hyphen.

—TONI MORRISON, *PLAYING IN THE DARK*

PREPARATION FOR SESSION 8

How does a suburban, White, middle-class American boy who was raised in a devout family of Methodist ministers grow up and decide the most important calling he can give his life to is becoming a soldier in the US Army? How do two White, God-fearing parents, who were once hippies protesting the war in Vietnam, casually allow their oldest son to sign up to protect and defend the United States against all enemies foreign and domestic? The answer to both questions is Christian nationalism. When I was seventeen, I joined the US Army imagining that I was offering my life in sacrificial service to "God and Country." I saw no difference or contradiction between giving my life to Jesus and giving my life to America; in my mind, at the time, they were one and the same.

For most Americans our dedication to and conflation of "God and Country" begin at a very young age. Not only was I raised in a church where an American flag graced the chancel and patriotic messages were regularly delivered every Fourth of July, but I was also a member of the Boy Scouts of America. One of the highest religious emblems (or merit badges) that a Boy Scout could achieve was the God and Country award that was symbolized by a white square knot on a purple background. God and country, church and state, religion and nationality were tied together for me and millions of other Americans during our most formative years. What it meant to be an American for me was synonymous with what it meant to be Christian, and what it meant to be an American Christian was synonymous with what it meant to be White.

Nationalism is an ideology that places individuals' loyalty to their nation-state above all other individual or group interests. While human beings have always had an attachment to their homeland, nationalism as an ideology is a relatively modern phenomenon that took root in the late eighteenth and early nineteenth centuries. Nationalism seeks to preserve and advance a nation's traditional culture and people. Some nations are defined ethnically and others civically, which leads to two different types of nationalism. Ethnic nationalism is focused on preserv-ing the purity of the original ethnic group of a particular nation, and civic nationalism is focused on preserving the values and principles its citizens are expected to uphold regardless of ethnicity. Both forms of nationalism seek to provide a unifying identity for a nation; however, they also tend to lead to the exclusion and oppression of people who do not fit into the dominant group. For instance, forms of ultra-nationalism (known as fascism), which wreaked havoc all over Europe in the late nineteenth and early twentieth centuries, scapegoated Jewish people, communists, immigrants, Gypsies, dissenters, the disabled, and many other groups, eventually culminating in the genocide of the Holocaust and the devastation of WWII.

Nationalism should be considered a blasphemous idolatry by Christians because Jesus did not intend for there to be any national, civic, or ethnic boundaries to separate the community of his followers. Further, Jesus proclaimed, "My kingdom is not of this world" (John 18:36) and went well beyond his own Jewish ethno-religious community to include the Gentiles, which laid the groundwork for the transnational nature of church. The apostle Paul famously said, "Our citizenship is in heaven" (Phil. 3:20) and "There is neither Jew nor Greek for all are one in Christ" (Gal. 3:28). Yet throughout history Christians have been highly susceptible to the temptation of nationalism. In fact, most fascist movements in Western history have claimed some Christian foundation. Christians have been so inclined to the seduction of nationalism that the term *Christian nationalism* was needed to describe and study the strange and troubling phenomenon that the vast majority of nationalist groups consider themselves to be religiously affiliated with Christianity.

American scholars Samuel Perry and Andrew Whitehead define Christian nationalism as an ideology that advocates a fusion of American life with a particular form of Christian identity.[1] In *Taking America Back for God,* Perry and Whitehead claim:

> Christian nationalism is a cultural framework—a collection of myths, traditions, symbols, narratives, and value systems—that idealizes and advocates a fusion of Christianity with American civic life. The Christianity of Christian nationalism represents something more than religion. . . . It includes assumptions of nativism, white supremacy, patriarchy, and heteronormativity, along with divine sanction for authoritarian control and militarism.[2]

Christian nationalism is so deeply engrained in our collective consciousness that most American Christians are unable to distinguish between what it means to be an American and what it means to be Christian. However, Christian nationalism is not Christianity but idolatry. American Christian nationalism is based on a story that replaces the

---

[1] Andrew L. Whitehead and Samuel L. Perry, *Taking America Back for God: Christian Nationalism in the United States* (New York: Oxford University Press, 2020), x.

[2] Whitehead and Perry, 10.

people of Israel with America in God's divine plan, and often leads to worshiping America as God. Instead of being a neutral or merely patriotic version of faith, American Christian nationalism is a dangerous, distorted, and monstrous accommodation of the Christian faith to the demands of American empire, or what Dorothee Sölle famously dubbed "Christofascism."[3]

The sad truth is that Christofascism has always been present in the United States in the form of Whiteness. As Alberto Toscano claims, the current analogies that are being made between "Trumpism" and European fascists often ignore the "distinctly American forms of authoritarianism" or "racial fascism" that have existed in our country since the first European (Christian) settlers arrived on these shores with enslaved Africans and began displacing and oppressing the indigenous peoples.[4] W.E.B. Du Bois and other leaders in the Black intellectual tradition often critiqued the fascism they saw in Europe in the late nineteenth and early twentieth centuries as simply the continuation of colonial dispossession and racial slavery that was consequential to the founding of America.

In recent years scholars and historians have uncovered that Adolf Hitler and the leaders of the Nazi Party were particularly inspired by the racial fascism they saw in America, such as racist immigration policies, concentration camps ("Indian reservations"), Jim Crow laws and segregation in the South, the eugenics movement, and the ideology of the American White supremacist Madison Grant. Hitler was deeply influenced by Grant and embraced his ideas wholeheartedly. Hitler personally wrote to Grant to thank him for writing the book *The Passing of the Great Race,* and he referred to it as "my Bible."[5] The fascism we Americans have prided ourselves on fighting against abroad was born and bred here and has always been a primary force corrupting our faith and politics.

Today we employ a constellation of terms like *Christian nationalism* or *racial fascism* to describe the same thing—Whiteness, or what Jonathan P.

---

[3] Dorothee Sölle, *Beyond Mere Obedience: Reflections on a Christian Ethic for the Future* (Minneapolis: Augsburg Publishing House, 1970).

[4] Alberto Toscano, "The Long Shadow of Racial Fascism," *Boston Review* online, October 28, 2020.

[5] Adam Serwer, "White Nationalism's Deep American Roots," *The Atlantic* online, April 2019.

Walton calls "White American Folk Religion."[6] American Christian nationalism is not simply the concretization of American nationalism and Christian piety, but the new religion of Whiteness that was born when European Christians felt they needed to justify settler-colonialism, indigenous genocide, and chattel slavery. The average person is willing to die for one of three things: family, country, or religion. White American folk religion combines all three of these deeply held affections in one sociopolitical religious belief system and tradition:

> Colonialism created a counter-faith I call White American Folk Religion (WAFR). It's a set of beliefs and practices grounded in a race, class, gender, and ideological hierarchy that segregates and ranks all people under a light-skinned, thin-lipped, blond-haired Christ. Americans of every color and racial assignment must reckon with the current and historic reality of a country and its churches rooted in White American Folk Religion. WAFR fuels ignorance, complicity, and willing participation in the patterns of injustice that perpetuate the death and degradation of brown, black, and indigenous women and men.[7]

Whiteness in America functions not only as a nationality but also like a religion—a false religion or idolatry masquerading as Christianity, but a religious system nonetheless. It is something White people are often willing to both kill and die for with religious fervor. Distinguishing Christianity, Judaism, and other religions from the false religion of Whiteness is extremely challenging but important work. Therefore, this week we will complete the course curriculum by reading Ta-Nehisi Coates's "The First White President," Toni Morrison's "Making America White Again," and Nell Irvin Painter's "What Is Whiteness?" We will also view Ryan Coogler's film about the police killing of Oscar Grant, *Fruitvale Station*. As we read and view these pieces may we all be like Abraham and cast down the idols of our forebears, leave our father's house behind, and set off for a new land where we can build a beloved community free from the American nationalist folk religion of Whiteness.

---

[6] Jonathan P. Walton, "The Perils of White American Folk Religion," *Christianity Today* online, July 17, 2020.

[7] Walton.

DEEP SOUL WORK

Read and View. Engage with these essays and this film slowly and carefully, taking time to stop and make notes as you go.
- Read "The First White President" by Ta-Nehisi Coates.[8]
- Read "Making America White Again" by Toni Morrison.[9]
- Read "What Is Whiteness?" by Nell Irvin Painter.[10]
- View *Fruitvale Station* by Ryan Coogler.[11]

Meditate and Reflect. *Spend some time in silent meditation after each of the readings or the viewing, and then write your answers these questions:*
1. How did the readings and viewing make you feel?
2. What was most meaningful to you?
3. What are you discovering about Whiteness?
4. Where do you see yourself in the readings and film?

Acknowledge and Confess. *Examine your own life story considering the readings and viewing this week and acknowledge what arises.*
- What stories from your life experience relate to what you read and viewed this week? (Be sure to include them in your racial autobiography.)
- What acknowledgments of Whiteness or personal confessions do you need to make based on this week's readings and viewing?
- Read Acts 10:34 and Galatians 3:28–29. What do these scriptures mean to you spiritually and theologically? One of the resounding themes of the New Testament is the full inclusion of Jews and Gentiles (that is, all the nations of the world) into the family of God. Jesus ate with Gentiles and welcomed them into his community. Peter came to realize God shows no partiality based on nations, tribes, countries, or ethnicities. Paul proclaimed, "There is neither Jew nor Greek" in Christ. In what ways have the American church and American Christianity failed to live up to what Jesus, Peter, and Paul all came to understand and called us to practice?

[8] Ta-Nehisi Coates, "The First White President," *Atlantic* (October 2017).

[9] Toni Morrison, "Making America White Again," *The New Yorker,* November 14, 2016.

[10] Nell Irvin Painter, "What Is Whiteness?" *The New York Times,* June 20, 2015.

[11] Ryan Coogler, *Fruitvale Station* (United States: The Weinstein Company, 2013).

- Reflect on this quotation from Frederick Douglass: "Between the Christianity of this land, and the Christianity of Christ, I recognize the widest possible difference—so wide, that to receive the one as good, pure, and holy, is of necessity to reject the other as bad, corrupt, and wicked. To be the friend of the one, is of necessity to be the enemy of the other. I love the pure, peaceable, and impartial Christianity of Christ: I therefore hate the corrupt, slaveholding, women-whipping, cradle-plundering, partial and hypocritical Christianity of this land. Indeed, I can see no reason, but the most deceitful one, for calling the religion of this land Christianity."[12]
- The prohibition against idolatry is referenced more than two hundred times in scripture. Reflect on the well-known and variously attributed phrase: "When fascism comes to America it will be carrying a cross and wrapped in the American flag." Perhaps we could replace the word *fascism* with *idolatry.*

Repent, Turn, and Transform. *Imagine a new creation and a new humanity for yourself and for our world.*
- What rituals and practices will be required to purge ourselves of the idolatry of Christian nationalism or racial fascism?
- How do our personal devotional practices, our worship, our rituals, our sacraments and ordinances, our governing model, our staff culture, our stewardship, and our facilities in the church need to change to combat Christian nationalism, the false religion of Whiteness, and the idolatry of Whiteness?
- Develop your own strategy for confronting Whiteness. Look at every aspect of your life—home, family, work, friends, church, hobbies, organizations, entertainment. What habits need to change?
- What kind of accountability do you need in your life to take responsibility for Whiteness as civil religion? How might you stand against Christian nationalism?
- What do you think could change if you apply what you've discovered this week in your sphere of power and influence?

---

[12] Frederick Douglass, *Narrative of the Life of Frederick Douglass, an American Slave* (1845), appendix, in Frederick Douglass and Harriet Jacobs, *Narrative of the Life of Frederick Douglass, an American Slave / Incidents in the Life of a Slave Girl,* intro. Kwame Anthony Appiah (New York: Modern Library Paperback Classics, 2010).

"The First White President"

Ta-Nehisi Coates

(2017)

IT IS INSUFFICIENT TO STATE the obvious of Donald Trump: that he is a white man who would not be president were it not for this fact. With one immediate exception, Trump's predecessors made their way to high office through the passive power of whiteness—that bloody heirloom which cannot ensure mastery of all events but can conjure a tailwind for most of them. Land theft and human plunder cleared the grounds for Trump's forefathers and barred others from it. Once upon the field, these men became soldiers, statesmen, and scholars; held court in Paris; presided at Princeton; advanced into the Wilderness and then into the White House. Their individual triumphs made this exclusive party seem above America's founding sins, and it was forgotten that the former was in fact bound to the latter, that all their victories had transpired on cleared grounds. No such elegant detachment can be attributed to Donald Trump—a president who, more than any other, has made the awful inheritance explicit.

His political career began in advocacy of birtherism, that modern recasting of the old American precept that black people are not fit to be citizens of the country they built. But long before birtherism, Trump had made his worldview clear. He fought to keep blacks out of his buildings, according to the U.S. government; called for the death penalty for the eventually exonerated Central Park Five; and railed against "lazy" black employees. "Black guys counting my money! I hate it," Trump was once quoted as saying. "The only kind of people I want counting my money are short guys that wear yarmulkes every day." After his cabal of conspiracy theorists forced Barack Obama to present his birth certificate, Trump demanded the president's college grades (offering $5 million in exchange for them), insisting that Obama was not intelligent enough to have gone to an Ivy League school, and that his acclaimed memoir, *Dreams from My Father*, had been ghostwritten by a white man, Bill Ayers.

It is often said that Trump has no real ideology, which is not true—his ideology is white supremacy, in all its truculent and sanctimonious power. Trump inaugurated his campaign by casting himself as the defender of white maidenhood against Mexican "rapists," only to be later alleged by multiple accusers, and by his own proud words, to be a sexual violator himself. White supremacy has always had a perverse sexual tint. Trump's rise was shepherded by Steve Bannon, a man who mocks his white male critics as "cucks." The word, derived from cuckold, is specifically meant to debase by fear and fantasy—the target is so weak that he would submit to the humiliation of having his white wife lie with black men. That the slur cuck casts white men as victims aligns with the dicta of whiteness, which seek to alchemize one's profligate sins into virtue. So it was with Virginia slaveholders claiming that Britain sought to make slaves of them. So it was with marauding Klansmen organized against alleged rapes and other outrages. So it was with a candidate who called for a foreign power to hack his opponent's email and who now, as president, is claiming to be the victim of "the single greatest witch hunt of a politician in American history."

In Trump, white supremacists see one of their own. Only grudgingly did Trump denounce the Ku Klux Klan and David Duke, one of its former grand wizards—and after the clashes between white supremacists and counterprotesters in Charlottesville, Virginia, in August, Duke in turn praised Trump's contentious claim that "both sides" were responsible for the violence. To Trump, whiteness is neither notional nor symbolic but is the very core of his power. In this, Trump is not singular. But whereas his forebears carried whiteness like an ancestral talisman, Trump cracked the glowing amulet open, releasing its eldritch energies. The repercussions are striking: Trump is the first president to have served in no public capacity before ascending to his perch. But more telling, Trump is also the first president to have publicly affirmed that his daughter is a "piece of ass." The mind seizes trying to imagine a black man extolling the virtues of sexual assault on tape ("When you're a star, they let you do it"), fending off multiple accusations of such assaults, immersed in multiple lawsuits for allegedly fraudulent business dealings, exhorting his followers to violence, and then strolling into the White House. But that is the point of white supremacy—to ensure that that which all others achieve with maximal effort, white people (particularly white men) achieve with minimal qualification. Barack Obama delivered to black people the hoary message that if they work twice as hard as white people, anything is possible. But Trump's counter is persuasive: Work half as hard as black people, and even more is possible.

For Trump, it almost seems that the fact of Obama, the fact of a black president, insulted him personally. The insult intensified when Obama and Seth Meyers publicly humiliated him at the White House Correspondents' Dinner in 2011. But the bloody heirloom ensures the last laugh. Replacing Obama is not enough—Trump has made the negation of Obama's legacy the foundation of his own. And this too is whiteness. "Race is an idea, not a fact," the historian Nell Irvin Painter has written, and essential to the construct of a "white race" is the idea of not being a nigger. Before Barack Obama, niggers could be manufactured out of Sister Souljahs, Willie Hortons, and Dusky Sallys. But Donald Trump arrived in the wake of something more potent—an entire nigger presidency with nigger health care, nigger climate accords, and nigger justice reform, all of which could be targeted for destruction or redemption, thus reifying the idea of being white. Trump truly is something new—the first president whose entire political existence hinges on the fact of a black president. And so it will not suffice to say that Trump is a white man like all the others who rose to become president. He must be called by his rightful honorific—America's first white president.

The scope of Trump's commitment to whiteness is matched only by the depth of popular disbelief in the power of whiteness. We are now being told that support for Trump's "Muslim ban," his scapegoating of immigrants, his defenses of police brutality are somehow the natural outgrowth of the cultural and economic gap between Lena Dunham's America and Jeff Foxworthy's. The collective verdict holds that the Democratic Party lost its way when it abandoned everyday economic issues like job creation for the softer fare of social justice. The indictment continues: To their neoliberal economics, Democrats and liberals have married a condescending elitist affect that sneers at blue-collar culture and mocks the white man as history's greatest monster and prime-time television's biggest doofus. In this rendition, Donald Trump is not the product of white supremacy so much as the product of a backlash against contempt for white working-class people. "We so obviously despise them, we so obviously condescend to them," the conservative social scientist Charles Murray, who co-wrote *The Bell Curve*, recently told the *New Yorker*, speaking of the white working class. "The only slur you can use at a dinner party and get away with is to call somebody a redneck—that won't give you any problems in Manhattan." "The utter contempt with which privileged Eastern liberals such as myself discuss red-state, gun-country, working-class America as ridiculous and morons and rubes," charged the celebrity chef Anthony Bourdain, "is largely responsible for the upswell of rage and contempt and desire to pull down the temple that we're seeing now."

That black people, who have lived for centuries under such derision and condescension, have not yet been driven into the arms of Trump does not trouble these theoreticians. After all, in this analysis, Trump's racism and the racism of his supporters are incidental to his rise. Indeed, the alleged glee with which liberals call out Trump's bigotry is assigned even more power than the bigotry itself. Ostensibly assaulted by campus protests, battered by arguments about intersectionality, and oppressed by new bathroom rights, a blameless white working class did the only thing any reasonable polity might: elect an orcish reality-television star who insists on taking his intelligence briefings in picture-book form.

Asserting that Trump's rise was primarily powered by cultural resentment and economic reversal has become de rigueur among white pundits and thought leaders. But evidence for this is, at best, mixed. In a study of preelection polling data, the Gallup researchers Jonathan Rothwell and Pablo Diego-Rosell found that "people living in areas with diminished economic opportunity" were "somewhat more likely to support Trump." But the researchers also found that voters in their study who supported Trump generally had a higher mean household income ($81,898) than those who did not ($77,046). Those who approved of Trump were "less likely to be unemployed and less likely to be employed part-time" than those who did not. They also tended to be from areas that were very white: "The racial and ethnic isolation of whites at the zip code level is one of the strongest predictors of Trump support."

An analysis of exit polls conducted during the presidential primaries estimated the median household income of Trump supporters to be about $72,000. But even this lower number is almost double the median household income of African Americans, and $15,000 above the American median. Trump's white support was not determined by income. According to Edison Research, Trump won whites making less than $50,000 by 20 points, whites making $50,000 to $99,999 by 28 points, and whites making $100,000 or more by 14 points. This shows that Trump assembled a broad white coalition that ran the gamut from Joe the Dishwasher to Joe the Plumber to Joe the Banker. So when white pundits cast the elevation of Trump as the handiwork of an inscrutable white working class, they are being too modest, declining to claim credit for their own economic class. Trump's dominance among whites across class lines is of a piece with his larger dominance across nearly every white demographic. Trump won white women (+9) and white men (+31). He won white people with college degrees (+3) and white people without them (+37). He won whites ages 18–29 (+4), 30–44 (+17), 45–64 (+28), and 65 and older (+19). Trump won whites in midwestern Illinois (+11), whites in mid-Atlantic New Jersey (+12), and whites in the Sun Belt's New Mexico (+5). In no state that Edison polled did Trump's white support dip below 40 percent. Hillary Clinton's did, in states as disparate as Florida, Utah, Indiana, and Kentucky. From the beer track to the wine track, from soccer moms to NASCAR dads, Trump's performance among whites was dominant. According to *Mother Jones*, based on preelection polling data, if you tallied the popular vote of only white America to derive 2016 electoral votes, Trump would have defeated Clinton 389 to 81, with the remaining 68 votes either a toss-up or unknown.

Part of Trump's dominance among whites resulted from his running as a Republican, the party that has long cultivated white voters. Trump's share of the white vote was similar to Mitt Romney's in 2012. But unlike Romney, Trump secured this support by running against his party's leadership, against accepted campaign orthodoxy, and against all notions of decency. By his sixth month in office, embroiled in scandal after scandal, a Pew Research Center poll found Trump's approval rating underwater with every single demographic group. Every demographic group, that is, except one: people who identified as white.

The focus on one subsector of Trump voters—the white working class—is puzzling, given the breadth of his white coalition. Indeed, there is a kind of theater at work in which Trump's presidency is pawned off as a product of the white working class as opposed to a product of an entire whiteness that includes the very authors doing the pawning. The motive is clear: escapism. To accept that the bloody heirloom remains potent even now, some five decades after Martin Luther King Jr. was gunned down on a Memphis balcony—even after a black president; indeed, strengthened by the fact of that black president—is to accept that racism remains, as it has since 1776, at the heart of this country's political life. The idea of acceptance frustrates the left. The left would much rather have a discussion about class struggles, which might entice the white working masses, instead of about the racist struggles that those same masses have historically been the agents and beneficiaries of. Moreover, to accept that whiteness brought us Donald Trump is to accept whiteness as an existential danger to the country and the world. But if the broad and remarkable white support for Donald Trump can be reduced to the righteous anger of a noble class of smallville firefighters and evangelicals, mocked by Brooklyn hipsters and womanist professors into voting against their interests, then the threat of racism and whiteness, the threat of the heirloom, can be dismissed. Consciences can be eased; no deeper existential reckoning is required.

This transfiguration is not novel. It is a return to form. The tightly intertwined stories of the white working class and black Americans go back to the prehistory of the United States—and the use of one as a cudgel to silence the claims of the other goes back nearly as far. Like the black working class, the white working class originated in bondage—the former in the lifelong bondage of slavery, the latter in the temporary bondage of indenture. In the early 17th century, these two classes were remarkably, though not totally, free of racist enmity. But by the 18th century, the country's master class had begun etching race into law while phasing out indentured servitude in favor of a more enduring labor solution. From these and other changes of law and economy, a bargain emerged: The descendants of indenture would enjoy the full benefits of whiteness, the most definitional benefit being that they would never sink to the level of the slave. But if the bargain protected white workers from slavery, it did not protect them from near-slave wages or backbreaking labor to attain them, and always there lurked a fear of having their benefits revoked. This early white working class "expressed soaring desires to be rid of the age-old inequalities of Europe and of any hint of slavery," according to David R. Roediger, a professor of American studies at the University of Kansas. "They also expressed the rather more pedestrian goal of simply not being mistaken for slaves, or 'negers' or 'negurs.'"

Roediger relates the experience, around 1807, of a British investor who made the mistake of asking a white maid in New England whether

her "master" was home. The maid admonished the investor, not merely for implying that she had a "master" and thus was a "sarvant" but for his basic ignorance of American hierarchy. "None but negers are sarvants," the maid is reported to have said. In law and economics and then in custom, a racist distinction not limited to the household emerged between the "help" (or the "freemen," or the white workers) and the "servants" (the "negers," the slaves). The former were virtuous and just, worthy of citizenship, progeny of Jefferson and, later, Jackson. The latter were servile and parasitic, dim-witted and lazy, the children of African savagery. But the dignity accorded to white labor was situational, dependent on the scorn heaped upon black labor—much as the honor accorded a "virtuous lady" was dependent on the derision directed at a "loose woman." And like chivalrous gentlemen who claim to honor the lady while raping the "whore," planters and their apologists could claim to honor white labor while driving the enslaved.

And so George Fitzhugh, a prominent 19th-century Southern pro-slavery intellectual, could in a single stroke deplore the exploitation of free whites' labor while defending the exploitation of enslaved blacks' labor. Fitzhugh attacked white capitalists as "cannibals," feeding off the labor of their fellow whites. The white workers were "'slaves without masters'; the little fish, who were food for all the larger." Fitzhugh inveighed against a "professional man" who'd "amassed a fortune" by exploiting his fellow whites. But whereas Fitzhugh imagined white workers as devoured by capital, he imagined black workers as elevated by enslavement. The slaveholder "provided for them, with almost parental affection"—even when the loafing slave "feigned to be unfit for labor." Fitzhugh proved too explicit—going so far as to argue that white laborers might be better off if enslaved. ("If white slavery be morally wrong," he wrote, "the Bible cannot be true.") Nevertheless, the argument that America's original sin was not deep-seated white supremacy but rather the exploitation of white labor by white capitalists—"white slavery"—proved durable. Indeed, the panic of white slavery lives on in our politics today. Black workers suffer because it was and is our lot. But when white workers suffer, something in nature has gone awry. And so an opioid epidemic among mostly white people is greeted with calls for compassion and treatment, as all epidemics should be, while a crack epidemic among mostly black people is greeted with scorn and mandatory minimums. Sympathetic op ed columns and articles are devoted to the plight of working-class whites when their life expectancy plummets to levels that, for blacks, society has simply accepted as normal. White slavery is sin. Nigger slavery is natural. This dynamic serves a very real purpose: the consistent awarding of grievance and moral high ground to that class of workers which, by the bonds of whiteness, stands closest to America's aristocratic class.

This is by design. Speaking in 1848, Senator John C. Calhoun saw slavery as the explicit foundation for a democratic union among whites, working and not:

> With us the two great divisions of society are not the rich and poor, but white and black; and all the former, the poor as well as the rich, belong to the upper class, and are respected and treated as equals.

On the eve of secession, Jefferson Davis, the eventual president of the Confederacy, pushed the idea further, arguing that such equality between the white working class and white oligarchs could not exist at all without black slavery:

> I say that the lower race of human beings that constitute the substratum of what is termed the slave population of the South, elevates every white man in our community. . . . It is the presence of a lower caste, those lower by their mental and physical organization, controlled by the higher intellect of the white man, that gives this superiority to the white laborer. Menial services are not there performed by the white man. We have none of our brethren sunk to the degradation of being menials. That belongs to the lower race—the descendants of Ham.

Southern intellectuals found a shade of agreement with Northern white reformers who, while not agreeing on slavery, agreed on the nature of the most tragic victim of emerging capitalism. "I was formerly like yourself, sir, a very warm advocate of the abolition of slavery," the labor reformer George Henry Evans argued in a letter to the abolitionist Gerrit Smith. "This was before I saw that there was white slavery." Evans was a putative ally of Smith and his fellow abolitionists. But still he asserted that "the landless white" was worse off than the enslaved black, who at least enjoyed "surety of support in sickness and old age."

Invokers of "white slavery" held that there was nothing unique in the enslavement of blacks when measured against the enslavement of all workers. What evil there was in enslavement resulted from its status as a subsidiary of the broader exploitation better seen among the country's noble laboring whites. Once the larger problem of white exploitation was solved, the dependent problem of black exploitation could be confronted or perhaps would fade away. Abolitionists focused on slavery were dismissed as "substitutionists" who wished to trade one form of slavery for another. "If I am less troubled concerning the Slavery prevalent in Charleston or New-Orleans," wrote the reformer Horace Greeley, "it is because I see so much Slavery in New-York, which appears to claim my first efforts."

Firsthand reports by white Union soldiers who witnessed actual slavery during the Civil War rendered the "white slavery" argument ridiculous. But its operating premises—white labor as noble archetype, and black labor as something else—lived on. This was a matter of rhetoric, not fact. The noble-white-labor archetype did not give white workers immunity from capitalism. It could not, in itself, break monopolies, alleviate white poverty in Appalachia or the South, or bring a decent wage to immigrant ghettos in the North. But the model for America's original identity politics was set. Black lives literally did not matter and could be cast aside altogether as the price of even incremental gains for the white masses. It was this juxtaposition that allowed Theodore Bilbo to campaign for the Senate in the 1930s as someone who would "raise the same kind of hell as President Roosevelt" and later endorse lynching black people to keep them from voting.

The juxtaposition between the valid and even virtuous interests of the "working class" and the invalid and pathological interests of black Americans was not the province merely of blatant white supremacists like Bilbo. The acclaimed scholar, liberal hero, and future senator Daniel Patrick Moynihan, in his time working for President Richard Nixon, approvingly quoted Nixon's formulation of the white working class: "A new voice" was beginning to make itself felt in the country. "It is a voice that has been silent too long," Nixon claimed, alluding to working-class whites. "It is a voice of people who have not taken to the streets before, who have not indulged in violence, who have not broken the law."

It had been only 18 years since the Cicero riots; eight years since Daisy and Bill Myers had been run out of Levittown, Pennsylvania; three years since Martin Luther King Jr. had been stoned while walking through Chicago's Marquette Park. But as the myth of the virtuous white working class was made central to American identity, its sins needed to be rendered invisible. The fact was, working-class whites had been agents of racist terrorism since at least the draft riots of 1863; terrorism could not be neatly separated from the racist animus found in every class of whites. Indeed, in the era of lynching, the daily newspapers often whipped up the fury of the white masses by invoking the last species of property that all white men held in common—white women. But to conceal the breadth of white racism, these racist outbursts were often disregarded or treated not as racism but as the unfortunate side effect of legitimate grievances against capital. By focusing on that sympathetic laboring class, the sins of whiteness itself were, and are still being, evaded.

When David Duke, the former grand wizard of the Ku Klux Klan, shocked the country in 1990 by almost winning one of Louisiana's seats in the U.S. Senate, the apologists came out once again. They elided the obvious—that Duke had appealed to the racist instincts of a state whose schools are, at this very moment, still desegregating—and instead decided that something else was afoot. "There is a tremendous amount of anger and frustration among working-class whites, particularly where there is an economic downturn," a researcher told the *Los Angeles Times*. "These people feel left out; they feel government is not responsive to them." By this logic, postwar America—with its booming economy and low unemployment—should have been an egalitarian utopia and not the violently segregated country it actually was.

But this was the past made present. It was not important to the apologists that a large swath of Louisiana's white population thought it was a good idea to send a white supremacist who once fronted a terrorist organization to the nation's capital. Nor was it important that blacks in Louisiana had long felt left out. What was important was the fraying of an ancient bargain, and the potential degradation of white workers to the level of "negers." "A viable left must find a way to differentiate itself strongly from such analysis," David Roediger, the University of Kansas professor, has written.

That challenge of differentiation has largely been ignored. Instead, an imagined white working class remains central to our politics and to our cultural understanding of those politics, not simply when it comes to addressing broad economic issues but also when it comes to addressing

racism. At its most sympathetic, this belief holds that most Americans—
regardless of race—are exploited by an unfettered capitalist economy.
The key, then, is to address those broader patterns that afflict the masses
of all races; the people who suffer from those patterns more than others
(blacks, for instance) will benefit disproportionately from that which
benefits everyone. "These days, what ails working-class and middle-class
blacks and Latinos is not fundamentally different from what ails their
white counterparts," Senator Barack Obama wrote in 2006:

> Downsizing, outsourcing, automation, wage stagnation, the
> dismantling of employer-based health-care and pension plans,
> and schools that fail to teach young people the skills they need to
> compete in a global economy.

Obama allowed that "blacks in particular have been vulnerable to these
trends"—but less because of racism than for reasons of geography and job-
sector distribution. This notion—raceless antiracism—marks the modern
left, from the New Democrat Bill Clinton to the socialist Bernie Sanders.
Few national liberal politicians have shown any recognition that there is
something systemic and particular in the relationship between black people
and their country that might require specific policy solutions.

In 2016, Hillary Clinton acknowledged the existence of systemic racism more explicitly than any of her modern Democratic predecessors.
She had to—black voters remembered too well the previous Clinton
administration, as well as her previous campaign. While her husband's
administration had touted the rising-tide theory of economic growth,
it did so while slashing welfare and getting "tough on crime," a phrase
that stood for specific policies but also served as rhetorical bait for white
voters. One is tempted to excuse Hillary Clinton from having to answer
for the sins of her husband. But in her 2008 campaign, she evoked the
old dichotomy between white workers and loafing blacks, claiming to
be the representative of "hardworking Americans, white Americans."
By the end of the 2008 primary campaign against Barack Obama, her
advisers were hoping someone would uncover an apocryphal "whitey
tape," in which an angry Michelle Obama was alleged to have used the
slur. During Bill Clinton's presidential-reelection campaign in the mid-
1990s, Hillary Clinton herself had endorsed the "super-predator" theory
of William J. Bennett, John P. Walters, and John J. DiIulio Jr. This theory

cast "inner-city" children of that era as "almost completely unmoralized" and the font of "a new generation of street criminals . . . the youngest, biggest and baddest generation any society has ever known." The "baddest generation" did not become super-predators. But by 2016, they were young adults, many of whom judged Hillary Clinton's newfound consciousness to be lacking.

It's worth asking why the country has not been treated to a raft of sympathetic portraits of this "forgotten" young black electorate, forsaken by a Washington bought off by Davos elites and special interests. The unemployment rate for young blacks (20.6 percent) in July 2016 was double that of young whites (9.9 percent). And since the late 1970s, William Julius Wilson and other social scientists following in his wake have noted the disproportionate effect that the decline in manufacturing jobs has had on African American communities. If anyone should be angered by the devastation wreaked by the financial sector and a government that declined to prosecute the perpetrators, it is African Americans—the housing crisis was one of the primary drivers in the past 20 years of the wealth gap between black families and the rest of the country. But the cultural condescension toward and economic anxiety of black people is not news. Toiling blacks are in their proper state; toiling whites raise the specter of white slavery.

Moreover, a narrative of long-neglected working-class black voters, injured by globalization and the financial crisis, forsaken by out-of-touch politicians, and rightfully suspicious of a return of Clintonism, does not serve to cleanse the conscience of white people for having elected Donald Trump. Only the idea of a long-suffering white working class can do that. And though much has been written about the distance between elites and "Real America," the existence of a class-transcending, mutually dependent tribe of white people is evident.

Joe Biden, then the vice president, last year:

> "They're all the people I grew up with. . . . And they're not racist. They're not sexist."

Bernie Sanders, senator and former candidate for president, last year:

> "I come from the white working class, and I am deeply humiliated that the Democratic Party cannot talk to the people where I came from."

Nicholas Kristof, *New York Times* columnist, in February of this year:

> "My hometown, Yamhill, Ore., a farming community, is Trump
> country, and I have many friends who voted for Trump. I think
> they're profoundly wrong, but please don't dismiss them as hateful
> bigots."

These claims of origin and fidelity are not merely elite defenses of an
aggrieved class but also a sweeping dismissal of the concerns of those
who don't share kinship with white men. "You can't eat equality," asserts
Joe Biden—a statement worthy of someone unthreatened by the loss of
wages brought on by an unwanted pregnancy, a background-check box
at the bottom of a job application, or the deportation of a breadwin-
ner. Within a week of Sanders lambasting Democrats for not speaking
to "the people" where he "came from," he was making an example of a
woman who dreamed of representing the people where she came from.
Confronted with a young woman who hoped to become the second
Latina senator in American history, Sanders responded with a parody
of the Clinton campaign: "It is not good enough for someone to say,
'I'm a woman! Vote for me!' No, that's not good enough. . . . One of the
struggles that you're going to be seeing in the Democratic Party is whether
we go beyond identity politics." The upshot—attacking one specimen of
identity politics after having invoked another—was unfortunate.

Other Sanders appearances proved even more alarming. On MSNBC,
he attributed Trump's success, in part, to his willingness to "not be politically correct." Sanders admitted that Trump had "said some outrageous
and painful things, but I think people are tired of the same old, same
old political rhetoric." Pressed on the definition of political correctness,
Sanders gave an answer Trump surely would have approved of. "What
it means is you have a set of talking points which have been poll-tested
and focus-group-tested," Sanders explained. "And that's what you say
rather than what's really going on. And often, what you are not allowed
to say are things which offend very, very powerful people."

This definition of political correctness was shocking coming from a
politician of the left. But it matched a broader defense of Trump voters.
"Some people think that the people who voted for Trump are racists and
sexists and homophobes and just deplorable folks," Sanders said later. "I
don't agree." This is not exculpatory. Certainly not every Trump voter

is a white supremacist, just as not every white person in the Jim Crow South was a white supremacist. But every Trump voter felt it acceptable to hand the fate of the country over to one.

One can, to some extent, understand politicians' embracing a self-serving identity politics. Candidates for high office, such as Sanders, have to cobble together a coalition. The white working class is seen, understandably, as a large cache of potential votes, and capturing these votes requires eliding uncomfortable truths. But journalists have no such excuse. Again and again in the past year, Nicholas Kristof could be found pleading with his fellow liberals not to dismiss his old comrades in the white working class as bigots—even when their bigotry was evidenced in his own reporting. A visit to Tulsa, Oklahoma, finds Kristof wondering why Trump voters support a president who threatens to cut the programs they depend on. But the problem, according to Kristof's interviewees, isn't Trump's attack on benefits so much as an attack on their benefits. "There's a lot of wasteful spending, so cut other places," one man tells Kristof. When Kristof pushes his subjects to identify that wasteful spending, a fascinating target is revealed: "Obama phones," the products of a fevered conspiracy theory that turned a long-standing government program into a scheme through which the then-president gave away free cellphones to undeserving blacks. Kristof doesn't shift his analysis based on this comment and, aside from a one-sentence fact-check tucked between parentheses, continues on as though it were never said.

Observing a Trump supporter in the act of deploying racism does not much perturb Kristof. That is because his defenses of the innate goodness of Trump voters and of the innate goodness of the white working class are in fact defenses of neither. On the contrary, the white working class functions rhetorically not as a real community of people so much as a tool to quiet the demands of those who want a more inclusive America.

Mark Lilla's *New York Times* essay "The End of Identity Liberalism," published not long after last year's election, is perhaps the most profound example of this genre. Lilla denounces the perversion of liberalism into "a kind of moral panic about racial, gender and sexual identity," which distorted liberalism's message "and prevented it from becoming a unifying force capable of governing." Liberals have turned away from their working-class base, he says, and must look to the "pre-identity liberalism" of Bill Clinton and Franklin D. Roosevelt. You would never know from this essay that Bill Clinton was one of the most skillful identity politicians of his era—flying home to Arkansas to see a black man, the lobotomized Ricky Ray Rector, executed; upstaging Jesse Jackson at his own conference; signing the Defense of Marriage Act. Nor would you know that the "pre-identity" liberal champion Roosevelt depended on the literally lethal identity politics of the white-supremacist "solid South." The name Barack Obama does not appear in Lilla's essay, and he never attempts to grapple, one way or another, with the fact that it was identity politics—the possibility of the first black president—that brought a record number of black voters to the polls, winning the election for the Democratic Party, and thus enabling the deliverance of the ancient liberal goal of national health care. "Identity politics . . . is largely expressive, not persuasive," Lilla claims. "Which is why it never wins elections—but can lose them." That Trump ran and won on identity politics is beyond Lilla's powers of conception. What appeals to the white working class is ennobled. What appeals to black workers, and all others outside the tribe, is dastardly identitarianism. All politics are identity politics—except the politics of white people, the politics of the bloody heirloom.

White tribalism haunts even more-nuanced writers. George Packer's *New Yorker* essay "The Unconnected" is a lengthy plea for liberals to focus more on the white working class, a population that "has succumbed to the ills that used to be associated with the black urban 'underclass.'" Packer believes that these ills, and the Democratic Party's failure to respond to them, explain much of Trump's rise. Packer offers no opinion polls to weigh white workers' views on "elites," much less their views on racism. He offers no sense of how their views and their relationship to Trump differ from other workers' and other whites'.

That is likely because any empirical evaluation of the relationship between Trump and the white working class would reveal that one adjective in that phrase is doing more work than the other. In 2016, Trump enjoyed majority or plurality support among every economic branch of whites. It is true that his strongest support among whites came from those making $50,000 to $99,999. This would be something more than working-class in many nonwhite neighborhoods, but even if one accepts that branch as the working class, the difference between how various groups in this income bracket voted is revealing. Sixty-one percent of whites in this "working class" supported Trump. Only 24 percent of Hispanics and 11 percent of blacks did. Indeed, the plurality of all voters making less than $100,000 and the majority making less than $50,000 voted for the Democratic candidate. So when Packer laments the fact that "Democrats can no longer really claim to be the party of working people—not white ones, anyway," he commits a kind of category error. The real problem is that Democrats aren't the party of white people—working or otherwise. White workers are not divided by the fact of labor from other white demographics; they are divided from all other laborers by the fact of their whiteness.

Packer's essay was published before the election, and so the vote tally was not available. But it should not be surprising that a Republican candidate making a direct appeal to racism would drive up the numbers among white voters, given that racism has been a dividing line for the national parties since the civil-rights era. Packer finds inspiration for his thesis in West Virginia—a state that remained Democratic through the 1990s before turning decisively Republican, at least at the level of presidential politics. This relatively recent rightward movement evinces, to Packer, a shift "that couldn't be attributed just to the politics of race." This is likely true—the politics of race are, themselves, never attributable "just to the politics of race." The history of slavery is also about the growth of international capitalism; the history of lynching must be seen in light of anxiety over the growing independence of women; the civil-rights movement can't be disentangled from the Cold War. Thus, to say that the rise of Donald Trump is about more than race is to make an empty statement, one that is small comfort to the people—black, Muslim, immigrant—who live under racism's boot.

The dent of racism is not hard to detect in West Virginia. In the 2008 Democratic primary there, 95 percent of the voters were white. Twenty percent of those—one in five—openly admitted that race was influencing their vote, and more than 80 percent voted for Hillary Clinton over Barack Obama. Four years later, the incumbent Obama lost the primary in 10 counties to Keith Judd, a white felon incarcerated in a federal prison; Judd racked up more than 40 percent of the Democratic-primary vote in the state. A simple thought experiment: Can one imagine a black felon in a federal prison running in a primary against an incumbent white president doing so well?

But racism occupies a mostly passive place in Packer's essay. There's no attempt to understand why black and brown workers, victimized by the same new economy and cosmopolitan elite that Packer lambastes, did not join the Trump revolution. Like Kristof, Packer is gentle with his subjects. When a woman "exploded" and told Packer, "I want to eat what I want to eat, and for them to tell me I can't eat French fries or Coca-Cola—no way," he sees this as a rebellion against "the moral superiority of elites." In fact, this elite conspiracy dates back to 1894, when the government first began advising Americans on their diets. As recently as 2002, President George W. Bush launched the Healthier US initiative, urging Americans to exercise and eat healthy food. But Packer never allows himself to wonder whether the explosion he witnessed had anything to do with the fact that similar advice now came from the country's first black first lady. Packer concludes that Obama was leaving the country "more divided and angrier than most Americans can remember," a statement that is likely true only because most Americans identify as white. Certainly the men and women forced to live in the wake of the beating of John Lewis, the lynching of Emmett Till, the firebombing of Percy Julian's home, and the assassinations of Martin Luther King Jr. and Medgar Evers would disagree.

The triumph of Trump's campaign of bigotry presented the problematic spectacle of an American president succeeding at best in spite of his racism and possibly because of it. Trump moved racism from the euphemistic and plausibly deniable to the overt and freely claimed. This presented the country's thinking class with a dilemma. Hillary Clinton simply could not be correct when she asserted that a large group of Americans was endorsing a candidate because of bigotry. The implications— that systemic bigotry is still central to our politics; that the country is susceptible to such bigotry; that the salt-of-the-earth Americans whom we lionize in our culture and politics are not so different from those same Americans who grin back at us in lynching photos; that Calhoun's aim of a pan-Caucasian embrace between workers and capitalists still endures—were just too dark. Leftists would have to cope with the failure, yet again, of class unity in the face of racism. Incorporating all of this into an analysis of America and the path forward proved too much to ask.

Instead, the response has largely been an argument aimed at emotion—the summoning of the white working class, emblem of America's hardscrabble roots, inheritor of its pioneer spirit, as a shield against the horrific and empirical evidence of trenchant bigotry.

Packer dismisses the Democratic Party as a coalition of "rising professionals and diversity." The dismissal is derived from, of all people, Lawrence Summers, the former Harvard president and White House economist, who last year labeled the Democratic Party "a coalition of the cosmopolitan elite and diversity." The inference is that the party has forgotten how to speak on hard economic issues and prefers discussing presumably softer cultural issues such as "diversity." It's worth unpacking what, precisely, falls under this rubric of "diversity"—resistance to the monstrous incarceration of legions of black men, resistance to the destruction of health providers for poor women, resistance to the effort to deport parents, resistance to a policing whose sole legitimacy is rooted in brute force, resistance to a theory of education that preaches "no excuses" to black and brown children, even as excuses are proffered for mendacious corporate executives "too big to jail." That this suite of concerns, taken together, can be dismissed by both an elite economist like Summers and a brilliant journalist like Packer as "diversity" simply reveals the safe space they enjoy. Because of their identity.

When Barack Obama came into office, in 2009, he believed that he could work with "sensible" conservatives by embracing aspects of their policy as his own. Instead he found that his very imprimatur made that impossible. Senate Minority Leader Mitch McConnell announced that the GOP's primary goal was not to find common ground but to make Obama a "one-term president." A health-care plan inspired by Romneycare was, when proposed by Obama, suddenly considered socialist and, not coincidentally, a form of reparations. The first black president found that he was personally toxic to the GOP base. An entire political party was organized around the explicit aim of negating one man. It was thought by Obama and some of his allies that this toxicity was the result of a relentless assault waged by Fox News and right-wing talk radio. Trump's genius was to see that it was something more, that it was a hunger for revanche so strong that a political novice and accused rapist could topple the leadership of one major party and throttle the heavily favored nominee of the other.

"I could stand in the middle of Fifth Avenue and shoot somebody and I wouldn't lose any voters," Trump bragged in January 2016. This statement should be met with only a modicum of skepticism. Trump has mocked the disabled, withstood multiple accusations of sexual violence (all of which he has denied), fired an FBI director, sent his minions to mislead the public about his motives, personally exposed those lies by boldly stating his aim to scuttle an investigation into his possible collusion with a foreign power, then bragged about that same obstruction to representatives of that same foreign power. It is utterly impossible to conjure a black facsimile of Donald Trump—to imagine Obama, say, implicating an opponent's father in the assassination of an American president or comparing his physical endowment with that of another candidate and then successfully capturing the presidency. Trump, more than any other politician, understood the valence of the bloody heirloom and the great power in not being a nigger.

But the power is ultimately suicidal. Trump evinces this, too. In a recent *New Yorker* article, a former Russian military officer pointed out that interference in an election could succeed only where "necessary conditions" and an "existing background" were present. In America, that "existing background" was a persistent racism, and the "necessary condition" was a black president. The two related factors hobbled America's ability to safeguard its electoral system. As late as July 2016, a majority of Republican voters doubted that Barack Obama had been born in the United States, which is to say they did not view him as a legitimate president. Republican politicians acted accordingly, infamously denying his final Supreme Court nominee a hearing and then, fatefully, refusing to work with the administration to defend the country against the Russian attack. Before the election, Obama found no takers among Republicans for a bipartisan response, and Obama himself, underestimating Trump and thus underestimating the power of whiteness, believed the Republican nominee too objectionable to actually win. In this Obama was, tragically, wrong. And so the most powerful country in the world has handed over all its affairs—the prosperity of its entire economy; the security of its 300 million citizens; the purity of its water, the viability of its air, the safety of its food; the future of its vast system of education; the soundness of its national highways, airways, and railways; the apocalyptic potential of its nuclear arsenal—to a carnival barker who introduced the phrase grab 'em by the pussy into the national lexicon. It is as if the white tribe united in demonstration to say, "If a black man can be president, then any white man—no matter how fallen—can be president." And in that perverse way, the democratic dreams of Jefferson and Jackson were fulfilled.

The American tragedy now being wrought is larger than most imagine and will not end with Trump. In recent times, whiteness as an overt political tactic has been restrained by a kind of cordiality that held that its overt invocation would scare off "moderate" whites. This has proved to be only half true at best. Trump's legacy will be exposing the patina of decency for what it is and revealing just how much a demagogue can get away with. It does not take much to imagine another politician, wiser in the ways of Washington and better schooled in the methodology of governance—and now liberated from the pretense of antiracist civility—doing a much more effective job than Trump.

It has long been an axiom among certain black writers and thinkers that while whiteness endangers the bodies of black people in the immediate sense, the larger threat is to white people themselves, the shared country, and even the whole world. There is an impulse to blanch at this sort of grandiosity. When W.E.B. Du Bois claims that slavery was "singularly disastrous for modern civilization" or James Baldwin claims that whites "have brought humanity to the edge of oblivion: because they think they are white," the instinct is to cry exaggeration. But there really is no other way to read the presidency of Donald Trump. The first white president in American history is also the most dangerous president—and he is made more dangerous still by the fact that those charged with analyzing him cannot name his essential nature, because they too are implicated in it.

"Making America White Again"

Toni Morrison

(2016)

The choices made by white men, who are prepared to abandon their humanity out of fear of black men and women, suggest the true horror of lost status.

This is a serious project. All immigrants to the United States know (and knew) that if they want to become real, authentic Americans they must reduce their fealty to their native country and regard it as secondary, subordinate, in order to emphasize their whiteness. Unlike any nation in Europe, the United States holds whiteness as the unifying force. Here, for many people, the definition of "Americanness" is color.

Under slave laws, the necessity for color rankings was obvious, but in America today, post-civil-rights legislation, white people's conviction of their natural superiority is being lost. Rapidly lost. There are "people of color" everywhere, threatening to erase this long-understood definition of America. And what then? Another black President? A predominantly black Senate? Three black Supreme Court Justices? The threat is frightening.

In order to limit the possibility of this untenable change, and restore whiteness to its former status as a marker of national identity, a number of white Americans are sacrificing themselves. They have begun to do things they clearly don't really want to be doing, and, to do so, they are (1) abandoning their sense of human dignity and (2) risking the appearance of cowardice. Much as they may hate their behavior, and know full well how craven it is, they are willing to kill small children attending Sunday school and slaughter churchgoers who invite a white boy to pray. Embarrassing as the obvious display of cowardice must be, they are willing to set fire to churches, and to start firing in them while the members are at prayer. And, shameful as such demonstrations of weakness are, they are willing to shoot black children in the street.

To keep alive the perception of white superiority, these white Americans tuck their heads under cone-shaped hats and American flags and deny themselves the dignity of face-to-face confrontation, training their guns on the unarmed, the innocent, the scared, on subjects who are running away, exposing their unthreatening backs to bullets. Surely, shooting a fleeing man in the back hurts the presumption of white strength? The sad plight of grown white men, crouching beneath their (better) selves, to slaughter the innocent during traffic stops, to push black women's faces into the dirt, to handcuff black children. Only the frightened would do that. Right?

These sacrifices, made by supposedly tough white men, who are prepared to abandon their humanity out of fear of black men and women, suggest the true horror of lost status.

It may be hard to feel pity for the men who are making these bizarre sacrifices in the name of white power and supremacy. Personal debasement is not easy for white people (especially for white men), but to retain the conviction of their superiority to others—especially to black people—they are willing to risk contempt, and to be reviled by the mature, the sophisticated, and the strong. If it weren't so ignorant and pitiful, one could mourn this collapse of dignity in service to an evil cause.

The comfort of being "naturally better than," of not having to struggle or demand civil treatment, is hard to give up. The confidence that you will not be watched in a department store, that you are the preferred customer in high-end restaurants—these social inflections, belonging to whiteness, are greedily relished.

So scary are the consequences of a collapse of white privilege that many Americans have flocked to a political platform that supports and translates violence against the defenseless as strength. These people are not so much angry as terrified, with the kind of terror that makes knees tremble.

On Election Day, how eagerly so many white voters—both the poorly educated and the well educated—embraced the shame and fear sowed by Donald Trump. The candidate whose company has been sued by the Justice Department for not renting apartments to black people. The candidate who questioned whether Barack Obama was born in the United States, and who seemed to condone the beating of a Black Lives Matter protester at a campaign rally. The candidate who kept black workers off the floors of his casinos. The candidate who is beloved by David Duke and endorsed by the Ku Klux Klan.

William Faulkner understood this better than almost any other American writer. In "Absalom, Absalom," incest is less of a taboo for an upper-class Southern family than acknowledging the one drop of black blood that would clearly soil the family line. Rather than lose its "whiteness" (once again), the family chooses murder.

"What Is Whiteness?"

Nell Irvin Painter

(2015)

The terrorist attack in Charleston, S.C., an atrocity like so many other shameful episodes in American history, has overshadowed the drama of Rachel A. Dolezal's yearslong passing for black. And for good reason: Hateful mass murder is, of course, more consequential than one woman's fiction. But the two are connected in a way that is relevant to many Americans.

An essential problem here is the inadequacy of white identity. Everyone loves to talk about blackness, a fascinating thing. But bring up whiteness and fewer people want to talk about it. Whiteness is on a toggle switch between "bland nothingness" and "racist hatred."

On one side is Dylann Storm Roof, the 21-year-old charged with murdering nine people at the Emanuel African Methodist Episcopal Church in Charleston on Wednesday. He's part of a very old racist tradition, stretching from the anti-black violence following the Civil War, through the 1915 movie "The Birth of a Nation," to today's white nationalists, neo-Nazis, and gun-toting, apocalyptically minded Obama-haters. And now a mass murderer in a church.

On the other side is Ms. Dolezal, the former leader of the Spokane, Wash., chapter of the N.A.A.C.P., who, it seems, mistakenly believed that she could not be both anti-racist and white. Faced with her assumed choice between a blank identity or a malevolent one, she opted out of whiteness altogether. Notwithstanding the confusion and anger she has stirred, she continues to say that she identifies as black. Fine. But why, we wonder, did she pretend to be black?

Our search for understanding in matters of race automatically inclines us toward blackness, although that is not where these answers lie. It has become a common observation that blackness, and race more generally, is a social construct. But examining whiteness as a social construct offers more answers. The essential problem is the inadequacy of white identity.

We don't know the history of whiteness, and therefore are ignorant of the many ways it has changed over the years. If you investigate that history, you'll see that white identity has been no more stable than black identity. While we recognize the evolution of "negro" to "colored" to "Negro" to "Afro-American" to "African-American," we draw a blank when it comes to whiteness. To the contrary, whiteness has a history of multiplicity.

Constructions of whiteness have changed over time, shifting to accommodate the demands of social change. Before the mid-19th century, the existence of more than one white race was commonly accepted, in popular culture and scholarship. Indeed, there were several. Many people in the United States were seen as white—and could vote (if they were adult white men)—but were nonetheless classified as inferior (or superior) white races. Irish-Americans present one example.

In the mid- to late-19th century, the existence of several white races was widely assumed: notably, the superior Saxons and the inferior Celts. Each race—and they were called races—had its characteristic racial temperament. "Temperament" has been and still is a crucial facet of racial classification since its 18th-century Linnaean origins. Color has always been only one part of it (as the case of Ms. Dolezal shows).

In the 19th century, the Saxon race was said to be intelligent, energetic, sober, Protestant and beautiful. Celts, in contrast, were said to be stupid, impulsive, drunken, Catholic and ugly.

The mass immigration that followed the Irish famine of the 1840s inflamed nativist, anti-Catholic bigotry that flourished through the end of the century. Then new waves of poor Eastern and Southern European immigrants arrived, inspiring new racial classifications: the "Northern Italian" race, the "Southern Italian" race, the "Eastern European Hebrew" race, and so on. Their heads were measured and I.Q.s assessed to quantify (and, later, to deny) racial difference. They were all white, members of white races. But, like the Irish before them, the Italians and Jews and Greeks were classified as inferior white races.

By the early 20th century, the descendants of the earlier Irish immigrants had successfully elevated Celts into the superior realm of northern Europeans.

Meanwhile, World War I dampened Americans' ardor for "Saxon"—given its German associations—and increased the popularity of a new term liberated from Germanic associations. The new name was "Nordic." Many German-Americans even altered their surnames during and after the war, but the notion of plural white races held on until World War II.

By the 1940s anthropologists announced that they had a new classification: white, Asian and black were the only real races. Each was unitary—no sub-races existed within each group. There was one Negroid race, one Mongoloid race, one Caucasoid race. Everyone considered white was the same as everyone else considered white. No Saxons. No Celts. No Southern Italians. No Eastern European Hebrews. This classification—however tattered—lives on, with mild alterations, even today.

The useful part of white identity's vagueness is that whites don't have to shoulder the burden of race in America, which, at the least, is utterly exhausting. A neutral racial identity is blandly uninteresting. In the 1970s, long after they had been accepted as "white," Italians, Irish, Greeks, Jews and others proclaimed themselves "ethnic" Americans in order to forge a positive identity, at a time of "black is beautiful." But this ethnic self-discovery did not alter the fact that whiteness continued to be defined, as before, primarily by what it isn't: blackness.

Ms. Dolezal seems to have believed that the choice to devote one's life to fighting racism meant choosing black or white, Negroid or Caucasoid. Black was clearly more captivating than a whiteness characterized by hate.

We lack more meaningful senses of white identity, even though some whites, throughout history, have been committed to fighting racism and advocating for social justice. In the 19th century, abolitionists like William Lloyd Garrison and John Brown helped end slavery. In the early 20th century, Mary White Ovington helped found the N.A.A.C.P. Lillian Smith depicted the South's nexus of "sin, sex, segregation" in her writings. White Communists, priests and rabbis stood beside the Rev. Dr. Martin Luther King Jr. during the civil rights movement. Where would America be without these white allies of black freedom fighters?

Given that the monolithic definition of whiteness is antithetical to social justice, perhaps we should encourage a rebellion against it. Just as blacks and whites joined together as "abolitionists" to bring down American slavery in the 19th century, anti-racist whites in the 1990s called themselves "race traitors," believing that social justice for all demands treason against white supremacy.

Eliminating the binary definition of whiteness—the toggle between nothingness and awfulness—is essential for a new racial vision that ethical people can share across the color line. Just as race has been reinvented over the centuries, let's repurpose the term "abolitionist" as more than just a hashtag. The "abolition" of white privilege can be an additional component of identity (not a replacement for it), one that embeds social justice in its meaning. Even more, it unifies people of many races.

9

Where Do We Go from Here?

PREPARATION FOR SESSION 9

Rewrite or add to your racial autobiography based on what you've discovered during this course. This time, spend more time attending to your formation into Whiteness. The personal racial history of our life did not begin when we first encountered a person of color. We were all assigned White at birth by parents, grandparents, family, friends, communities, pastors, churches, teachers, schools, books, movies, and television shows that formed us in Whiteness. Again, the goal is not to be comprehensive but to create a basic timeline using short stories and vignettes as snapshots of your most memorable experiences and discoveries of race at different points throughout your life.

This rewritten autobiography should include your early formative experiences of race—perceptions and perspectives on race you inherited from your family of origin and childhood; experiences with race in school, extracurricular activities, work, church; and the emergence of your self-awareness of your own race.

Writing our racial autobiographies is one of the most important and practical tools for engaging in the deep inner work of confronting Whiteness. Consider your racial autobiography an ongoing work. The most powerful racial autobiographies will serve you for the rest of your life as a living spiritual document. Please continue to add stories long after the course is completed, and consider sharing them with your families and friends.

RENEWING BAPTISMAL COVENANTS
TO RENOUNCE WHITENESS

The baptismal rite in the *Roman Ritual* preserves three questions that are among the earliest practices of the church. A celebrant asks a candidate for baptism, "Do you renounce Satan? And all his works? And all his attractions?" The candidate replies, "I renounce Satan and his works and his attractions." This formal renunciation of evil goes back to the very beginnings of organized Christian worship and continues in some form in most baptismal vows to this day.

If Whiteness is an evil lie, idolatry, and a false religion that terrorizes and possesses people like a demonic principality or power, then should we not renounce Whiteness at our baptisms? In a class at Duke Divinity School, theologian Willie James Jennings once said that when pastors of White-dominant churches baptize children who were assigned White at birth, as they come up out of the water they should say, "You are no longer White, you are now a Christian." Theologian J. Kameron Carter echoed this call when he wrote:

> Is this not the baptismal calling, sustained by the Eucharist real-
> ity of Christ's Jewish flesh, to exit the ways in which whiteness
> has crafted an intellectual, socio-economic, political, and, even,
> a "pseudotheological" reality for us to inhabit? Oh, for the day
> when after a child's baptism the minister or priest might utter the
> words, "Having been baptized, having left Ur of the Chaldees, I
> now declare you no longer white!"[1]

What would it mean for each of us to reaffirm or remember our baptisms by renouncing Whiteness? We can proclaim, "I renounce White-ness and all its works and its attractions and its worship and its angels and its inventions and all things that are under it!" Or, modifying the baptismal vows of the Methodist tradition, we can proclaim: "I renounce the spiritual forces of Whiteness, reject the evil power of Whiteness in this world, and I repent of my sin. I accept the freedom and power God gives me to resist Whiteness, injustice, and oppression in whatever forms

---

[1] J. Kameron Carter, "Whiteness as a False Reality: The Baptismal Identity of 'The Now, But Not Yet,'" *Comment* online, September 15, 2006.

they present themselves." Our baptismal vows form a covenant between us and God and us and our neighbors.

Spend some time in meditation remembering and reaffirming your baptismal vows by renouncing Whiteness and all its works in the world. Then write a covenant with God and your neighbors describing the ways you are going to live into this covenant with great courage and curiosity. Be sure to include what you imagine your responsibility is to God and neighbor as well as what you expect their responsibility is to you. Once you've completed your covenant, offer a prayer, a song, an image, or a symbol to represent the covenant and consecrate the agreement in your own unique ritual. Who or what will hold you accountable for the covenant you have made? Consider adding the accountability element as a sign and a seal of your intention to fulfill the obligations of the vows that you have made.

Conclusion

From Color-Blind Racism to Responsibility

Congratulations! You have completed the journey of *Confronting White-ness*. This work can feel like walking through hell, which makes sense because Whiteness is hellacious. For people assigned Whiteness, looking at ourselves through the eyes of people of color is never easy. It is often extremely heart-wrenching and exhausting, especially because we have been trapped in an insidious lie that we have profited from while the same lie has harmed so many others. Of course, nothing worth doing is ever easy. We can't overcome four hundred years of systemic racism and oppression by reading a book or saying a prayer. It will require tremendous effort and labor for many years. Completing the *Confronting Whiteness* course is both an ending and a new beginning. It marks the end of this stage of the journey but the beginning of a lifelong journey. Whiteness is not only an ideology that needs to be confronted; it must be divested from and dismantled. If you have not yet realized that this process will require hard work and constant vigilance for the rest of your life, then you haven't yet completed the course. Confronting Whiteness is a lifelong calling.

Many people who have completed the course have described the journey as the deepest and most profound examination of their own racial identity. Others have described the experience as a complete worldview shift, a spiritual conversion, a rude awakening, a transfor-mation, a reckoning, an intervention, or a diagnosis of cancer. In every case we are not the same people we were when we began the journey. We are different. We are being made new. This change is important on its own, but if it is to make an impact on the Whiteness that pervades our world with injustice and evil, then the change we've experienced demands something of us. A new theory requires new practices. A new worldview necessitates a new rule of life. We must show up differently and live more courageously.

241

As we conclude this journey and begin the one that will take the rest of our lives, we must each ask, "What am I going to do in my sphere of influence and power?" First, we must spend some time in discernment to discover what our sphere of power and influence is (family, neighborhood, church, religious community, school, work, city, non-profit boards). Once we discover our sphere of influence, we understand where our power can make a difference in the world. However, the stakes get higher when we move from learning about racial justice to trying to live an anti-racist life.

The following are the three most important commitments for White people:

1. *Truth.* It is no coincidence that the same people who deny the existence of systemic racism tend also to deny climate change, COVID-19 vaccines, and the results of the 2020 election. Denial is a dangerous and contagious drug. We must commit ourselves to the truth and living in reality, no matter how uncomfortable or painful it is. Only the truth can set us free.

2. *Accountability.* We must engage in spaces and practices of accountability. We need friends, family, neighbors, colleagues, small groups, communities, associations, clubs, and organizations to hold us accountable for continuing the lifelong practice of confronting our Whiteness and ideologies of Whiteness in the world.

3. *Responsibility.* We must take personal and collective responsibility for the harm that Whiteness has caused and work to repair the harm and heal the damage. Whiteness, at its core psychological level, is denial and the abdication of responsibility. Resisting those dangerous temptations is a good place to begin.

Willie James Jennings offered a new anti-racist moral imperative when he said that before every choice we make we should ask how this decision will affect the lives of poor Black and brown women and their children. One practice that can have tremendous impact is to fund and follow Black and brown women who are doing the work of confronting and divesting from Whiteness. Support Black- and brown-women-led organizations that are working for racial justice.

Because Black and brown women, especially Queer Black and brown women, live at the site of intersecting forms of oppression (Whiteness, imperialism, patriarchy, and homophobia), they have the wisdom and tools to lead us out of the mess that we've made. It is of the utmost importance for people racialized as White to sit at the feet of Black and brown women and fund their work like the women who provided for Jesus's ministry. In addition to funding and following Black and brown women, it is important for White people to support Black- and brown-led movements for racial justice with our time, talents, and money, especially those movements focused on the most urgent problems of mass incarceration and policing. But we must not try to lead these movements; we need to observe, listen, and learn.

THOMAS MERTON, JAMES BALDWIN, AND LIBERATION FROM WHITENESS

When the famous Trappist monk, spiritual mystic, and theologian Thomas Merton read the prophetic work of James Baldwin, he had a crisis of conscience that became the catalyst for a profound moral awakening and spiritual transformation. Merton published a book that was born from his encounter with Baldwin entitled *Seeds of Destruction,* in which he reflected on Dr. King, the civil rights movement, and the topic of "Black Revolution." Merton described Baldwin and other Black intellectuals' message to White people in the following way: "White society has sinned in many ways. It has betrayed Christ by its injustices to races it considered 'inferior' and to countries which it colonized."[1] Merton continued,

> These Negroes are not simply judging the white man and rejecting him. On the contrary, they are seeking by Christian love and sacrifice to redeem him, to enlighten him, so as not only to save his soul from perdition, but also to awaken his mind and his conscience, and stir him to initiate the reform and renewal which may still be capable of saving our society. . . . The Negro problem is really a *White* problem: that the cancer of injustice and hate which is eating white society and is only partly manifested in racial segregation with all its consequences, *is rooted in the heart of the white man himself.*[2]

---

[1] Thomas Merton, *Seeds of Destruction* (New York: Farrar, Straus and Giroux, 1964), 66.

[2] Merton, 45, 46.

Merton died three years later, yet Baldwin's words had ushered him into a process of confronting Whiteness. Merton's transformative struggle with Baldwin and Whiteness had a tremendous impact on his theological vision. Baldwin put up a mirror for Merton and gave him the eyes to see his own moral and spiritual situation—as well as the moral and spiritual situation of all White people—more clearly and truthfully. Hauntingly, Merton wrote:

> There has generally been no conception at all that the white man had anything to learn from the Negro. And now the irony is that the Negro (especially the Christian Negro of the heroic stamp of Dr. King) *is offering the white man a "message of salvation," but the white man is so blinded by his self-sufficiency and self-conceit that he does not recognize the peril in which he puts himself by ignoring the offer.*[3]

To summarize Merton, in the civil rights movement, the broader freedom movement, and the call for justice, Black people in America were offering people trapped in the lie of Whiteness the opportunity for salvation and liberation, but we ignored the offer.

Today, White Christians (and people racialized as White in general) are suffering from the horrific consequences of this tragic decision to reject salvation and liberation when they have been offered to us. However, with the resurgence of the Black freedom movement as embodied by Black Lives Matter and the Movement for Black Lives, our neighbors of color may be offering us salvation and liberation again. Barbara Holmes has described the Black Lives Matter movement as "contemplative activism" and "deeply spiritual resistance."[4] So the question is, what will we choose this time? Will we ignore the offer again or will we choose salvation? Will we choose freedom? Will we choose justice? Will we choose liberation?

At the end of our journey we must return to first things such as our mantra and mission statement. Like a broken record, I have quoted from Baldwin, who said that White people "are, in effect, still trapped in a history which they do not understand; and until they understand it,

---

[3] Merton, 63–64.

[4] Barbara Holmes, *Joy Unspeakable: Contemplative Practices of the Black Church* (Minneapolis: Fortress Press, 2017), 141.

they cannot be released from it."[5] Why? It may seem as though Baldwin was offering people racialized as White some very bad news; however, implied within his famous words is the good news of the Gospel.

The only way to repair a systematic problem is with systematic interventions. Whiteness is a lie created to steal economic resources and political power from other people; therefore, the remedy must involve giving and sharing economic resources and political power. There is no hope in Whiteness, but there is hope that people who were assigned Whiteness will begin to believe that it is no longer working for them or anyone else in our world. You are now a part of a very small circle of brave people who made the hard choice to do the difficult work of confronting your Whiteness. Remember that you are not alone. There are others out there like you who want the world to be different. We must always believe what Amoja Three Rivers said, "White people have not always been 'white,' nor will they always be 'white.' It is a political alliance. Things will change."[6]

We can be released from our history if we try to understand it. We can be delivered from Whiteness if we work diligently to stand against it. We can be saved and liberated from evil if we choose to stand in solidarity with the oppressed. Whiteness is a way of death, and my hope is that *Confronting Whiteness* offers us all a path toward life. May we choose life so that we and all who come after us can truly live.

> See, I have set before you today life and prosperity, death and adversity. If you obey the commandments of the LORD your God that I am commanding you today, by loving the LORD your God, walking in his ways, and observing his commandments, decrees, and ordinances, then you shall live and become numerous, and the LORD your God will bless you in the land that you are entering to possess. But if your heart turns away and you do not hear, but are led astray to bow down to other gods and serve them, I declare to you today that you shall perish; you shall not live long in the land that you are crossing the Jordan to enter and possess. I call heaven and earth to witness against you today that I have set

[5] James Baldwin, "The Fire Next Time," in *James Baldwin: Collected Essays*, ed. Toni Morrison (New York: Library of America, 1998), 294.

[6] Amoja Three Rivers, quoted in David Roediger, *Black on White: Black Writers on What It Means to Be White* (New York: Schocken, 1998), 1.

before you life and death, blessings and curses. Choose life so that you and your descendants may live, loving the LORD your God, obeying him, and holding fast to him; for that means life to you and length of days, so that you may live in the land that the LORD swore to give to your ancestors, to Abraham, to Isaac, and to Jacob. (Deuteronomy 30:15–20)

Bibliography

Allen, Theodore W. *The Invention of the White Race,* vols. 1 and 2. New York: Verso, 1994.

Anderson, Carol. *White Rage: The Unspoken Truth of Our Racial Divide.* New York: Bloomsbury, 2016.

Arendt, Hannah. *Eichmann in Jerusalem: A Report on the Banality of Evil.* New York: Penguin, 2006.

Baldwin, James. "As Much Truth as One Can Bear." *The New York Times Book Review,* January 14, 1962; republished in *The Cross of Redemption: Uncollected Writings.* Edited by Randall Kenan. New York: Vintage International, 2011.

———. *James Baldwin: Collected Essays.* Edited by Toni Morrison. New York: Library of America, 1998.

Berry, Lucretia. *What Lies between Us: Fostering First Steps toward Racial Healing.* Second edition. CreateSpace Independent Publishing Platform, February 23, 2017.

Bonilla-Silva, Eduardo. *Racism without Racists: Colorblind Racism and the Persistence of Racial Inequality in America.* Lanham, MD: Rowman and Littlefield, 2014.

———, and David Dietrich. "The Sweet Enchantment of Color-Blind Racism in Obamerica." *The Annals of the American Academy of Political and Social Science.* vol. 634, *Race, Racial Attitudes, and Stratification Beliefs: Evolving Directions for Research and Policy* (March 2011).

Carter, J. Kameron. *Race: A Theological Account.* New York: Oxford, 2008.

Cash, W. J. *The Mind of the South.* New York: Knopf, 1941.

Coates, Ta-Nehisi. *Between the World and Me.* New York: Spiegal and Grau, 2015.

———. "The First White President." *Atlantic,* October 2017.

————. *The Water Dancer.* New York: One World, 2019.

Cone, James. *A Black Theology of Liberation.* Maryknoll, NY: Orbis Books, 1986.

————. *The Cross and the Lynching Tree.* Maryknoll, NY: Orbis Books, 2013.

————. *Said I Wasn't Gonna Tell Nobody.* Maryknoll, NY: Orbis Books, 2018.

Desmond, Matthew. "In Order to Understand the Brutality of American Capitalism, You Have to Start on the Plantation." *The New York Times Magazine,* August 18, 2019.

DiAngelo, Robin. *White Fragility.* Boston: Beacon, 2018.

————. "White Fragility." *International Journal of Critical Pedagogy* 3, no. 3 (2011): 54–70.

Douglas, Kelly Brown. *Stand Your Ground: Black Bodies and the Justice of God.* Maryknoll, NY: Orbis Books, 2015.

————. "What Does Jesus Have to Do with Whiteness?" *Feminism and Religion* (December 20, 2013).

Douglass, Frederick. *Narrative of the Life of Frederick Douglass, an American Slave* (1845). In Frederick Douglass and Harriet Jacobs, *Narrative of the Life of Frederick Douglass, an American Slave / Incidents in the Life of a Slave Girl,* intro. Kwame Anthony Appiah. New York: Modern Library Paperback Classics, 2010.

————. *What to a Slave Is the Fourth of July?* Rochester, NY, 1852.

Du Bois, W.E.B. *Black Reconstruction in America: An Essay toward a History of the Part Which Black Folk Played in the Attempt to Reconstruct Democracy in America, 1860–1880.* New York: Oxford University Press, 2007.

————. *Darkwater: Voices from within the Veil.* New York: Schocken Books, 1969.

Dyer, Richard. *White.* New York: Routledge, 2017.

————. "White." *Screen* 29, no. 4 (Fall 1998): 44.

Ellis, Marion. *By a Dream Possessed: Myers Park Baptist Church.* Charlotte, NC: Myers Park Baptist Church, 1997.

Emerson, Michael O., and Christian Smith. *Divided by Faith: Evangelical Religion and the Problem of Race in America.* New York: Oxford University Press, 2000.

Feagin, Joe. *The White Racial Frame: Centuries of Racial Framing and Counter Framing.* New York: Routledge, 2010.

Fikes, Robert, Jr. "Escaping the Literary Ghetto: African American Authors of White Life Novels, 1946–1994." *Western Journal of Black Studies* 19, no. 2 (1995): 105–12.

Fletcher, Jeannie Hill. *The Sin of White Supremacy.* Maryknoll, NY: Orbis Books, 2017.

Frankenberg, Ruth. *White Women, Race Matters: The Social Construction of Whiteness.* New York, Routledge, 1994.

Gramsci, Antonio. *Selections from the Prison Notebooks.* London: International Publishers, 1978.

Gulati-Partee, Gila, and Maggie Potapchuk. "Paying Attention to White Culture and Privilege." *The Foundation Review* 6, no. 1 (2015).

Haider, Asad. *Mistaken Identity: Race and Class in the Age of Trump.* New York: Verso, 2018.

Harris, Cheryl I. "Whiteness as Property." *Harvard Law Review* 106, no. 8 (June 1993): 1707–91.

Hart, Drew. *Trouble I've Seen.* Harrisburg, PA: Herald Press, 2016.

Helms, Janet. *A Race Is a Nice Thing to Have: A Guide to Being a White Person or Understanding the White Persons in Your Life.* San Diego: Congnella, 2018.

Hill, Daniel. *White Awake: An Honest Look at What It Means to Be White.* Downers Grove, IL: InterVarsity Press, 2017.

hooks, bell. *Black Looks: Race and Representation.* New York: Routledge, 2015.

———. "Representing Whiteness in the Black Imagination." In *Displacing Whiteness: Essays in Social and Cultural Criticism,* edited by Ruth Frankenberg. Durham, NC: Duke University Press, 1997.

Jennings, Willie James. "Can White People Be Saved?: Reflections on the Relationship of Missions and Whiteness." In *Can "White" People Be Saved: Triangulating Race, Theology, and Mission,* edited by Love L. Sechrest, Johnny Ramirez-Johnson, and Amos Young. Downers Grove, IL: IVP Academic, 2018.

———. *The Christian Imagination,* New Haven, CT: Yale University Press, 2010.

———. "To Be a Christian Intellectual." *Yale Divinity School News,* October 30, 2015.

Johnson, James Weldon. *The Autobiography of an Ex-Colored Man.* New York: Dover Publications, 1995.

Kendi, Ibram X. *How to Be an Antiracist.* New York: One World, 2019.

———. *Stamped from the Beginning.* New York: Bold Type Books, 2016.

King, Ruth. *Mindful of Race: Transforming Racism from the Inside Out.* Boulder, CO: Sounds True, 2018.

Lipsitz, George. *The Possessive Investment in Whiteness.* Philadelphia: Temple University Press, 2006.

Lomax, Louis E. "A Summing Up: Louis Lomax Interviews Malcolm X. In *When the Word Is Given: A Report on Elijah Muhammad, Malcolm X, and the Black Muslim World.* Westport, CT: Praeger, 1979.

Magee, Rhonda V. *The Inner Work of Racial Justice: Healing Ourselves and Transforming Our Communities through Mindfulness.* New York: Tarcher Perigee, 2019.

———. "Taking and Making Refuge in Racial [Whiteness] Awareness in Racial Justice Work." In *Buddhism and Whiteness: Critical Reflections,* edited by George Yancy and Emily McRae, 277–92. Lanham, MD: Lexington Books, 2019.

———. "Teaching Mindfulness with Mindfulness of Race and Other Forms of Diversity." In *Resources for Teaching Mindfulness: An International Handbook,* edited by Donald McCown et al., 225–46. Switzerland: Springer International Publishing, 2016.

McClintock Fulkerson, Mary, and Marcia Mount Shoop. *A Body Broken, a Body Betrayed.* Eugene, OR: Cascade, 2015.

Menakem, Resmaa. *My Grandmother's Hands: Racialized Trauma and the Pathway to Mending Our Hearts and Bodies.* Central Recovery Press, 2017.

Morrison, Toni. "Making America White Again." *The New Yorker,* November 14, 2016.

———. *Playing in the Dark: Whiteness and the Literary Imagination.* New York: Vintage Books, 1992.

Painter, Nell Irvin. *The History of White People.* New York: Norton, 2010.

———. "What Is Whiteness?" *The New York Times,* June 20, 2015.

Perkinson, James W. "Reversing the Gaze: Constructing European Race Discourse as Modern Witchcraft Practice." *Journal of the American Academy of Religion* 72, no. 3 (2004).

———. *White Theology: Outing Supremacy in Modernity.* New York: Palgrave-Macmillan, 2004.

Roediger, David R. *Black on White: Black Writers on What It Means to Be White.* New York: Schocken, 1998.

————. *The Wages of Whiteness: Race and the Making of the American Working Class.* New York: Verso, 1991.

————. *Working toward Whiteness: How America's Immigrants Became White.* New York, Basic Books, 2005.

Rose, Julie. "Myers Park HOA Pays $17,500 to Settle Dispute with NAACP." *WFAE* [Charlotte's NPR news source], January 17, 2011.

Solzhenitsyn, Aleksandr I. *The Gulag Archipelago.* New York: Harper Perennial Modern Classics, 2007.

Stovall, Natasha. "Whiteness on the Couch." *Longreads,* August 2019.

Thandeka. *Learning to Be White.* New York: Continuum, 1999.

Tisby, Jemar. *The Color of Compromise: The Truth about the American Church's Complicity in Racism.* Grand Rapids, MI: Zondervan, 2019.

Vivian, C. T. *Black Power and the American Myth: 50th Anniversary Edition.* Minneapolis: Fortress Press, 2021.

Wallis, Jim. *America's Original Sin: Racism, White Privilege, and the Bridge to a New America.* Grand Rapids, MI: Brazos Press, 2016.

Watson, Veronica. *The Souls of White Folk: African American Writers Theorize Whiteness.* Jackson: University Press of Mississippi, 2013.

Wink, Walter. *The Powers That Be.* New York: Doubleday, 1998.

X, Malcolm. *The Autobiography of Malcolm X.* New York: Bantam Doubleday Dell Publishing Group, 1998.

————. "God's Judgment on White America." December 4, 1963.

————. "UC Berkeley Interview." October 11, 1963.

Index